G000256742

# EAGLE'S WAR

# EAGLE'S WAR

The War Diary of an Aircraft Carrier

PETER C. SMITH

CRÉCY BOOKS

Published in 1995 by Crécy Books Ltd.
© Peter C. Smith 1995

First published in 1995

ISBN 0 947554

*This book is copyright. No part of it may be reproduced in any form without permission in writing from the publishers except by a reviewer who wishes to quote brief passages in review written for inclusion in a newspaper, magazine, radio or television broadcast.*

Printed in Great Britain by
Bookcraft (Bath) Limited,
Midsomer Norton, Avon BA3 2BX

# Contents

# DEDICATION

For DAVID JOHN SMITH
my brother and my friend,
deeply missed.

# Acknowledgements

In order to give the full flavour of life aboard one of HM aircraft carriers in time of war I have sought the views and memories of those who served to supplement the dry hard facts gleaned from dusty records, battle reports and signals held at the Public Record Office and similar reference centres. Many of these gallant gentlemen have asked me to allow them to remain anonymous, but I would like to extend to them my sincere gratitude for their permission to quote from their memoirs, yarns and stories of the 'Real' Navy. The following individuals have also given me help, information and their valuable time and are equally deserving of my thanks and debt:

Oliver J. Barritt; Jack Bean; Jack Bryant; Mr Bushnell; Alfred H. Carpenter; Douglas Clare; Les 'Nobby' Clark; Donald J. Clist; R.J. 'Jumper' Collins; R. C. Cosh; George E. Cox; T.C. Crawford; Roland A. Dakin; Fred R. Davenport; Charles Davis; Gordon 'Ginger' Drake; A.S. Evans; Jack Farminer; Reginald W. G. Few; Jack 'Windy' Gale; A. Les O. Goodenough; Alf Gray; Dick Greenwood; Norman Greenwood; E. Hodgson; Harry W.M. Kempshall; Eddie Kemp; E. Kenward; Albert W. Leyster; Arthur 'Patty' Lloyd; E.B. Mackenzie; Phillip McLean; J. Milne; John B. Murray; E. Newman; R. Northover; Les Owen; Don Perkins; Ken Pierce; Bill Prime; Harry Rathbone; Joseph Routledge; Thomas C. Sprake, B.E.M.; Alf Thomas; Ray Thrower; Ken Timmins; K. Timms; E.W. Tyler; Edwin R. Walker; D. Walling; Ray Wallmark; Fred White; Sam White; Cyril Williams; E. Williamson; Wilfred Wiley; W. F. 'Tug' Whymark.

Particular acknowledgement to Mr L.F. Davenport for making available the war diary of R.F. Williams which proved invaluable in checking dates and times with official statements and fallible fading memories.

I hope they will all enjoy the memories of their famous old

7

ship that this book will evoke. They say any warship is only as good as her crew. *Eagle* was without a doubt a valiant and doughty ship!

Peter C. Smith
Riseley, Bedford.

# CHAPTER ONE

# A Quiet Number!

On 24 June 1939, the British troopship *Dilwara* sailed from Southampton docks bound for the distant waters of the Far East. Her decks were crowded with sailors, soldiers and a few airmen bound for the garrisons and bases of the British Empire which in those days, not long ago in terms of actual years but an eternity away from the nation's present fourth-rate status, girded the globe and upheld the peace. Her voyage was destined to take her to Malta, Aden, Bombay, Colombo, Singapore and Hong Kong and at each of these ports a proportion of her service passengers disembarked to join the various fleets, regiments and squadrons serving there.

Quite a large batch of these passengers carried on the trooper for that particular peacetime journey as she made her leisurely way eastward were men of the Royal Navy bound for her final port-of-call. They were a fresh draft of the crew of the aircraft carrier HMS *Eagle*, at that time based in the Far East and due to re-commission after an absence from home of two years. It was a popular drafting, eagerly sought-after from the men of the regular navy who had previously spent time in exotic places like China, Japan and Malaya and who could tell tales that thrilled the many youngsters on their first trip to distant seas.

In Europe and in the Far East the war clouds hung heavily. Hitler was busy occupying what remained of Czechoslovakia, so naively sacrificed by British Prime Minister Chamberlain the previous September. The Führer's pale and portly shadow, Mussolini, the Italian braggart, was puffing himself up over his latest bloodless conquest, Albania. Japanese troops were deep into northern China extending their hold on that unhappy land and British civilians were humiliated in Chinese cities by the troops of Nippon. The march of Fascism and the cringing thoughtless disarmament, with the nation's defences cut to the

bone by the faceless men of the Treasury, had meant that Great
Britain had neither the political will, nor the military
wherewithal, to oppose the steady expansion of the dictators'
empires. Only recently had a change of mood come upon the
country and guarantees had been issued to Poland that Britain
would fight for them should they be threatened by Hitler.
What the Government had refused democratic and well-armed
Czechoslovakia the year before, it now committed Britain to do
for a clerical-Fascist regime whose army was built upon cavalry
and the lance.

The thoughts of balmy days in the far-distant South China
sea upon a stately and elderly aircraft-carrier must have
seemed like an ideal escape from the harsh realities of Europe
bracing itself for another blood-letting in the manner of the
Great War. The other side of the world where the sun always
shone was definitely what 'Jack' would term 'a quiet number!'

Initially indeed this would appear to be the case. Aircraft
carriers were not rated highly in the navies of the 1930s; the
battleship remained the final arbiter of sea power with no real
proven challenger. The exponents of air power had been
shrilly and persistently claiming that the bomber had replaced
the battleship but no firm proof had been forthcoming. More
quietly a few dedicated naval pilots in the navies of Great
Britain, Japan and the United States had been experimenting
and perfecting techniques that were to show that the torpedo –
and dive-bomber (as distinct from the altitude bomber of the
land-based air forces) did *indeed* have the potential to usurp
that centuries-old tradition, but it was still all theory in June
1939.

Other than the *Eagle*, British sea power in the Far East was
represented by a squadron of cruisers, one destroyer and one
submarine flotilla and a few escort vessels. It was hardly a
credible deterrent to a navy like that of Japan with ten
battleships, eight aircraft carriers and whole squadrons of
lesser ships. But it was not really meant to be. The American
Pacific Fleet was supposed to be the counter to that, but they
were based thousands of miles from Japan, at Hawaii.

The British main fleet had for years concentrated in home
waters and the Mediterranean. Should war come, the theory
went, this great fleet would steam eastward and in seventy days
concentrate at the huge new naval base at Singapore to defend
the Empire. Until then it remained close to home.

There were a few snags to this. Firstly the pious hope that Japan would give seventy days' notice of her intentions to go to war. When she had gone to war with Russia in 1904 she had announced her intentions with a surprise destroyer attack on the enemy fleet *before* the declaration of war. The British view that she would be more 'sporting' 35 years later was to prove illusory! Secondly, to send the whole British fleet east assumed that Britain would not be busy in an existing war with either Germany or Italy at the same time. In the event she was to be heavily engaged with both! Thirdly, unlike the Japanese, Germans, and the Americans, the Royal Navy had not developed ship-to-ship refuelling techniques or the necessary ships, equipment and hardware to provide a floating 'Fleet Train' to keep such a fleet operational across the huge distances of the eastern ocean.

So *Eagle* and her companions were by no stretch of the imagination a deterrent; rather they were a 'show the flag' and peace-keeping force, ideal for anti-piracy patrols, for the hunting and rounding-up of mercantile raiders and convoy escorting where the threat of submarines did not exist. Indeed the first two roles had dominated the *Eagle*'s previous commission from 1937 and the latter roles were to prove an ideal *raison d'être* for the first nine months of the war.

For such duties no fighter aircraft were necessary and so the sole aircraft outfit of the *Eagle* was two squadrons of Fairey Swordfish biplanes. These totalled just eighteen aircraft, nine each of Nos. 813 and 824 Squadrons, FAA (Fleet Air Arm – Although this term had been officially abandoned on 29 May 1939 in favour of 'Air Branch', the old name stuck and was used throughout the war until re-introduced in 1953, and so this is the term that will be used in this book).

These wire-and-struts aircraft were quite new even although they looked incredibly obsolete against the sleek modern monoplanes that equipped the Japanese and American navies. That they showed little advance over the aircraft of two decades earlier was due to two main factors. The first and most pernicious was the heavy hand of the Treasury upon financial resources of the services. Lack of funding proved to be a very false economy but it has always been the tradition of Great Britain to neglect its armed forces in times of peace, and the state of present-day navy bears testimony that the same policy persists as it did fifty years ago. Secondly, for two decades the hand of neglect and lack of interest lay heavily over the development of modern aircraft for the fleet. This was due not to the Admiralty, who were busy building seven modern carriers for the fleet, but to the uncaring indifference of the Royal Air Force. The latter service was for twenty years responsible for the aircraft provided for the fleet and they woefully failed to discharge that duty. Indeed a mix of Royal Navy and RAF personnel still existed aboard *Eagle* at this time, and continued into the war, as a legacy of this black period of dual control. This had only been finally and thankfully terminated when the Inskip recommendations had been implemented the month before the trooper had left home waters.

What of the carrier herself? She displaced just over 22,600 tons according to the Navy List for February 1939. She had an overall length along her flight deck of 652 feet, and its width was 96 feet She was old, she was slow and she was a conversion from a battleship, as indeed had been most (but not all) the early aircraft carriers of the three principal fleets. It is not proposed to give a rivet-by-rivet description of this famous old ship, for our story is more concerned with what she and her crew achieved in three years of all-out war. For those who enjoy the minutia of construction and development the excellent *Profile* compiled by David Brown is recommended as being the most detailed and accurate. Suffice it to say here that she was converted from the hull of the battleship *Almirante Cochrane*, laid down for the Chilean Navy at Elswick in February 1913, but was not finally completed and fully utilised for sea as a British aircraft carrier until February 1924. Her speed was therefore never much more than 24 knots in her heyday and that was long past. Ideally aircraft carriers were found to require at least ten knots more speed than this but of course many of her contemporaries were similarly handicapped.

She did prove, along with the smaller but custom-built *Hermes*, the standard layout on which most subsequent aircraft carriers down to the present day have been based, the 'island' superstructure with funnels, bridge, masts and range-finders huddled amidships on the starboard side of the ship, leaving the flight-deck free of encumbrance for flying off and landing on operations. There were lifts fore and aft to 'strike down' the aircraft to capacious hangars below for maintenance, arming and repair; large stocks of aircraft torpedoes, bombs and aviation fuel for the aircraft complement which made them extremely vulnerable ships to both accident and enemy action, and sprinkler systems were installed that automatically sprayed the hangars with salt water in case of fire.

Being built on a battleship's hull she had a 4–5-inch armoured belt at sea level and was also fitted with anti-torpedo 'bulges' early on. These were meant to pre-empt the main force of the explosion of a 750 lb warhead should she be hit. Both systems gave her an exaggerated and, in the event, totally illusory reputation of being well-protected from attack from both on and below the surface. From the air she was wide open. The armoured-deck aircraft carrier was then a new concept and the first one, *Illustrious*, was still building. *Eagle* had 1.5 inch thick main and hangar decks and a flight-deck 1 inch thick in places, but any modern bomb of 250 lb upward could have pierced it with ease, let alone the 1,000 lb the Luftwaffe were then employing.

Her defensive armament was puny. For protection against surface attack she still carried nine of the old single MkXVII 6 inch guns in open shields. These had a maximum range of 16,400 yards. Against air assault her defences were pitiful, and had actually been *reduced* earlier so that in June 1939 she merely carried four single 4 inch Mk V HA guns and two multiple 2-pdr 'Pom-Poms' for close-range defence, along with an assortment of fairly useless light machine guns of the .303 calibre, pathetically inadequate against modern aircraft.

Since her completion she had served in the Mediterranean Fleet between 1923 and 1931, had undertaken a cruise to South America, where she had shown the flag at Buenos Aires. She then had a refit and joined the China Fleet between 1933 and 1934. Another refit, then back to the Mediterranean in 1935, on to China once more in 1937 for a commission. Now she was expecting to re-commission for a further two-year stint in those waters after a refit at Singapore dockyard.

What of her crew? She nominally carried a ship's crew of about 750 officers and men, plus her squadron officers and men which of course varied. But once the war commenced and modifications were added, her numbers vastly increased and she was always a badly over-crowded vessel in which to serve.

We shall be seeing the *Eagle* largely through the eyes of her crew in these pages, which is how it should be. Some loved her with a fierce pride, to others she was 'just another ship', while some positively loathed her. All shades of opinion on *Eagle*'s merits and deficiencies are recorded in this book so the reader can make his own judgement about just what life was like aboard a Royal Navy fighting carrier in World War II.

How did HMS *Eagle* first strike the newcomers? D.J. Clist remembered:

Unlike present-day aircraft carriers *Eagle* was unique in having an upper deck round which you could walk from stem to stern and so enjoy the benefits of sea breezes and see what was going on – like a Mediterranean cruise! Having taken a walk round the ship it was easy for me to visualise much of what the various dockyard refits had finally achieved. Upon what had been mainly the normal upper deck level of the old battleship had been emplaced, along practically the whole length of the ship, steel plating supported by girders to form the deck of two hangars. There were no gangways from the hangar to below decks; these were from the walk. On the same level as the hangars were the quarterdeck and forecastle. These latter two positions enjoyed an abundance of fresh air, therefore they were very popular for sleeping billets for both officers and men. The peculiar positions in which the hammocks were slung gave one a certain amount of surprise as to their comfort – but not one of those persons would vacate such a billet for one below decks.

All the messdecks on the old *Eagle*, except where the artisans, miscellaneous petty officers and senior ratings lived, were immediately below the hangar spaces and thus did not provide very much fresh air in the tropics. These messes stretched the whole width of the ship. One comforting factor was the lack of compartment doors – no knee raising or head ducking but, of course, wartime standards demand numerous doors for safety purposes.

The first time I saw the old *Eagle* was at a place in North China called Wei-hai-wei. This place of course no longer 'exists' so far as the British Navy is concerned, but it is an island situated between the Gulf of Pehida and the Yellow Sea, south of the well-known former Russian base of Port Arthur of 1904 fame, and more recently the Korean war – being only a stone's throw from North Korea itself. The climate there varied to the extreme – heavy snowfalls regularly in winter, but very hot in summer. The China Fleet (as our Far East squadron was known pre-war) used to leave Hong Kong annually when the summer approached and sail for Wei-hai-wei, where, although it was hot, the heat was not so trying as at Hong Kong which is further south and hemmed in by hills.

While there the fleet carried out numerous exercises, gun shoots, submarine detection by aircraft and asdic, smoke screening of convoys and escort duties. The aircraft also practised flying on and off the carrier during daylight and at night. There were also numerous recreational activities.

The stay at Wei-hai-wei usually terminated sometime in August and the fleet returned to Hong Kong either direct or by way of a short cruise around the Balis. Usually during a commission the ship would of course visit the northern Chinese port of Shanghai, a great commercial centre in those days, where the entertainment value was first rate.

In July 1939, we returned directly to Hong Kong without any intermediate visits to such ports because we were due to re-commission with a seven-eighths new crew on 4 August. This involved an evolution not before attempted on the China Station because of the numbers forming the ship's company. The troopship *Dunera* and an old submarine depot ship HMS *Lucia*, brought to Hong Kong the new ship's complement and the whole operation was carried by having the *Eagle* on one side of a jetty and the *Dunera* and *Lucia* on the opposite. The old (relieved) portion of the ship's company of *Eagle* walked down the for'ard gangway and the new members walked up the after gangway. In the middle of the jetty were two Royal Marine bands playing music for the spirits of those joining the ship – the ratings going home needed no 'spiriting!'

Only a few days' respite were allowed the new ship's company before sailing for Singapore where *Eagle* was to undergo a lengthy refit.

They sailed from Hong Kong on 12 August. For the very young and the very green a warship the size of Eagle as one's first ship could either be daunting or inspiring. For R.J. Collins it was, happily, the latter:

I joined HMS *Eagle* in Hong Kong in August 1939 as a 5th class ERA, and had never served afloat before, so it was quite an experience. I shall always remember one Sunday morning, while most people were at 'Divisions', I was employed repairing the ship's syren which was attached to one of her funnels. It was a lovely sunny morning, the Royal Marine band was playing on the flight deck and I thought, 'This *is* the life!' From my lofty perch I watched the Royal Marine band beat retreat and it was a grand sight and one that stayed with me all my life.

'Tug' Whymark recalls that a short period was spent in hard work, getting organised and slotting into his place in the new team:

I was detailed to the gunnery division, which included all aspects of the ship's own armament, magazines and bomb rooms. We worked under the supervision of the ship's gunnery officers and we had commissioned gunners, gunners' mates, chief and petty officers, an ordnance chief petty officer and numerous gunnery 'rates'. I qualified for seaman gunner during my period in the gunnery division which under normal circumstances would have meant a draft back to the UK for a term at the notorious Royal Navy Gunnery School on Whale Island in Portsmouth harbour, HMS *Excellent*. Of course the outbreak of hostilities changed all that. Providing there were qualified gunnery instructors aboard your vessel and adequate armaments available one could then do the course afloat and qualify.

Her commanding officer was Captain C. Moody, who had been appointed I/C (in command) of HMS *Eagle* on 1 January 1937. Captain Moody was later relieved by Captain A.R.M. Bridge, CBE (16 June 1939). When he became the Director of Naval Air Division at the Admiralty, he was in turn replaced by Captain E.G.N. Rushbrooke, DSC (24 April 1941) who was formerly the captain of the netlayer *Guardian*, while her final commanding officer was to be Captain L.D. Mackintosh, DSC, who took command in June 1942. Telegraphist Air Gunner Ginger Tyler recalled:

When *Eagle* re-commissioned at Hong Kong on 4 August, 1939, the captain, Clement Moody, personally said goodbye to every member of the ship's company with a handshake (the first time I had experienced this) and Captain A.R.M. Bridge took over command. He was a different kettle of fish. As I had only been in the ship for about eight months I had to carry on with the new commission, which ended when I left the ship in December 1941.

With her squadrons embarked from Kai Tak, the ship left for Singapore on 12 August, and is the custom with a newly commissioned ship, we went into an intensive 'shake-down' routine, designed to bring the ship, her crew and the squadrons, up to a state of full efficiency. Gunnery drills, action stations, and flying off and recovery of aircraft were exercised. The squadrons carried out navigation exercises, air firing, dive bombing on a towed target and dummy torpedo attacks on the ship. By the time we arrived in Singapore, and the aircraft had been disembarked to Seletar, the raw ship's company had been pretty well licked into shape.

My old pilot, Lieutenant R.M. Smeeton, had left the ship, and I flew from now on for a period with Sub-Lieutenant Collins, pilot, and Lieutenant Campbell-Meiklejohn, observer. We functioned very well as a crew, and had no problems. Collins was an aggressive but very competent pilot. Meiklejohn was a meticulous and accurate navigator. I hope they had the same confidence in me as I had in them.

With squadrons re-embarked, *Eagle* left Singapore on 31 August and headed westward. The gunnery and torpedo sections were busily engaged fusing bombs and fitting warheads to aircraft torpedoes.

In August 1939 the ship's commander was Commander R. Oliver-Bellais and he was relieved by Commander T.C. Hampton (22 May 1939) and later by Commander B.J. de St Croix (5 November 1941). The outstanding Commander (Flying) was Commander C.L. Keighley-Peach, an inspirational figure.

Number 813 Squadron personnel included Lieutenant-Commander (P) N. Kennedy, (1 September 1938) with Lieutenant (P) R.M. Smeeton (18 January 1937) and Flight Lieutenant R.C. Gashell,RAF. (18 January 1937). Later the squadron was led firstly by Lieutenant-Commander (P) N. Kennedy (1 April 1939), then by Lieutenant-Commander (P) D.H. Elles, by Lieutenant-Commander (O) A.V. Lyle and finally by Lieutenant (O) C. Hutchinson (I/C March 1942).

Number 824 Squadron was initially led by Flying Officer C.S. Cooper, with D.O.F. Lumsden, F.G.R. Thomas, J. Compton,

and Squadron Leader R.G. Forbes. Later, command of the
squadron was held firstly by Lieutenant-Commander (O) A.J.
Debenham (15 June 1939), then by Royal Marine Captain (later
Major) (P) F.W. Brown (11 August 1941).

The arrival of the new crew in August included Surgeon
Lieutenant E.B. Mackenzie, (1 April 1939) and he added to his
responsibilities the job of 'unofficial photographer'. Many of
his original prints he kindly made available enabling us to have
a unique record of the first years of *Eagle*'s wartime operations.

The Royal Navy commissioned its ships from its three main
naval bases in those days, Portsmouth, Plymouth and Chatham
and *Eagle* was a Devonport ('Guz') ship.

This then was part of *Eagle*'s team on the eve of war. The
ship herself arrived at Singapore on 19 August 1939. The crew
were full of talk of cruises to Bali, of lovely Chinese girls of the
'alongside crews' at Shanghai, of leisurely days under the
tropical sun. But for them and HMS *Eagle* the new commission
was not to be 'A Quiet Number'. For them all, as for the rest of
the world, time was running out far more rapidly than they
realised. On that very same day the Soviet Union's opportunist
and cynical pact with the hitherto hated Nazi Germany was
announced by Stalin to the Politburo. When the news broke it
caused a sensation. It did more, it made war inevitable.

CHAPTER TWO

# Indian Ocean Patrols

HMS *Eagle* had arrived at Singapore in mid-August to carry out a short refit. What an evocative name that is to any man who served in the pre-war Navy. One such Donald Clist and he remembers *Eagle*'s visit there on the eve of war most vividly:

*Singapore* – what it is like nowadays I have no idea, but pre-1939 it was a really wonderful place in which to spend weeks of all night leave! The night clubs and cabarets were most enjoyable and it was possible to be provided with a permanent bed and breakfast billet, with other meals and dhobying thrown in for an inclusive weekly charge!

The climate is very sticky and one is continuously sweating, thus being bothered with sweat rash, prickly heat or dhoby itch – very irksome and once you acquire this complaint it takes a fancy to you and refuses to leave you.

We were going to spend Christmas 1939 in dock at Singapore and sail in January for a cruise to Bali and the ports of Indo-China but the news from the UK became more tense with each broadcast. Each day on board ship thanks to the wireless department we were provided with a news sheet. The sparkers listened out during hours when the rest of the crew were asleep. At breakfast time the messes were able to sit down, read and discuss the events just the same as if at home – except for the pools of sweat! On some occasions, when convenient to working hours and the W/T department the tannoy system was switched on so as to permit the hearing of the news direct from the BBC Overseas Service. The tannoy in our ship I should mention, was a real 'Heath Robinson' affair; one shudder from the ship and the whole system fell over. However, it behaved itself when we were switched on to hear the statement broadcast by the then Prime Minister, Neville Chamberlain, that we were at war

with Germany. Actually, we had come out of the Graving
Dock about 72 hours before this broadcast – the buzz having
been passed of course from UK to the local C-in-C.
Therefore, within a few hours of this historical broadcast we
were at sea.

Our first instructions were to patrol through the Malacca
Strait. The stocks of food which we had taken on board at
Singapore would last us for six weeks, but the fuel situation
of course soon deteriorated and very quickly we were obliged
to regularly refuel at sea from one of the RFA (Royal Fleet
Auxiliary) tankers, *Cherryleaf*. A few days after the first such
refuelling we set course for Ceylon, covering at the same
time a small convoy of Commonwealth ships bringing food
and troops to the UK, the first actual convoy from the
Australasian area.

'Tug' Whymark gives this recollection of the abrupt transition
from peace to war aboard the *Eagle*:

On arrival at Singapore *Eagle* berthed alongside the naval
base and shore leave was granted on both 1 and 2 September
(two watches) and I was on second watch leave which was due
to expire at 2200. But the recall was received in the middle of
a session of alcoholic consumption at the naval canteen and
immediately we returned to ship wondering what all the fuss
was about! As soon as we reached the top of the gangway we
knew. There they all were. 'Jimmy' (the first lieutenant), duty
officer, chief gunner's mate 'Jaunty' and the 'Crushers', not
forgetting the gunnery officer himself (Commissioned
Gunner). Every man jack of us was detailed to various parts
of the ship and began ammunitioning. Shells and bombs
were armed, time fuses set on ready-use ammunition, fuel
and stores loaded etc. All the ship's company worked through
the night. Those of us who had knocked back a few pints of
'Tiger' beer damn soon sweated it out of the system. I myself
was down in the depths of the starboard 6-inch magazine.

We reported to the watch PO (petty officer) and after
checking the graph and temperature reading of the
magazine, we secured it. Not too soon either because we were
knackered! We climbed up through the zig-zagged
hatchways and into the main seamens' messdeck. What a
relief, and up the main ladders onto the upper decks. It was
around daybreak. Thank God for beautiful fresh air, after

being stripped down to the waist, sweat literally pouring away from us. That particular magazine was to be my battle station for the next few months, except for harbour night action station which alternated one watch in the ship's magazines and one watch on the twin Lewis gun on the front deck.

In the early hours the ship reported ready for sea, all hawser and springs were let go and we were soon on our way out and down the Jahore Straits heading, I suppose, for the South China Sea. The captain cleared lower deck and announced that our country was now at war with Germany. *Eagle* was at first degree readiness and war evolutions began in earnest, gun drill, aircraft sorties, torpedoes and bombs primed, shells fused and primed. Most of the aircraft's technical staff in those early days were still RAF and were among the last to be phased out and replaced by FAA personnel. From then on it seemed to us that only the captain and coders knew where *Eagle* was going at any particular time, or why!

The first merchant ship *Eagle* intercepted was not an enemy at all but a Dutch passenger ship. The very indignant Dutch captain didn't know Holland was about to be invaded by German forces but was nonetheless given his orders and changed course.

Of course the Germans were invading Poland, not Holland, in September 1939; the Dutch had to wait another eight months for their turn. So this incident caused a bit of a stink as the little European neutrals couldn't see further than the ends of their noses and were most upset.

*Eagle* had sailed from Singapore in company with the light cruiser *Birmingham* and the destroyer *Daring* in accordance with Rear-Admiral 5th CS's (Cruiser Squadron's) sailing order of the day before. The positions of most German merchant ships had been plotted and recorded well before the outbreak of war and the Royal Navy was determined to scoop up as many potential blockade-runners as they could right at the outset of hostilities.

The *Daring* had to turn back to Singapore at 1945 due to an engine-room defect but the carrier and the cruiser continued through the Malacca Straits and to the northward of Sumatra, subsequently turning southward to approach the Mentawa Islands.

The Swordfish aircraft diligently searched along the west coast of Sumatra and the off-lying islands between Sabang and Bengulen throughout 4, 5 and 6 September. On 5 September while at sea, *en route* from Singapore to Colombo, they 'crossed the Line' for the first time in war conditions. Early on the morning of the latter date, one of the TSRs (Torpedo/Spotter/Reconnaissance) spotted five ships in Padang, three of which had HAL funnel markings. This aircraft subsequently reported a suspicious merchant ship south of Padang and outside territorial waters. The senior officer in *Birmingham* ordered this vessel to steer south-west but this order was not complied with in spite of the dropping of smoke floats as a warning signal. The ship then hoisted a swastika flag and proceeded into Dutch territorial waters but the *Birmingham*, not standing any nonsense of that kind, followed her in under the rules of 'Hot Pursuit' and discovered she was the German freighter *Franken*. Leaving the cruiser to deal with her, *Eagle* was sent off to carry out further aircraft searches at dawn on 7 September to the north and west of Siberu Strait, a distance of 130 miles, to detect any ships which might have escaped from Padang during the previous night. None was found and *Eagle* proceeded on her way to Colombo, where she arrived at 0500 on 10 September.

The repercussions of her first interception rumbled on and were summarised by the Director of Naval Air Division on 12 December thus:

> The incident ... has been previously reported through diplomatic channels as a dastardly attack on a merchant ship inside Dutch territorial waters. A suitable reply to the Dutch protest is understood to have been sent.

The Director of Naval Intelligence scrawled an eloquent 'Noted' on this. Adolf Hitler was to violate the protesting nations' boundaries rather more seriously than *Eagle* had done ere many weeks had passed by.

As usual when approaching Colombo all *Eagle*'s aircraft were flown off to the neighbouring RAF airfield at Ratmalana to prepare for NDL (Night Deck Landing) training and torpedo dropping at night. Fresh drafts from home were required to bring all the warships in distant waters up to wartime complement and the liner *Dunera* had brought out a large number of ratings to join the *Eagle* earlier. Shore leave was granted between 1600 and 2200 next day but all too soon the delights of Colombo had to be forgotten and at 1730 the following afternoon, the carrier set sail on her next major war patrol heading north-west up towards the west coast of India. They sailed towards Bombay and rendezvoused with the light cruiser *Liverpool* escorting a merchant vessel at 1700 on Monday, 25 September. These three ships then returned to Colombo in company and arrived there at 1130 on Thursday, 28 September.

Only a solitary night was allowed before *Eagle* was off once more, putting to sea at 0730 next day and patrolling to the south-west of Colombo and down past the Maldive Islands throughout Saturday and Sunday. The equator was touched but not crossed on 2 October before they turned back north and anchored at Colombo again at 0800 on Thursday, 5 October. Here they remained until Wednesday, 11 October and in the interim leave was granted daily between 1600 and 2200. They finally left Colombo at 1645 on the latter date and proceeded to Trincomalee off which they rendezvoused with the cruiser *Cornwall*. Neither ship was able to enter the harbour owing to a fierce storm which had blown up and which forced them to circle round outside, as it was too risky to try entering in the heavy seas then running. An unpleasant night was had by all!

Trincomalee is one of the largest natural harbours in the world. It was large enough to accommodate all the Allied Naval ships then operating in the Far East and more besides. The entrance was not readily visible from the sea and once inside that entrance numerous bays and coves provided wonderful cover for the ships. The water in the harbour is very deep and at that time it was surrounded by virgin jungle. It was well sheltered and provided excellent sailing had time permitted. For the matelot sailing was the most popular pastime at Trincomalee because there were no other entertainment facilities. Football and hockey were the only recreations and then were only available on a limited scale, four pitches for the whole fleet. During the latter part of the war that all changed of course but in 1940 conditions were basic.

It was expected that the Germans would sail surface ship raiders to attack Allied shipping routes, in the same manner that they did in World War One. In anticipation, the British Admiralty formed a series of Hunting Groups to track them down. The German warships that might be encountered could vary from the pocket battleships (14,000-ton ships armed with six 11-inch guns and a speed of 27 knots), heavy cruisers (12,000-ton ships armed with 8-inch guns and a speed of 32 knots) or disguised merchant ships fitted with concealed 5.9-inch guns and other weapons. The threat was therefore both nebulous and uncertain. All that could be known was that the Germans already had such ships prepared and that a certain percentage of them would escape the British blockade in home waters and reach the distant oceans.

Because of the importance of Australian troops reaching the Mediterranean the Indian Ocean was considered particularly vulnerable. The vast distances involved meant that searches for such enemy surface ships, and their supply ships and tankers, resembled finding the needle in the haystack. Close protection could be given to selected convoys, like the troop convoys, but the independently-routed merchant ships in waters far distant from Europe could not be convoyed; there were insufficient warships to do the job. Nor could shore-based air patrolling do much other than offer a thin screen, so few aircraft were available then and those aircraft were often far from suitable, having only short range and largely untrained aircrew for the maritime protection role.

Here HMS *Eagle* really came into her own. She might be small and old compared with Japanese and American aircraft-carriers, she might not carry fighter or dive bomber aircraft to influence the battles of major fleets, but she had embarked the highly trained and highly skilled Fairey Swordfish TSR aircraft and could carry them around the vast Far Eastern zone to where she was most required. The so-called 'focal areas', general areas where merchant shipping tended to funnel through and thus provide a natural point of ambush for any potential raider, were given priority for patrol activity by the Royal Navy. These areas were around Ceylon itself where the Indian east coast shipping and Bay of Bengal traffic from Burma congregated on their way west, the deep water channels that funnelled the shipping from Australia and the Far East through the island barriers of the Maldives and Seychelles and off the Cape of Good Hope. Her air searches could thus find suspect vessel, examine and scrutinise them at a safe distance and send back details for London to check. Then, should the contact seem worthy of closer inspection, they could direct more suitable warships, normally cruisers, to make a closer inspection and bring the enemy to book.

Carrier/cruiser combinations made perfect hunting groups and one of the first decisions taken concerning *Eagle*'s wartime deployment was contained in signals dated 5 and 31 October. These instructed her to form Force 'I' which was to be based on Colombo, Ceylon (now Sri Lanka) and to hunt for German raiders on the trade routes in the Indian Ocean area. Her companions in the Force were to be the heavy cruisers, *Cornwall* and *Dorsetshire* (10,000-tons, eight 8-inch guns, 31 knots.) It was in accordance with these commands that *Eagle* finally entered Trincomalee harbour at 0800 on 13 October and, after refuelling, both she and the *Cornwall* sailed again, arriving back at Colombo two days later. They refuelled and sailed at 2000 the same evening with their companion and patrolled south of Colombo, meeting the light cruiser *Gloucester* on Tuesday 17 October. All three ships remained in company until Friday, 20 October, when *Gloucester* left them. *Cornwall* and *Eagle* continued their vigilant search, once more passing the Maldive Islands on their port bow on Sunday, 22 October, while returning northward and carrying out a full-calibre shoot with their main 6-inch guns the next morning off the coast before anchoring at Colombo again at 1400.

Among the statistics announced for this time was that *Eagle*'s two Swordfish squadrons had, between the declaration of war on 3 September and 16 January, searched one million square miles of ocean for raiders and submarines. When it recalled that the old 'Stringbag' could only stagger through the air at a *maximum* speed of 90 knots, was an obsolescent biplane, all wires and struts like a World War I machine, and had a crew of three, it makes such achievements memorable. But they were to do much more in the months ahead.

Consider also conditions below in the tropics: the engine room staff performed wonders considering both the age of the vessel and the heat they had to work in. R.J. Collins was at that time a very fresh-faced 5th Class ERA. He recounts his early experiences after joining *Eagle* in August 1939:

I had training on the evaporators but when we put to sea I was given watch keeping in the boiler rooms. We had four boiler rooms, A,B,C and D. A boiler room had three boilers while the others each had six apiece, 21 in all. I had never been in a boiler room before in my life and as I went down in the lift to A boiler room I stared out to my left and thought to myself that I knew very little about all this!

Anyway, when I got out of the lift the chief stoker came over to me and asked me if I knew what to do. I told him that I had no idea. He then gave me a run-down on my duties. I must confess I felt very inadequate but I am happy to say that I soon found my way round and after a few months became good at my watch-keeping duties, although I did find it very hard at times. I hardly knew whether it was Christmas or Easter, I just kept on working the same. The warrant officers continually chased me up and kept plying me with questions about the systems and how things worked until my head split. The threat of having one's leave stopped if one could not answer was a constant threat. There is no doubt that they wanted the maximum effort at all times from us.

I can still recall that my duties included connecting the 21 boilers up ready for leaving harbour, main and auxilliary steam valves. It was a very hard task and by the time you got to the last boilers you could just about lift the wheel spanner, the heat was terrible. I am happy to say that I never passed out on duty while connecting up, but some of my mates did. The chief stokers used to keep me going by always having a fanny of oatmeal and water waiting for me to drink at the end. As one drank it it used to run out of your shoes. It used to take me about an hour to come round to normal sometimes. I used to rest in the flats where it was cool. On occasions one would shiver up in the heat and get spots before your eyes. Anyway I settled down and accepted it all as part of my duty.

Dick Greenwood has similar recollections:

I joined *Eagle* in August 1939 and quite a number of the stokers' branch were 2nd class and, of course, it was their first time abroad, and especially in the tropics. Still, it then being peace-time we should have, as a new commission, gone on a winter's cruise to become familiar with the ship. But events proved otherwise and we set sail to Singapore with the war clouds very dark indeed. Arriving at Singapore naval base, we all had to assemble on the flight deck to be told by the captain to have a look and see who the captain was and that the cruise would not take place because war was imminent.

At about 1800 the decks were cleared again with this news

and we had to proceed to sea. From then on it was all sea time in the Indian Ocean and the fresh young stokers were falling over like ninepins. No one could be spared. Each time we put into Colombo after days at sea six boilers had to be cleaned. The doors were knocked down immediately, the boilers were blown down and one crawled into the red hot steam drums to clean tubes, burning our exposed bare skin. Then, once the boilers had been cleaned, box everything up and away again.

The sick bay was full of stokers and when I collapsed on the first watch in the boiler room I remember looking up from the deck where I had fainted with faces looking down at me without an ounce of sympathy especially from the stoker who had been called from the messdeck to take my place! I had to get myself to the sick bay as best I could being sick and feeling feverish. The sick bay was full and I was told to go right back to the stokers' deck for my hammock. How I did this with a stoker holding me up I can't think. The stoker wouldn't attempt to carry the hammock for me of course. Then I did not have the energy to sling it when I got there and collapsed on a stool.

No help or advice was given us young stokers; all the engine room and boiler crews were in the same boat. The upper deck commander at one stage decided to go down to the boiler room and see for himself why so many were going sick. He came down one forenoon watch, down the lift, with the chief Buffer trailing behind him in their beautiful white tropical rigs. They walked down three of the 21 boilers we had, away from me because I was tending the first two boilers from the lift base. He came back looking altogether different. They shot back into the lift smothered with blobs of oil raining down from the worn-out bearings of the force draft fans way above. The commander, who was a very nice humane person, gave me a sympathetic smile as he flew past me with the black-bearded Buffer trying to beat him out. In this particular boiler room, one of four, we all used to come off watch smothered in oil and sweat. Incidentally the commander was promoted to captain when we reached the Mediterranean and took command of one of the anti-aircraft cruisers. He was killed on her bridge in the Battle for Crete.

Their stay in harbour this time was for four days and then they were off once more. This time they sailed in company with the

light cruisers *Dauntless* and *Durban*. This mission took them
back eastward across the Indian Ocean once more; they passed
the Nicobar Islands on Monday, 30 October. Air patrols
continued and at 0715 on the Wednesday morning one of the
Swordfish had a mishap and was forced to land in the water. All
the crew were picked up unhurt, however, and the squadron
reached the great Singapore Naval base at midday on 1
November. Next morning at 0730 the carrier went into the
floating dock there, and remained there until 2330 on
Saturday.

The *Eagle* remained at anchor in Singapore harbour until
1600 on 8 November when she sailed in company with the
Australian light cruiser *Hobart* to Colombo, which they reached
at 0800 on 12 November after an uneventful passage. A quick
refuelling then off again with *Dorsetshire* and *Cornwall* at 0930
on the Monday, with another 6-inch sub-calibre shoot being
conducted on the way out to sea. Again their patrol took them
down to the Maldive Islands, but this time it was to call, for they
dropped anchor off Mahe at 1740 on Wednesday, 15
November. One of *Eagle*'s crew observed:

> *Cornwall* and *Dorsetshire* have been winding their way in and
> out of the Islands all day. This is a strange sight from a
> distance as the cruisers are taller than most of the land.

They sailed from the Maldives at 2130 that evening and carried
out a night encounter exercise with their two companions firing
star shells in a spectacular display. The whole of Force 'I' was
back at Colombo at 0800 on Saturday, 18 November. On 23
November *Eagle* was at Colombo with Force 'I' and she and her
two heavy cruisers sailed in company with the Australian
destroyer *Waterhen* at 0800 on 25 November to meet and escort
a French convoy coming into Colombo. The presence of the
destroyer was welcomed, especially by the crew of another
Swordfish which was forced to ditch some six miles from the
carrier at 1040 on 27 November. All the aircraft were picked
up by the *Waterhen* and transferred back on board safely.

The whole force was steering towards Madagascar at this
time in an intensive search for a suspected raider. With both
the pocket battleships *Admiral Graf Spee* and *Admiral Scheer*
rumoured to be at large, tension was high that a fight could
result. This tension was further screwed up a notch or two
when a report was received of some suspicious activities taking

place in the Chagos Islands a few days earlier. The squadron turned south on Friday, 1 December to investigate. Next day *Eagle* flew off sixteen air searches to scour the Chagos Archipelago thoroughly for any raiders that might be lurking there among the islands, but nothing was seen. After checking out this area Force 'I' made course towards Madagascar once again and on Sunday, 3 December, *Dorsetshire* was detached to Mauritius.

Again tropical storms provided difficulties, especially for the aircrew in their frail struts and fabric biplanes out in the vastness of the southern ocean. Finding their parent flight deck in the thousands of square miles of nothing during periods of storm activity was no sinecure even for the trained and experienced men of *Eagle*'s air group. Two experiences graphically brought home to everyone how small their ship was and how large the ocean.

On Tuesday the normal air searches were flown but two of the aircraft failed to find the ship on their return. There were anxious moments as their fuel ran low and no sight of them was seen from the ships bridge or the flight deck. Eventually a smoke screen was laid down by the ships and both pilots were able to spot this at long range and homed in on it, landing safely. The tropical storms came out of nowhere with a suddenness and fierceness that made them treacherous. The next day the same thing occurred, and one aircraft failed to find the ship at sunset. The ships shone their searchlights into the sky and again smoke was laid. These ruses again, thankfully, proved successful and once more the Swordfish got back aboard in one piece. On 7 December they arrived at Diego Suarez at 1100, and they found the *Gloucester* already there.

On 8 December *Eagle* was in company with both *Gloucester* and *Cornwall* when they sailed at 1100 and on this date she was ordered to sail for Simonstown, South Africa. Here she was to undergo seven days' boiler cleaning. On that date another signal ordered her to proceed instead to Durban to have the job carried out and she duly arrived at the latter port at 1130 on 12 December. Leave was granted and here her boilers were due to be seen to and the barnacles that grow so abundantly in tropical seas were to be scraped from her hull. However, next day, Wednesday, all leave was abruptly cancelled and she sailed at 0815 on 14 December for Cape Town. Whatever prompted this rapid deployment ended as soon as it began when, at 0230 on the Friday, they reversed course and returned to Durban at 21 knots. This time the work was carried out without further alarms and for the next six days the crew was able to explore the wonderful countryside adjacent to the port. Many of the ship's crew were taken to The Valley of a Thousand Hills and similar tourist attractions and were given every hospitality by the friendly South African people. Donald Clist recalled:

> Our next stop was Durban. This was very much looked forward to – after all that had been said and written about the hospitality of the people. It was certainly true and many a heart was broken when it came to the time of leaving. A wonderful climate coupled with such grand friendship made us forget all about trials and hardships of cruising around the oceans in the course of a major war – and the stifling heat. Personally, I did not enjoy very much of shore time – yes, the hard-pressed scribes again! – thanks to a Board of Enquiry on a couple of lost aircraft.

This much welcomed but the too short break was soon over and at 0630 on Friday, 22 December, *Eagle* was back to work again. She was escorted to sea by *Cornwall* and *Gloucester* and headed for Mauritius to conduct further patrols over the Christmas period. The heavy cruiser was detached on 24 December for the Cape. Christmas Day found them at sea at action stations, not the happiest of Christmas Days for the bulk of her crew. On Boxing Day she put into Port Louis, Mauritius, at 0615 but this was merely to oil and collect mail and they sailed the same day, again with the *Gloucester*, heading for the Seychelles Islands. On 27 December air searches were flown over the Cargados (Carajos Islands) and next day they searched Cortivy. 1230 on 29 December found her at anchor in the Seychelles and leave was granted, although both ships were anchored one mile from the shore. Both ships sailed at 0430 on Sunday, 31 December, with Colombo again their destination and they duly arrived there at 1645 on 4 January.

One of the first signals received by *Eagle* following this Christmas break was early notice that she was to act as escort for convoy US1 during its passage from Colombo to Aden. The carrier duly proceeded to Colombo and here she joined forces with the battleship *Ramillies* and other escorts. An eyewitness recorded that:

Colombo harbour is full of ships from all countries and the harbour is very congested. HMS *Kent* (a heavy cruiser), submarine *P.84* (HMS *Odin*) and the French cruiser *Suffren* which has just come out of dry dock are also here. *Eagle* was attached to 5th Cruiser Squadron but is now attached to 4th Cruiser Squadron. *Sussex* (heavy cruiser) is most likely to join us.

The latter in fact arrived the next day with the C-in-C East Indies' flag flying. He duly announced he would be inspecting the *Eagle* the next day which was a prompt for a load of bull all over the ship! Meanwhile *Gloucester* went into dry dock and *Kent* sailed on 8 January, her place being taken by *Hobart* which arrived on 10 January. Another arrival to join this impressive concentration was the light cruiser *Birmingham* which had come west from the far distant China Station but she only put in to refuel at 0930 and had sailed again for the UK by 1800 as had the AMC *Carthage*.

*Eagle* herself sailed from Colombo in company with *Sussex* and *Hobart* at 0645 on Monday, 15 January, for a patrol south of the island. Another full-calibre shoot of the 6-inch guns was conducted two days later and they were back at Colombo later the same day. Here they remained until 25 January when in company with the same two cruisers they sailed for Trincomalee which was reached at 1555 on 26 January.

They remained at Trincomalee for five days during which time the *Sussex* sailed east to meet the Australian troop convoy. *Eagle* only made one brief excursion at 0830 on 29 January to land on one of her aircraft which had flown ashore several days earlier. They were back in harbour by 1045. That night an amphibian aircraft from the cruiser *Hobart* carried out a night bombing exercise over the port which kept everyone alert (and awake!).

At 0725 on the last day of the month *Eagle* and *Hobart* sailed and the next day they rendezvoused with the French cruiser *Suffren* and the *Sussex* and soon after the top hamper of the battleship *Ramillies* hove into view. She and the heavy cruiser *Kent* were escorting the convoy which consisted of twelve large liners packed to the gunnels with Australian soldiers. The full list of the liners was:

*Strathaird* (22,284 tons, P & O); *Strathnayer* (22,283 tons, P & O); *Orion* (23,371 tons, Orient); *Orcades* (23,371 tons, Orient);

*Orford*, (20,043 tons, Orient); *Otranto* (20,026 tons, Orient);
*Empress of Canada* (21,517 tons, CPR); *Empress of Japan* (26,032
tons, CPR); *Athos II* (15,276 tons, Fr.MM); *Rangitata* (16,737
tons, NZS Co); *Dunera* (11,162 tons, B.I) and *Sobieski*, a Polish
liner. They made a brave sight. Where, one wonders, could one
raise a fraction of such an assembly nowadays to transport a
whole division of troops in just one convoy?

As *Eagle* and *Hobart* joined the escort so *Kent* and *Suffolk*
returned to Ceylon to refuel. The whole assembly, convoy and
heavy escort (one battleship, one aircraft carrier, three heavy
cruisers, one light cruiser), then proceeded west without incident for the next few days. Their destination was Aden and then
up the gulf to Suez and the Middle East. On Saturday, 3
February, at 1715 in the afternoon, *Eagle* herself cruised up and
down the lines of the convoy at the request of the Australian
troops who had never seen an aircraft carrier close up before.
Her Royal Marine band played on the flight deck and she was
met with loud cheers as each liner passed by. This 'review' lasted
45 minutes and was much appreciated by both sides.

Next day another Swordfish had to make a forced landing a
few miles out from the convoy but again the crew were rescued
safely by the returning *Sussex*. On 6 February an additional
escort joined the convoy; this was the destroyer *Westcott* on her
way home from the China Station. She refuelled underway from
the *Sussex*. Otherwise their passage proved uneventful and they
reached Aden safely at 1800 on 8 February 1940 while the
convoy carried on to Port Suez.

By the time they reached Aden *Eagle*'s aircraft had searched
365,150 square miles between 1 January and 10 February and
since the outbreak of the war the ship herself had steamed
34,889 sea miles. With these types of mileages being notched up
the old lady began to show her age, as Donald Clist recalls:

> After so much steaming our engines began to misbehave and
> also the fresh water evaporators did not operate to their full
> extent – consequently we were restricted with our fresh
> water supplies. The fresh water was switched on first thing in
> the morning for about one hour and about the same period
> in the Dog Watches only.

One can imagine what that meant to conditions aboard in
the tropics! *Eagle* herself sailed from Suez at 0430 on 9 February
and carried out a patrol in the Gulf of Aden the same

day with the destroyer *Westcott* covering the ships of Group 2 of US1 for the final leg of their journey. *Eagle* returned to Aden at 1715 that afternoon. The same routine was repeated the following day after which she remained in harbour with *Ramillies* and *Hobart* until Saturday, 17 February, when she sailed in company with *Sussex* for Colombo having, on 13 February, been instructed to resume her duties with Force 'I'. The proven usefulness of this type of warship, and the loss of the carrier *Courageous* early in the war, meant that aircraft carriers were in constant demand, even old aircraft carriers. On 21 February it was proposed that *Eagle* sail for home waters where there was much pressure on the Home Fleet. It was further proposed on 25 February, the day she arrived back once again at Colombo, that *Eagle* be sent to replace the heavy cruiser *Kent* as escort for the second Australian troop convoy, US2.

They anchored at Colombo along with *Ramillies* and *Hobart* until 0800 on Tuesday, 5 March, carrying out a full calibre shoot of her 6-inch guns on the way out as usual. Next day, while at anchor off Trincomalee, signals were received that *Eagle* should continue operating in the Ceylon area with Force 'I' for six days more and on 12 March would be detached to Singapore naval base for docking. On completion of this much-needed refit she would probably be required to escort convoy US2 from Fremantle, Australia, to Aden. However fate decreed otherwise.

After swinging round the buoy at Trinco, *Eagle* sailed with *Hobart* for Singapore at 0930 on 12 March. A report was received of a suspicious vessel in the southern part of the Bay of Bengal and *Eagle* was sent to investigate.

On the afternoon of 14 March, while steaming eastward and passing between the island of Pulo Rondo and the Nicobar Islands, ready-use 250 lb bombs were being struck down, boxed and fused, in their bomb room. These bomb rooms consisted of three upper rooms, D, E and F from port to starboard in that order, between stations 178 and 189, and the engine room and boiler rooms. These three rooms were connected by doors. Underneath these three bomb rooms were, from port to starboard, the firework magazine, B and C bomb rooms and the 4 inch shell magazine.

There were handling rooms above D and F rooms on port and starboard sides respectively and these connected with the hangar (via the bomb lifts), the mess deck (through a watertight door) and the flight deck (through a trunk on the starboard side only).

The 250 lb bombs were stowed in D bomb room and the route used to strike them down was from flight deck by whip through vertical trunk to the starboard handling room; thence by second whip from starboard handling room to F bomb room. Across F and E rooms to D.

The ratings handling the bombs in handling and bomb rooms consisted of two leading seamen and ten able seamen under the charge of Mr R.R. Keech, MVD the ship's gunner. The exact stationing of these men at the time was not known but the majority would have been in the bomb rooms handling the bombs across from F through E to D room. Some would have been in the starboard handling room.

Just after 1400 a loud explosion was heard throughout the ship, and smoke and fumes were at once seen coming up the trunk on to the flight deck and out of the hangar on to the quarterdeck. Simultaneously a flash from the upper bomb rooms came up through the port handling room. This flash vented into the port side of the hangar via the port bomb lift, setting fire to a wing of one of the Swordfish there and thence on to the mess deck through the watertight door, injuring some ratings, four of them seriously, one of whom later died.

Immediately all bomb rooms and the firework and 4 inch magazines which formed one magazine group, were flooded. At the same time the hangar was completely sprayed, extinguishing the fire in the wing of the burning aircraft. Two Swordfish which happened to be in D hangar were pulled out in time to avoid the effects of the chemical spray. The heat in and around the bomb room area was intense and the ship's company were sent to general fire quarters at once.

Once the heat had subsided as a result of the flooding and it became clear that the fire danger was over, pumping out of the flooded compartments commenced usng a portable submersible pump placed in the telephone exchange. At 1630 the ship's company were mustered and the number killed, all of whom were in the bomb rooms or starboard handling room – Mr Keech, two leading seamen and ten able seamen, was established.

Some graphic eyewitness memoirs of this ghastly accident illustrate its seriousness. Perhaps E. Kenward was one of the luckiest men during this tragedy, as he told me:

We were ordered to put all the ready-use bombs into the magazine in readiness for us entering dry dock at Singapore. I was actually one of those in the magazine striking down the bombs into the bomb room. Because of the intense heat we were only able to stay in the bomb room for a fairly brief period at any one time and my turn came for a rest. On returning to my messdeck almost immediately the fire bells sounded. On rushing to the hangar, which seemed to be on fire, I was told that a bomb had exploded in the bomb room. The tragic outcome was that some fourteen of my shipmates were killed and if my memory is correct nine were from my mess alone, along with several injured. The dead were buried at sea off Singapore.

Donald Clist:

We had been at sea only two days – we were then in the vicinity of Pulo Rondo and the Nicobar Islands – when a mysterious explosion was heard at 1345 – everyone was at that time enjoying their afternoon rest. Each department was called upon to report any incident because no one had reported an actual mishap. The engine room reported that the source appeared to be close by them. Immediately an investigation was carried out amidships in the bomb rooms. In the meantime one of the officers on duty on the bridge saw a rating, covered in smoke and his clothes burning running headlong for the bows of the ship – obviously with the idea of jumping overboard. This turned out to be Chief Petty Officer Strudwick and he had been in charge of the gunner's party striking down 250 lb bombs after the aircraft had landed.

The whole of the ship's company was cleared with the exception of engine room and W/T department ratings who were actually on watch for mustering on the flight deck. It was quickly ascertained that fourteen members of the gunner's party were missing, including the officer in charge. A hush descended throughout the ship when it was announced that the safety of the ship had been endangered by this explosion – it was too early as yet to investigate the effect it had had below.

At 1800 that day, a party of volunteers, actually the remainder of the gunner's party, made their way towards the bomb room. Remember the state of affairs down there was not known, the ship alone in tropical waters, there were no lights in the bomb room area and hundreds of gallons of sea water were also in the compartments (as soon as any excess heat or untoward disturbance occurred in a bomb room, automatic water sprinklers came on until switched off by hand). Therefore, with just swimming trunks this party commenced to go below. Pumping out operations at a slow pace was also commenced. This operation continued throughout the night. The bodies and remains of other bodies were brought up on deck and the sailmaker commenced the gruesome duty of covering them up and sewing them in separate 'bundles'. Burial at sea took place the following afternoon.

During the evening, as the pumping continued, a preliminary survey of the damage was undertaken. There was a considerable amount of heavy distortion and piercing of all bulkheads and decks between 178 and 189 stations. This resulted in the Nos. 3 and 4 dynamos being put out of action. The turbo bilge pump in D boiler room was put out of action likewise by splinters. The damage to all the aircraft save one was slight. All were tested and found fit to fly ashore on arrival at Singapore. Flying had to be discontinued on the afternoon of the accident but aircraft were able to fly anti-submarine patrols during the following day, and one aircraft was used to take messages to the naval Officer in Charge at Penang for onward transmission to avoid the ship breaking wireless silence.

However, if some aircraft were OK their radio sets did not survive their immersion in the spray nor was their electrical wiring totally immune and all required careful checking once ashore.

It was hard to establish the cause of the accident with any total certainty but a Board of Enquiry later made the following findings. There was a hole a few feet away from the landing place in the deck of F bomb room, and the whole deck of this room was very badly bent downwards. There was little doubt therefore that the 250 lb bomb exploded on landing in the bomb room pointing at a downward angle. These bombs were all boxed and fused, but should have been entirely safe provided that their vanes had not revolved, thus keeping the fuses armed. There were two devices fitted to prevent this happening. A safety pin, taken out before flight and re-inserted after the aircraft had landed back on, and a safety clip, which also prevented the vanes from revolving. The latter remained on during flights and was only extracted, by an electro-magnetic device, when the pilot released the bomb during an attack.

After each flight the bombs were inspected on return and should the safety clip be found not to be in place the bomb was regarded as dangerous and the fuse was lowered overboard. On some rare occasions bombs sustained damage on landing, either through coming off or through the aircraft crashing on deck. On such occasions the bombs were thoroughly inspected and if any doubt existed regarding their safety they were disposed of at once.

The fact remains, however, that this particular 250 lb bomb was in a dangerous state and it was assumed that at some time previously the vanes had revolved. How this could have occurred was impossible to conjecture, nor could any error or fault be traced to any particular person or group. It was one of the war's tragic accidents of which there were so many. But it did highlight the vulnerability of both men and machines operating in combat conditions on what were considered normal routine tasks.

Miraculously the remaining bombs remained stable. One eyewitness described how decks, bulkheads and deckheads were bent up like paper. The bomb room had to be flooded. After three hours the water was pumped out and the dead carried to the forecastle. The ship's spraying system came into action and put out this blaze but, in the process the corrosive chemicals used put almost all the other aircraft out of action and the carrier was reduced to four flyable machines as a result. Other fires were extinguished in under an hour by normal damage control measures and flooding of affected areas. These operated a makeshift round-the-clock anti-submarine patrol as the carrier headed for harbour.

She at once proceeded to Singapore for repairs. Nor was that the end of their woes, as an eyewitness recorded that next day the following sombre scenes took place:

This morning a mass burial was performed on the quarterdeck. The injured ratings are all on the danger case list. One is receiving oxygen. This morning a Swordfish, while landing, partly frayed out the arrestor wire, overshot the flight deck, hit the for'ard pom-pom and crashed into the sea. The crew of three escaped with a few cuts.

*Eagle* arrived at Singapore Naval Base at 0745 on Saturday 16 March, where she docked for a detailed examination and to carry out an enquiry into the cause of the disaster. All the aircraft had been flown ashore and Royal Marine, Fleet Air Arm and RAF personnel were also disembarked. The injured men were put ashore to the base hospital immediately but, at 1800, one of these died there. An eyewitness related later:

> On arrival at Singapore further volunteers were called for to unload the affected bomb room. Numerous splintered bombs remained. Plenty of volunteers came forward and with the assistance and guidance of NASO experts the ship suffered no further damage.

While repairs took place *Eagle* herself had to be relieved from her intended escort duties with US2. One of the most ticklish jobs was removing the remaining potentially dangerous bombs from the affected weapons area, a job for stout hearts and steady hands.

Repairs at Singapore were confirmed on 17 March as being extensive and her earliest completion date for sailing back to war was confirmed as 14 April. Even this gloomy forecast had to be modified next day. The repairs could not commence at all before 21 March and would take an estimated six weeks. The dangerous task of disembarking all remaining bombs at Singapore was completed by 23 march and work proceeded.

The carrier was finally towed into dry dock on Wednesday, 27 March. The bulk of the ship's company was then disembarked and moved in the brand-new barracks, in many cases still not fully completed, known as the Fleet Shore Accommodation (FSA to the ship's company, a play on the more normal SFA and equally appropriate!) While here leave was granted from 1315 to 0700 the following day; most nights and short weekends were granted from 1315 Saturday to 0700 Monday as well. The remaining ship's company at any time were taken to and from the ship as required in lorries each day to carry out repairs, operating duties etc. One AB wrote:

The barracks in which we are living are the first to be built at Singapore. The buildings occupy a very large area; there being nine blocks, three storeys each. There is plenty of recreation to be had as there is a cinema, billiard hall, soda fountain, reading and writing rooms, beer canteen, swimming pool, football and cricket pitches and so on.

On 28 April a signal indicated that *Eagle* might be urgently required in the Mediterranean. Worsening relations with the Fascist Government of Italy, led by that boastful braggart Benito Mussolini, and the cutting off of British coal supplies to that nation, caused the Admiralty to take some cautious early steps to prepare for war in that area. The main Mediterranean Fleet was under the command of Admiral Sir Andrew Cunningham, and based at Alexandria, Egypt. It had been much reduced as the call for its warships in more active zones of combat, especially in Norway, had whittled it down. Reinforcements would have to be brought back from all over the world and the need for a carrier to replace the Med Fleet's own *Glorious*, which had been sent to Norway, meant the need to get *Eagle* back to sea as quickly as possible. The Admiralty therefore instructed that if *Eagle* was in the time-honoured phrase 'in all respects ready for sea', she should be sailed from Singapore to Colombo at the earliest date practicable.

As a consequence the repair work carried out to the carrier was to some extent rushed through in order to get her away to sea again. One eyewitness recorded:

A new 'top' has been fitted to the *Eagle*, cylindrical in shape called a homing beacon which enables aircraft to find the ship if visibility is poor. If aircraft lose their bearings the beacon projects rays which the aircraft pick up, so enabling them to find the ship. Before, if an aircraft lost its direction, the ship and aircraft had to use wireless, thus giving away our position. The beacon does away with that sort of thing.

On Saturday 20 March, *Eagle* was finally taken out of dry dock and placed alongside the dock under the 250 ton crane. But the ship's company remained for another five weeks still at the FSA. Not until Monday, 6 May, was she towed out into midstream and moored. The carrier finally sailed for Colombo at 1400 on 9 May.

She was beset with severe weather conditions on entering the Indian Ocean and monsoon rains were encountered throughout the next few days which made life aboard uncomfortable. Having put into Colombo on 14 May, *Eagle* spent five days there and then proceeded onward. The only incident to enliven her journey westward occurred at 2200 on 1 May when a merchant ship failed to answer *Eagle*'s challenge and was duly shaken up by searchlights *et al*. She turned out to be a very sheepish British vessel! *Eagle* duly arrived at Aden at 1745 on 22 April and sailed at 1900 the same day, proceeding up the Red Sea to Port Said with the cruisers *Gloucester*, *Liverpool* and the Australian *Sydney* in company. It was rumoured that Italy's uncertain attitude might mean unprovoked and surprise submarine attacks at any time, *prior* to any official declaration of war as well as clandestine minelaying to block the canal itself. They were now keeping a stricter watch than hitherto. The heat was recorded as 'almost unbearable' as they proceeded up the Gulf at twenty knots, being 109 degrees in the shade. *Hobart* relieved *Liverpool* on 23 May and both she and *Gloucester* parted company the day after. *Eagle* herself reached Port Suez at 1800 on 26 May, anchored then entered the canal after dark following the *Sydney* as the next day she passed slowly northward through the Suez Canal, reaching Port Said at 1130 on Sunday, 26 May. Next day she was met by the destroyers *Hereward* and *Hero* and escorted to Alexandria which they reached at 1900. Here they joined the Mediterranean Fleet under the inspired and heartening leadership of Admiral Sir Andrew Cunningham.

A new and exciting phase of her wartime life was now to begin.

# CHAPTER THREE

# Eye of the Storm

The harbour at Alexandria was full of ships on the morning of Tuesday, 28 May. One eyewitness from *Eagle* noted in his diary some of the stirring names he could see close by his own vessel: The battleships *Ramillies*, *Warspite*, *Royal Sovereign*, *Malaya* and *Lorraine* (French); the cruisers *Sydney* (Australian), *Leander* (New Zealand), *Gloucester*, *Liverpool* and *Orion*; depot ships *Resource* and *Medway*, and hordes of destroyers including *Diamond*, *Dainty*, *Decoy*, *Voyager*, *Vampire*, *Mohawk*, *Jervis* and *Janus* to name but those immediately visible, along with minesweepers, submarines, patrol vessels and MTBs. The *Eagle's* days of lonely voyaging with either no companions or just the odd cruiser for company were clearly over for the time being. On 26 May the C-in-C had signalled that *Eagle* would be administered by RA 1st BS (Rear-Admiral in Command, 1st Battle Squadron). There was an expectant feeling running through the fleet as Mussolini dithered and fussed. Everyone knew that, with France and the Low Countries down and out and Great Britain seemingly on the ropes, the Duce would grab his chance to cash in on Hitler's victories without too much effort on his own part. The question was: when would he jump?

While they waited they prepared. The Italians had a large modern fleet, with four old battleships which had been modernised and four brand new battleships just completing, all of which had a huge margin of speed over Cunningham's veterans, all of which dated back to before Jutland! *Eagle* was the only carrier and many so-called 'experts' had predicted that no carrier could survive in the Mediterranean in the face of the thousands of long-range bombers and torpedo aircraft the Regia Aeronautica could deploy. Admiral Cunningham thought otherwise. The enemy also outnumbered him in heavy cruisers (twelve and he had none), light cruisers (two to one), destroyers (by more than four to one) and had a huge submarine fleet (larger than Germany's). However none of this overawed the British matelot or their indomitable leader. All were 'burning to get at the enemy' and, in Cunningham's words, 'to test the flavour of the ice cream!'

Leave was granted between 1330 and 2200 each day between 28 May and Sunday, 2 June, but on Monday, 3 June, *Eagle* sailed in company with the fleet flagship *Warspite*, battleships *Malaya*, *Royal Sovereign* and *Lorraine*, and destroyers to carry out combined manoeuvres. The carrier herself carried out a full 6-inch calibre shoot and the whole force returned to harbour at 1800.

Next day they sailed once more at 0730 and carried out HA (High Angle 4-inch anti-aircraft) and pom-pom (multiple 2pdr anti-aircraft) practice against a drogue target. No 813 Squadron's Swordfish had taken up depot at Dekheila airfield (known as HMS *Glebe*) from 21 May and a few of them landed aboard this day. Telegraphist Air Gunner 'Ginger' Tyler recalls life for the air crews ashore in Egypt in the waiting period:

Commanding in the Eastern Mediterranean was Admiral Sir Andrew Cunningham, 'Cutts' to the lower deck, flying his flag in the recently modernised *Warspite*.

The local airfield at Dekheila had been prepared, and soon we and the aircraft were established there whilst the ship remained in harbour. While based ashore our squadrons carried out training in dive bombing and torpedo attacks, and carried out all the usual services for the fleet, such as towing targets for high angle AA firing and close-range pom-pom shoots.

For some reason I had been saddled with the target-towing job, whenever this was required, flying mainly with Lieutenant (A) Drummond. He had a very short temper and was prone to venting his anger when things were going badly by pushing and pulling on his control column so that I was often thrown about in the back of the aircraft and unable to do my job. On one occasion whilst towing the sleeve with all seven thousand feet of wire reeled out, I had to give him a real, fruity blast through the speaking tube, to 'Get on and do your job properly'. Strange to say he complied, and ever after, while I was flying with him, he was quite subdued.

Having had so much practice, whenever dropping the

sleeve on *Eagle*'s flight deck, I was able to place it right down the forward ift on most occasions.

Life ashore at Dekheila proved to be somewhat irksome, we were accommodated in a tented camp, and had a large marquee as a mess and canteen. Millions of flies swarmed around the area and made conditions very trying. Dust and sand crept into our clothes, our food and into our beds, but we shrugged off the inconveniences, and had some very hilarious times while we were there.

All was now ready and final preparations made. *Eagle* lay waiting events until the expected announcement of Italy's entry into the conflict came.

Cunningham, despite Churchill's doubts, determined on taking the offensive immediately according to long drawn-up plans. At 1840 on 10 June *Eagle* had left Alexandria but she returned at 2330, refuelled and at 0215 next morning, in company with the *Warspite* (flag), *Malaya* and destroyers *Nubian*, *Janus*, *Juno*, *Ilex*, *Hasty*, *Dainty*, *Stuart*, *Voyager* and *Vampire*, proceeded to sea preceded by the five cruisers of the 7th CS (Cruiser Squadron), heading for a position approximately 80 miles south of Cape Matapan, Greece, to effect a concentration in the central basin ready to take the war to the Italian fleet. Hostilities officially commenced at 1010, 11 June (0001 BST, British Standard Time). At 1800 the *Stuart*, *Voyager* and *Vampire* of the Australian flotilla were replaced by the *Havock*, *Hero*, *Hereward*, *Hostile*, *Hyperion* and *Imperial*. They steered north-west and then along the south coast of Crete to reach a position approximately 80 miles south of Cape Matapan at 1200/12.

They were to the south of Crete during the next day and *Eagle*'s aircraft conducted intensive searches for enemy shipping without making any sightings. Petrol consumed during these patrols amounted to 3,200 gallons. A rendezvous was made here with the 7th Cruiser Squadron returning from an attack on enemy patrols off Benghazi and Tobruk, during which they had sunk an Italian gunboat. The cruisers, except for *Neptune*, were then sent on ahead at 1230 to conduct a sweep of their own up to a point 120 miles south-east of Cape Santa Maria di Leuca, while the fleet provided them with cover which continued on a north-westerly course at 16 knots to a position south-west of Zante. The fleet altered course at 2345 and the cruisers rejoined at midday on 13 June when just west of Crete.

The first shock of war came in the early hours of Thursday and it was first blood to the Italians. A submarine penetrated the destroyer screen and torpedoed the light cruiser *Calypso* at 0230. She was able to carry on until 0430 but then had to be abandoned and sunk. A destroyer went alongside her and rescued the bulk of the crew but 38 ratings had been killed. It was a nasty shock but fortunately the Italian submarines were rarely as efficient as that athough by no means to be despised.

During the afternoon of 13 June the cruisers were again detached for an eastward sweep along the North African coast and they again rejoined at 1530 next day when the fleet returned to harbour at 1845 on 14 June. They were led in by the 2nd DF (Destroyer Flotilla) using their TSDS (two speed destroyer sweeps, high speed minesweeps). *Eagle* remained at Alexandria until 21 June, when they had their first air raid.

On 20 June it was proposed that some Fairey Swordfish TSR aircraft based at Malta might form a useful reserve for *Eagle*'s limited striking force. Clearly there was also a striking requirement for fighter aircraft to defend the fleet while at sea also. Few were available but three Gloster Sea Gladiator biplanes were eventually found crated at Dekheila and were duly embarked. Volunteers from the Swordfish crew for 'fighter' pilots were answered and led by the Commander (Flying) Commander L.P. Keighley-Peach; a total of four pilots was found. Practice began on interceptions. The standard Italian heavy bomber, the three-engined Savoia-Marchetti SM79, flew in close formations at a great height and bombed in patterns on the command of their leaders. At the enormous heights they flew they were little troubled by AA fire from the ships, nor did the Gladiators have the performance to reach them without a great deal of warning. However by trial and error lessons were learnt and by positioning the Gladiators in good time a few surprises were to be delivered to the hitherto complacent Italian aircrew in the days ahead.

TAG Tyler had an airborne view of one of these Gladiator 'kills', as he relates.

On the following morning I went off with my usual pilot and observer, Leatham and Grieve. As we climbed through a thin layer of early morning haze, there, right on our starboard beam, about three miles aways was a huge Cant reconnaissance seaplane. Pointing out the target to the observer, I immediately rattled off a brief sighting report on the radio. This completed, I stood up and readied my gun for possible action. We were heading at top speed for the Cant, but within what appeared to be just a few seconds, one of *Eagle*'s Gladiators streaked by and immediately tore into action. The Italians didn't know what hit them, and soon they were spiralling down into the sea trailing a great black plume of smoke.

Keighley-Peach had done it again, and hopefully the shadower had been downed before he had time to signal our position back to his base. But it was wishful thinking on our part, for, from about eleven o'clock in the forenoon until about six in the evening the fleet was subjected to ten more bombing attacks, again without suffering any damage or casualties.

During one air attack I was lucky enough to be in the air, on anti-submarine patrol just ahead of the fleet. Suddenly we saw the guns of the fleet open up, and we watched fascinated as a mass of bombs burst all around the old *Eagle*. The ship was completely blanketed by huge waterspouts as the bombs burst, and it looked certain that she was at last to catch a packet, but no; as the water towers cleared, there she was again. She seemed to have a charmed life.

We had another aircrew casualty on 1 August, when we were at sea just outside Alexandria for a practice shoot. 824 Squadron was ranged on the flight deck with engines running, waiting to take off on a dawn patrol. The front machine, with a faulty engine, had to be taxied to the forward lift, and as the observer and TAG were getting out to transfer to another machine, the pilot revved up his engine to move. The slipstream caught the TAG, Goodyear, and blew him into the airscrew of the next aircraft. He was terribly injured and died in the sick bay about one hour later.

Fortunately the Italian air forces' addiction to altitude bombing of ships under way at sea was to prove as abortive as similar methods practised by the RAF. The arrival of the German dive bombers immediately changed things for the worse, for they hit what they aimed at, but at this period they were busy finishing off France and attacking the evacuation ships in the English

Channel, so high-level bombing was all the British ships had to face most of the time. This could be very accurate but the chances of a bomb actually hitting such a small target were remote indeed.

The next move came on the afternoon of 22 June when the *Eagle* put to sea at 1700 followed three hours later by battleships *Royal Sovereign*, *Ramillies* and destroyers to conduct operation BQ, a sweep in force in the area between southern Italy and Libya with a possible night bombardment of Port Augusta and a raid into the Straits of Messina coupled with the sailing of a convoy from Malta to Alexandria. However, the Admiralty got cold feet and ordered the operation to be deferred and Cunningham therefore signalled the ships to return to harbour, *Eagle* arriving early on 23 June.

At 1230 on Friday, 28 June, saw *Eagle* sailing again in company with the battleships *Ramillies* and *Royal Sovereign* with a screen of seven destroyers: *Hyperion*, *Havock*, *Hero*, *Hereward*, *Hasty*, *Juno*, and *Janus* as Force 'B'. This sortie was to cover convoy AS1 from the Aegean Sea to Alexandria and Port Said and also one from Malta to Alexandria. The 7th Cruiser Squadron was already at sea on offensive sweeps and clashed with Italian destroyers that afternoon. This caused the Malta convoy to be cancelled again.

*Eagle* again patrolled south of Crete during the next two days. At 1230 she was 50 miles south-west of Gavdhos Island, and during the following night course was shaped well to the south of Vallera. Again the presence of Italian submarines was widespread. Many were detected and attacked on 29 June. In the morning one of the anti-submarine patrols spotted and bombed the submarine *Argonauta* which was destroyed. Another, *Uebi Scebeli*, was sunk by the destroyers *Dainty* and *Ilex* at 1230 and several more depth-charged as the fleet cruised to the most westerly point of Crete before returning eastward. The whole force returned to Alexandria from the west at 1015 on 2 July.

Meanwhile France was in her death agonies and seeking a separate peace despite the original binding Allied treaties. What the fate of the French fleet was to be under control of Mussolini and Hitler was uncertain. The French Admiral Darlan trusted the dictators' word that they would not be taken over, but Britain did not have quite so much simple faith in the words of such men. She intended to keep fighting and was prepared to use force to make sure that the already heavy odds against her were not made greater by the French warships sailing under the Axis flags.

At Alexandria this involved patient and careful negotiations between Admiral Cunningham and the French Admiral Godfroy. The latter refused to continue the fight against the occupiers of his country but was persuaded not to use force against his former friends. It was a tense period, made worse when at Mers-el-Kebir at the other end of the Mediterranean, Admiral Somerville's Force 'H' was forced to open fire and sink several of the French ships based there.

In anticipation of the worst, all leave was cancelled, and three British destroyers were deployed across the mouth of the harbour with torpedo tubes loaded and ready to block any attempt at a break-out. The *Malaya* dropped anchor across the bows of the French battleship *Lorraine*, and *Warspite*, *Royal Sovereign*, *Ramillies* and *Eagle* also trained their heaviest guns on the French ships at point-blank range. The French did likewise. Not until a compromise was reached, in which the French landed the breech blocks of their guns and discharged their oil fuel to demilitarise themselves, could the British relax. The bulk of the French sailors elected for a return to France leaving behind but a skeleton crew on each of their ships.

On 5 July there was a combined Fleet Air Arm and RAF attack on the Italian supply port of Tobruk on the North African coast. No.813 Squadron was to carry out a dusk torpedo attack on warships and shipping in the port while the RAF carried out a general bombing of the fortress facilities. All nine of the squadron's Swordfish had been disembarked to operate from desert air strips in support of the Army. This operation was duly carried out with great panache and skill. Seven of the aircraft were able to launch their torpedoes against targets in the harbour and hit four ships. The Italian destroyer *Zeffiro* was torpedoed and sunk as was the liner *Liguria* (15000 tons), while the other hit blew the bows off the *Euro* which had to be towed to Taranto for repairs. The freighter *Manzoni* was also torpedoed and sunk and two other merchant ships damaged and beached. But this was just a warm up.

Two days later *Eagle* took part in Operation MA5. The fleet sailed in three groups and she was part of Force 'C' along with battleships *Royal Sovereign* (Flag) and *Malaya*, and destroyers

*Hyperion, Hostile, Hasty, Ilex, Imperial, Dainty, Defender, Juno, Janus, Vampire,* and *Voyager* which left harbour between 1320 and 1445, *Warspite* having gone on ahead. The whole fleet was out to cover various convoy movements to and from Malta. So was the Italian fleet, consisting of two battleships, sixteen cruisers and 32 destroyers, covering their own convoys to Libya. Neither was initially aware of the other and this led to the first full-scale clash between the two fleets at the Battle of Calabria.

They passed south of Crete once more on 8 July, but this time did not turn back. The enemy air force quickly found them and mounted attack after attack. By 1820 that evening *Eagle* had come through three high altitude attacks unscathed but badly shaken. Heavy bombs had fallen within yards of her old hull, and bomb splinters and shrapnel came across the flight deck like rain sometimes. The 4 inch guns barked away ceaselessly but the enemy were but tiny silver specks high in the cloudless sky and did not seem inconvenienced by them. Submarine alarms were also constant and the Swordfish and destroyers made counter-attacks while the fleet changed course.

It was a similar story on 9 July with the bombing continuing as the two fleet drew close together. Here, for the first time, the young Fleet Air Arm pilots of Nos. 813 and 824 Squadrons showed their mettle in a full blooded fleet action. They followed the many peacetime practices that had occupied the torpedo bomber aircrew for hours in the 1930s. The reconnaissance of the enemy fleet and regular reporting of its composition, size, speed and course, was done by 813 Squadron, while the initial torpedo striking force, twice sent off to try to hit and slow down the two reluctant enemy battleships so that the slower British heavy ships could bring them to battle, were conducted most gallantly by 824 Squadron's nine machines.

The first launch was at 1145 when it was decided to despatch a torpedo bomber striking force to slow them down so that the British battleships could bring them to fight. Nine Swordfish were launched at this time from *Eagle*. Each was armed with a single torpedo. The launch position was about 90 miles from the last reported position of the Italian fleet but this took them an hour to cover, by which time the position was widely inaccurate as the enemy had in the interim reversed course and the shadowing aircraft had lost touch.

Commander John B. Murray gave me this graphic account of the opening moves in their search:

Briefing for the attack was elementary as far as I remember; it just reiterated the standard squadron attack, which was to approach the target at reasonable height, about 8,000 ft., split into three sub-flights when in position, and coordinate the attack so that each sub-flight made its final dive to dropping positions from a different sector on the target at the same time. This procedure had been practised *ad infinitum* over the years, always against a specified target ship.

In the event we took off in brilliant cloudless weather with unlimited visibility, possibly 50 or so miles from the Italian fleet, and clambered laboriously to gain sufficient height (a Swordfish with a torpedo climbs very slowly at about 60 knots).

Nonetheless the Swordfish did stumble on the rear elements of the Italian fleet at 1252, consisting of two 8 inch cruiser divisions and their escorting destroyers. Throughout the approach these big cruisers were mistaken by the airmen for the main battleship force of the enemy. The striking force worked its way round steadily to a favourable attacking position but the difference in their relative speeds was only about 60 mph and it took a long time. Not until 1315 were the torpedo bombers ready to go in against what they still thought to be the enemy capital ships. Commander Murray:

The final dropping conditions were a height of 50 feet, a range of 1,000 yards and a maximum speed of 90 knots. To achieve these conditions after a near vertical dive from 8-10,000 ft required practice: too low was dangerous, too fast and the torpedo would not enter the water correctly and would not run properly and too high would again cause damage to the torpedoes.

A heavy flak barrage was encountered by the Italian vessels through which the old 'Stringbags' flew with their usual incredible immunity. The Italians reported that the British biplanes came in at heights of about 80 feet, dropping their torpedoes at ranges of around 3,000 feet. It was the large cruisers *Fiume, Pola, Trieste*, and *Zara* that were the main objects of their attack. The nine torpedoes were launched about equally against all these ships.

Aboard the *Pola* one of the Italian admirals described the attack thus:

Two of the aircraft made a determined effort to attack the head of our line, coming up from astern, and one of these, having penetrated our destroyer screen and avoided the fire of all our escort, unleashed a torpedo in a beautiful manoeuvre against the *Pola* from the left at an angle of about 70 degrees, and at a distance of between 1,000 to 1,500 metres.

The cruiser turned hard left at full power, engaging this aircraft with every gun which could be brought to bear. Commander Murray recalled that:

The Italians put up a heavy barrage well before we were in range and kept this up during the approach and dive to dropping position. I think we were all a bit confused with the large number of enemy ships, and this no doubt led to aircraft attacking different targets instead of concentrating on one specific ship. Low down on the water at 50 feet the barrage was very heavy and came from all angles as we were by then in the middle of the fleet. One factor which disturbed our aim was the disturbing use by the enemy ships of their main armaments firing at very low angle, the splashes made by these projectiles was most disconcerting.

Other Italian accounts pay due tribute to the bravery and gallantry of the attacking Swordfish crews, but every one of their torpedoes was avoided and not a single cruiser was so much as scratched. The Swordfish bore equally charmed lives and all returned safely to the *Eagle* by 1434 that afternoon.

A second nine-plane striking force was readied and despatched from the *Eagle* arriving over the Italian ships at 1545. Once again they mistook the heavy cruisers, now leading the Italian fleet which was retiring at high speed and being chased by the *Warspite*. She had scored one hit on the enemy flagship and was looking to land a few more. These Italian cruisers were fully engaged with their British opposite numbers with their main guns firing full astern, but their flak guns switched to the Swordfish and laid down another heavy barrage. All the torpedo bombers penetrated this and launched from the starboard bow and beam of the leading enemy ship at close range. From splashes and spray they were convinced that at least one torpedo had hit home on this ship, which they identified as a *Bolzano* Class cruiser.

Their target was in fact the name ship itself, which was leading the line of the 3rd Cruiser Division. She reported the Swordfish making their attack between 1610 and 1615 and only violent jinking at high speed enabled her to avoid all the many missiles aimed at her, a good piece of seamanship indeed. She claimed to have destroyed two of her attackers in return and other cruisers made similar claims but once more the Swordfish came through the wall of flak bursts unscathed and all returned safely to the carrier.

Commander Murray summed up to me the feelings of the young pilots after the two strikes had failed to achieve their objectives: 'Looking back, it does seem that we failed miserably, but it was the first time that we had experienced anything quite like it. A Swordfish is a slow aeroplane.'

It was thought that they had scored one hit on a cruiser but this was not so.

Although the enemy was chased to within a few miles of his own coastline and *Warspite* scored a hit with a single 15-inch shell at extreme range, and the British cruisers damaged the heavy cruiser *Bolzano*, the enemy managed to escape and gain the shelter of his ports.

Their fleet would not fight but their bombers were relentless and unending in their attempts to redress the balance. Non-stop altitude bombing continued for three days and many near-misses were recorded on most of the major ships. Fortunately from the hundreds of bombs aimed at the fleet only one hit; the cruiser *Gloucester* was damaged on her bridge the day before the battle, but she kept with the fleet and acted as *Eagle*'s close escort during the surface action. One eyewitness recorded in his diary:

While this engagement lasted, Italian bombers made desperate attempts to sink our ships; the *Eagle* seems to be the main objective. Our own aircraft have given the Italians something to think about so it is definitely us they are trying for. During yesterday's attacks *Gloucester* was hit with a bomb on the bridge. The damage sustained was enough to keep her out of the present surface action. Like the *Eagle* she stayed well to the rear and being so close to us, nearly had another salvo of bombs on her decks! We are now cruising close to the Italian coast waiting to see if they will come out and give battle again.

As the enemy would not come out of harbour 813 Squadron despatched a torpedo striking force of nine Swordfish to seek them out in harbour. A raid on Port Augusta was mounted on the evening of 10 July but found only small fry. They scored one torpedo hit on the destroyer *Leone Pancaldo* and another on an oil tanker.

It was during 11 July that *Eagle* endured much particularly severe bombing while in company with the battleships *Royal Sovereign* and *Malaya*. Italy had a single squadron of twin-engined SM85 dive bombers based in Sicily and although the squadron was sent out and returned having failed to hurt the British fleet at all, it would appear from eyewitness accounts that one of these machines managed to carry out a determined attack this day.

> We are at sea proceeding back to Alexandria. Today a dive bomber scored a *very* near miss in *Eagle*'s vicinity. The ship was shaken and about a ton of rust has come off her bottom! Enemy bombers have been attacking all day.

However, next day he was recording in his diary: 'Bombing less violent' and on 13 July, 'Quiet Day'. *Eagle* had come through her baptism of fire with honour although Cunningham later confessed he was very worried when he saw her surrounded by towering bomb splashes. 'One salvo of those eggs on her unprotected decks would have sent her straight to the bottom!'

But at least she could now hit back. On 14 July it was reported that two Sea Gloster Gladiator biplane fighters from the FAA Reserve, embarked aboard *Eagle* and piloted by Keighley-Peach and Lieutenant L.K. Keith, had shot down four Italian bombers during attacks on the fleet and damaged three others. Keighley-Peach himself was wounded by return fire from the SM79's but got back aboard safely.

Cunningham made several requests to London following this action. He asked for an armoured carrier, some modernised battleships with better speeds, a couple of heavy cruisers and many more destroyers. Admiral Sir Dudley Pound sent him all these, even though Britain faced imminent threat of invasion. The carrier *Illustrious*, with an armoured deck and Fairey Fulmar monoplane fighters was to reinforce *Eagle*; battleships *Barham*, *Queen Elizabeth* and *Valiant* eventually replaced *Royal Sovereign*, *Ramillies* and *Malaya*; heavy cruisers *York* and *Kent* were also sent, with as many destroyers as could be spared.

Meanwhile the Med Fleet kept up the offensive. *Eagle* sailed again on 19 July returning the next morning. A Swordfish striking force from the ship's No.824 Squadron was disembarked the same day and six aircraft and moved to the front line airstrip at Sidi Barrani with torpedoes ready to attack Tobruk that evening, following the encounter off Cape Spada between Italian cruisers and our light forces. Again their night assault in the early hours of 20 July was a brilliant success and their torpedoes scored hits on the destroyers *Nembo* and *Ostro* in brilliant moonlight.

Meanwhile their parent ship lay at Alexandria until 26 July, refitting and resting. This period of relative calm was shattered by a night bombing of the harbour by the Italians on 25 July. A freighter, the *Arrow*, lying directly for'ard of *Eagle* got the bombs meant for her and burnt for most of the night before sinking. Another night-time air raid was in progress when she put to sea with the *Warspite*, *Malaya*, *Ramillies Neptune*, *Sydney*, destroyers *Jervis*, *Janus*, *Nubian*, *Mohawk*, *Garland*, with *Hereward*, and *Imperial* joining the screen from Port Said. The fleet sailed at 0330 on 27 July.

*Eagle* was at sea with the three battleships to give distant cover to convoy AS2. She was attacked by aircraft between 1830 and 1930 but there were no hits. Fighters from the *Eagle* shot down one bomber during attacks on AS2 on 29 July. Sunday found them south of Crete again where they met this convoy and provided escort. Air attacks from Libyan and Rhodes airfields were not as intense as earlier and seemed half-hearted by comparison. *Eagle* now had all four Sea Gladiators embarked and at least two Italian bombers were thought to have been destroyed by them this day. However, the following day saw one of the British fighters written off. Fortunately the pilot was picked out of the water by the *Sydney*. The fleet returned to Alexandria at 0830 the following day.

They sailed from Alexandria on 31 July with *Royal Sovereign*, *Malaya* and destroyers *Jervis*, *Hero*, *Hereward*, *Hasty*, *Hostile*, *Imperial*, *Ilex* and *Vendetta*. (Force 'B') for Operation MA9, to carry out a diversionary sortie to draw enemy attention away from Operation 'Hurry', the flying of fighter aircraft to Malta from the carrier *Argus* from Gibraltar. The whole force returned to Alexandria on 1 August, due to condenser trouble in *Malaya*. A full calibre shoot of the 6 inch guns was conducted at sea on the last day of July. While at anchor in Alexandria harbour they suffered another fatality next morning when an air gunner was caught by a Swordfish airscrew and killed outright.

This day also commemorated the first anniversary of the commission during which time *Eagle* had steamed 54,671 miles, visited thirteen different ports, her aircraft had searched 1,851,586 square miles of ocean and the Italians had aimed 503 heavy bombs at her. In return at least ten bombers were claimed destroyed.

Night flying operations were conducted on 5/6 August. While the ship was thus idle it must be remembered that her squadrons were not. They flew ashore to Dekheila just before the ship entered harbour and from there were sent out on frequent sorties to Tobruk and the surrounding area in support of the army. This proved difficult for the aircrew and on conclusion of the exercise at 0210, five aircraft had been damaged, one seriously, but all the crews were safe.

Three Swordfish from *Eagle*'s 824 Squadron, led by Captain O. Patch, Royal Marines, cooperated with RAF units, and attacked enemy ships off Bomba (Jezirat-el-Marakael) at 0800 on 22 August. The Italian submarine *Iride* and the depot ship *Monte Gargano* were sunk and the destroyer *Calipso* had a torpedo pass directly under her hull.

The FAA were again prominent during diversionary operations to cover Operation Hats. The *Eagle* sailed from harbour at 0340 on 30 August in company with *Warspite*, *Malaya*, *Sydney*, *Orion*, *Kent*, *Gloucester*, *Liverpool* and destroyers *Stuart*, *Voyager*, *Vampire*, *Vendetta Decoy*, *Defender*, *Hereward*, *Imperial*, *Garland*, *Hyperion*, *Ilex*, and *Hasty*. They gave distant cover to convoy MF2. The Italian fleet, with five battleships, six cruisers and 27 destroyers, was at sea and so another round was hoped for but never materialised for they were recalled at 1400 on 1 September when it was known the British fleet was out.

Late on the afternoon of 31 August, the convoy was subjected to heavy bombing attacks and one of the ships was hit. Her steering gear was damaged but she kept going. At 2200 a striking force of Swordfish was readied fully armed on the flight deck ready for an attack on the enemy fleet which was understood to be 180 miles to the south. Throughout Sunday widespread searches were conducted; one of the Swordfish failed to return and was presumed lost. At 1545 the Italian fleet was finally discovered making at full speed for Italy. The fleet closed the convoy and kept on towards Malta itself.

On 2 September the whole fleet cruised disdainfully off Malta while some cruisers and destroyers were sent in to refuel. The convoy arrived safely and at 0900 *Illustrious, Valiant,* the AA cruisers *Coventry* and *Calcutta* along with four destroyers reinforced Cunningham's fleet from the west after an uneventful passage through the whole Mediterranean Sea, Mussolini's much-vaunted 'Mare Nostrum'! At 1600 the combined fleet turned back eastward before splitting into two groups and prepared a series of air attacks on Italian airfields at Rhodes.

Fighters from the carrier, part of Force 'I', shot down one shadowing enemy aircraft at 1500 on 2 September. At 1513 her aircraft located two enemy battleships, seven cruisers and some destroyers, west of Cape Matapan.

On 4 September, passing to the south of Crete, an enemy dive-bombing attack was made on *Eagle,* at sunset (1900). The bombs fell very close, close enough in fact to put the dynamo out of action for lighting and supplying power to the pom-pom mounting. Consequently this weapon could not open fire for several vital minutes. An emergency call was sent to *Illustrious* for fighter protection and three Fulmars still in the air duly arrived and were greeted by being fired on by *Eagle's* AA guns! These proved so effective that the Fulmars had to land on owing to damage.

At the subsequent red-faced inquest it was decided that this error was probably due to the fact that the Fulmars did not have their mainplanes painted black, and consequently they were mistaken for Italians. One of *Eagle's* own Sea Gladiators made a crash landing the same evening, smashing all mainplanes; the aircraft was not written off but was inoperational. One Italian bomber was claimed brought down by AA fire.

All this delayed the launch of *Eagle's* own Swordfish which were in the ship's hangars 'bombed up' and ready for the take-off. Thus they did not get the twelve aircraft away until 0315. Two of the main hangars at Maritza, Rhodes, were hit. Unfortunately these delays in launching the strike led to a night attack arriving over the heavily defended base in daylight. The Italians were pre-warned by *Illustrious's* strike against neighbouring Collato field and could thus assemble a strong force of defending Fiat C42 biplane fighters to meet them. Four of

*Eagle's* aircraft were destroyed, their greatest ever loss in one mission.

The attack on Rhodes was to be *Eagle's* aircrews worst casualty list. The bleak statements contained in TAG Tyler's diary reveal in their stark simplicity what this meant to a close-knit team like the Swordfish squadrons:

> September 9th: Took off at 0400 with six other bombers. Six of 824 Sqdn took off later. Just before we attacked we saw the aircraft from *Illustrious* attacking Calato, which was badly bombed about. We dived down and attacked Maritza. Plenty of AA fire but a hell of a lot of machine gun fire with tracer and 'Flaming Onions'. Hangars, workshops and barracks blown up and set afire by incendiaries. We left the place blazing merrily but were met by fighters (CR.42's).
>
> We lost four aircraft from our squadron but the enemy paid dearly for it. The missing planes and their crews were – 4C, Lieutenant Drummond, Midshipman Todd and L.A. Derwent; 4H, Lieutenant Collier, DSC, PO (A) March and N.A. Wilson; 4K, Lieutenant Hook, Lieutenant Bell and L.A. White; 4M, Lieutenant Hain, Sub-Lieutenant Smith and N.A. Taylor.
>
> Later we heard that Drummond, Bell, Todd and Derwent had been killed and that the rest were POWs.

*Eagle* arrived back at Alexandria with *Warspite* and the rest of the fleet from Operation 'Hats' on 5 September. She was scheduled to go into the floating dock on her return to have the effects of all those near misses on her ancient hull evaluated. Five Italian bombers were claimed as definitely shot down, but the Italian radio broadcasts that day boasted of how *Eagle* had been hit by a heavy bomb and had been left in a sinking condition. Photographs taken by the Italian aircraft were published 'proving' this lie. The subsequent attack on Rhodes did nothing to abate this sort of propaganda.

As *Eagle* was placed in the floating dock at 0945 the same day she arrived at Alexandria, all night leave was granted to the bulk of the crew, although night-time air raids took some of the edge from that. She left the floating dock again at 1000 on 7 September. Her Gloster Sea Gladiator fighter aircraft were also airborne on war patrols the following day in defence of a Red Sea convoy. The carrier remained at Alexandria until 21 September when she conducted daylight deck landing trials.

On 30 September the 8 inch cruiser *York* arrived to offset the damage to the *Kent*. Italian torpedo bombers had been becoming more active in dusk attacks and one such had landed a torpedo on *Kent*. The magazines blew up under 'X' turret, killing 32 men and wounding many more. Her propeller shafts and engines were also damaged but she got back to port for repairs. Another arrival that day was the famous light cruiser *Ajax* newly commissioned after her River Plate exploits. The whole fleet was at sea except for *Eagle*, *Ramillies*, *Malaya*, and the two newcomers.

These three heavy ships, along with *Ajax* and *Coventry*, sailed from Alexandria at 0100 escorted by the destroyers *Voyager*, *Vendetta*, *Vampire*, *Waterhen*, *Dainty*, *Decoy*, *Defender*, and *Diamond* and steered towards Crete to cover convoys to Crete and to threaten the Italian convoy routes to Libya. On 3 and 4 October they cruised off that island. 'We have been lying in wait for the enemy close to the lofty mountainous south-western coast of Crete for the last thirty-six hours', wrote one seaman at this time. 'Their convoy must have been informed of our presence and presumably hastened back. We are now starting back to Alexandria.'

They returned to Alexandria a.m. on 6 October on conclusion of this sortie. The next two days were spent in oiling and ammunitioning and then, at 1115, the entire fleet, *Warspite*, *Valiant*, *Malaya*, *Ramillies*, *Illustrious*, *Eagle*, cruisers *Gloucester*, *York*, *Ajax*, *Orion* and *Sydney* and destroyers *Hyperion*, *Ilex*, *Havock*, *Hero*, *Hasty*, *Hereward*. *Imperial*, *Vampire*, *Vendetta*, *Dainty*, *Decoy*, *Defender*, *Jervis*, *Juno*, *Janus* and *Nubian*, once more sailed westward and steered toward Malta covering another series of complex through-Mediterranean operations which showed their dominance of this land-locked sea. There were numerous submarine alarms and depth charge attacks throughout 10 October but otherwise their passage was quiet and next day they cruised off Malta itself while various cruisers and destroyers were detached thither to fuel. One of these, the destroyer *Imperial*, was mined during this period and badly damaged. She was still afloat and was able to proceed into harbour under her own power.

The following day, Saturday, 11 October, they reversed course for Alexandria once more. Although the main fleet was hardly molested at all, the cruisers, steaming in a search line some 60 to 80 miles from the *Eagle*, had a field day. At 0230 on

12 October the *Ajax* caught a division of Italian destroyers and at once steered to attack. She destroyed two of them, *Airone* and *Ariel*, with her 6 inch guns and the other made off. Shortly afterwards another group of destroyers was located by the same ship and again *Ajax* made short shrift of them damaging one before the others made off. The 8 inch cruiser *York* had meanwhile come up in support but there was no continuation of the action due to the darkness. At dawn the next day however, the *Eagle*'s Swordfish conducted a search and located the damaged enemy destroyer, the *Artigliere*, with a huge rent in her portside hull and fo'c'sle, being towed by a sister ship. *Ajax* went off at high speed to the reported position and on her arrival the tow was slipped and the other destroyer high-tailed it for home. The *York* came up and the crew of the *Artigliere* hastily abandoned ship. Half an hour was given for them all to get clear and then *York* despatched her with a well placed salvo of 8 inch shells which caused her to explode in a spectacular eruption of smoke and flame. *York* then dropped further carley rafts for the Italian crew before making off to rejoin her companions.

An eyewitness aboard *Eagle* recorded that:

> *Ajax* received four hits with 4.7 inch shells, she is steaming directly astern of the *Eagle*, but does not appear to be damaged very much. There is a large hole underneath her bridge on the hull of the ship. As she is steaming, this is being welded by her crew and a new plate fitted. At 0915 the third destroyer which *Ajax* damaged was blown absolutely to bits with one salvo from HMS *York*. This was visible from the *Eagle*. Enemy bombers are trying in vain to bomb us out of the water but so far they have been very unsuccessful.

On 13 October *Illustrious*, *Liverpool*, *Gloucester*, *York* and four destroyers parted company to carry out a raid on Leros, one of the Dodecanese islands. This was done satisfactorily but while recovering her aircraft in the darkness, with all her deck lights on, the carrier attracted the attentions of Italian torpedo bombers. They attacked and one of their missiles caught the *Liverpool* in her bows. She was soon burning fiercely. Great damage was caused and eventually her whole bows as far back as 'A' turret dropped off. She was then taken in tow and brought safely back to Alexandria. Nor was this the end of their woes for the *Illustrious* had a fire in one of her hangars in which at least four Swordfish were destroyed.

*Eagle* returned to harbour at 1115 and here found the damaged *Kent* now out of floating dock and being prepared for sea. Her shafts, two out of three propellers and 'Y' gun turret were out of action and she was secured alongside the jetty astern of the submarine depot ship *Medway*. Here a submarine leaving her parent ship rammed the poor old *Kent* in her bows and caused slight damage and much indignation.

There followed another brief spell in harbour, the only excursion being trial deck landings, both day and night, conducted on 20 October. She proceeded to sea at 1015 escorted by the destroyers *Hasty*, *Havock*, *Ilex*, *Decoy* and *Hereward* returning at 0915 the following day.

A very vivid and personal memoir of what life was like aboard *Eagle* at this exciting period of her life, was given me by Doug Clare:

I joined her as a signal boy in May 1940 and left her eighteen months later in November 1941 as a leading signalman. My first six months onboard were spent in the boys' messdeck. Normally this would have meant strict supervision by boys' instructors, but because of the conditions prevailing and Italy entering the war, that virtually fell by the wayside, all boys being required for more or less men's duties. Seamen boys formed part of guns' crews just as we signal boys were employed on the flag deck and sometimes on the bridge. On being rated ordinary signalman I transferred to the real(!) signalmen's mess where I spent a very happy twelve months.

In those days almost all messages between ships in company and to/from shore, were passed by 'visual' means such as flags, flashing light, semaphore, morse flag and even on occasion heliograph, though this latter was mainly for landing parties. Some years before World War II a system of manoeuvering ordered by 'equal speed signals' had been devised, mainly to train officers of the watch in ship manoeuvering. Signalmen had to know these signals and consequent manoeuvres off pat. Very frequently whilst in harbour at Alexandria we signalmen from ships such as *Eagle*, *Warspite*, *Barham* and others, would land at Ras El Tin football ground where we'd all march about and as a particular equal speed signal was ordered we'd manoeuvre as if we were ships. Often wondered what the watching Egyptians made of it all! Now that war had come there were no such training manoeuvres at sea and many a signalman had a good natter about the need to keep up the knowledge though it was still required as a skill for examinations for promotion.

*Eagle*'s flag-deck was one deck from and overlooking the compass platform, and was completely open to the elements except for a thigh-high strip of canvas stretched around the outboard stanchions. A 20 inch signalling projector (carbon arc) was fitted in each port and starboard wing and 10 inch SP's outside them. Signal halyard for hoisting countless flags everywhere of course, and woe betide anyone who let a loose end with Inglefield Clip float up without means of hauling it down again for it meant a hazardous climb out on the yards to retrieve it. Those on the mainmast were even worse for they were of wire and the mast covered in soot from the funnels, and while at sea quite hot and swirling in noxious fumes.

Immediately below the flag-deck was the main signal office, where all necessary signals were collated, copied and distributed. We had been very heavily bombed for days on end, and only a short time previously a massive bomb had landed just ahead of *Eagle* drenching the ship with oily water and debris. The fan trunking had sucked in quite a lot of cordite smell and very fine water causing a gas 'scare' with everyone dashing around with handkerchiefs pressed to nose and mouth looking for gas masks. I had just gone into the MS for a drink of 'Kai' when a further raid occurred with one plane dive-bombing us with guns firing, and I elected (?) to stay in the MSO, though of course I should have been on the flag-deck (not that the MSO would have been any help for its deckhead was only thin strip metal with corticene on top for deck of flag-deck). I well remember the leading signalman of the watch shouting down the voice pipe for me to get back on the flag-deck, and when I got there telling me something I've never forgotten: 'We're all bloody scared, even the captain out there on the compass platform is probably as scared as anyone, but he makes sure he doesn't show it and so must you! Now, grab your telescope and get to work.' The leading signalman was one of the real old school, and that is a perfectly true story. Countless times afterwards his words came to mind. I mention this to illustrate the steadying influence of the 'older school' on a young boy of just seventeen and as something else I have to thank the old *Eagle* for.

Yet another instance of 'thanks' for which the *Eagle* is to be credited comes to mind. At the time of Italy's entry into the war none of Cunningham's main Mediterranean Fleet was fitted with RDF. Consequently the arrival of HMS *Valiant* in the Eastern Med was like manna from heaven, she being fitted with surface-to-air RDF (or at least what she had was being utilised as such). In those days there was no voice net between ships and all day long *Valiant* would be signalling by all round masthead flashing lights, her ADR's (aircraft detection reports) and I spent many an hour with either telescope or binoculars trained on *Valiant* through the daylight hours reading these reports with someone alongside writing them down and passing them to the compass platform. One would be doing this under air attack of course and with our own guns belting away. It turned out to be superlative training for later incidents.

As long as our Fairey Swordfish could be seen, even if they were only a speck on the horizon, we communicated by 20 inch SP, moving to smaller apparatus as they closed. At flying stations/landing-on, we had several flags on long halyard stretching from the island to the 'nets' on the port side, and if urgent warning was required to be given to aircraft waiting to land, then we signalmen would have to dash across the flight deck with the particular flag usually on the direction of Commander Flying. Our old commander (F), Keighley-Peach, is still with us and I can picture him to this day in my mind. I often wonder if he was told of the terrific cheer that went up when, in his Sea Gladiator, he shot down the first Italian bomber over the fleet at sea. The Italians usually flew above effective height of AA fire certainly that of *Eagle*'s antiquated 4 inch weapons. These guns initially had absolutely no protection whatsoever for their crews, but then neither did anyone else on the upper deck have any.

During daylight hours, when we were usually attached to the 'Second Eleven', we followed the Rear-Admiral embarked in *Royal Sovereign* and later *Barham*. Messages at sea were usually sent by semaphore in those conditions. I well remember one of the battleships Yeoman of Signals atop 'B' turret (so he could be easily seen by all the squadron), vigorously sending us semaphore while Eytie bombs were falling all round both ships!

Usually the Admiral's Night Intention were signalled before dusk, but any subsequent other orders or changes of course and speed at night would be signalled by a Hether lantern. This was a contraption which clipped onto the Barr & Stroud binoculars with a lead to a battery secured around the waist by a harness with a morse key on the lantern and a blue shaded lens with small aperture and brilliance of light as low as possible. In some cases the message was not to be answered so there was no sure indication that it had been received, a very good lookout with binoculars therefore was essential. It's a wonder that things went as smoothly as they usually did!

'Tug' Whymark has similar memories of this period:

I can remember that once Italy had declared war our patrols became more interesting and we spent more time at first degree readiness instead of the previous second degree of readiness. When we closed up at our battle stations I was stationed at the forward 4 inch HA gun and we were constantly in action in those early months. The Italian bombers nearly always came over at very high level, and during the first attacks were fired off some 750 plus rounds of 4 inch in defence of the ship. *Eagle* was kept very active at the start and periods in harbour at Alexandria long enough for leave were rare. Even when, later on, we were in harbour more, there were only limited facilities ashore there. During these periods our aircraft were put ashore and kept in action supporting the troops in the desert.

As the Mediterranean war hotted up so we spent more time at Suda Bay in Crete and carried out many air raids against the enemy in North Africa, Tripoli, Benghazi and the like, also against the islands of Leros and Rhodes, as well as escorting troop convoys to Greece. Several times we caught the enemy unawares, as I understand it from those who went up in the Swordfish on these raids, but once or twice we got caught and spanked.

Heavy units of the Italian Navy did not show themselves too much after Calabria, and when they did sail seemed to always keep close to land, Taranto and so on. On the first occasion they were visible through binoculars and gun sights I believe. Our heavy units straddled them several times and got a hit. After that we didn't see them at all. Instead we used to send our Swordfish off with torpedoes to try and stop them but they seldom scored any hits.

On one occasion I can recall us steaming for Malta from the direction of the Crete area and there was a gas alert. The ship was closed up at action stations at this time and respirators were ordered to be worn, so someone was expecting the worst! However, within a short time a gas – all clear was given. I do not really know at this distance in time what had caused the original alert, neither side actually used gas. At the time we ratings believed that what sparked the alarm was that it was a very warm morning as the weather was perfect and the breeze almost motionless. The fumes from the collective ships's smoke, or from a smokescreen being laid, lay heavy on the sea and someone mistook it for gas. I suppose a toxic smell could have resulted and hung around but in all my years at sea I never experienced a similar alert at all.

As the air attacks increased so we got counter-measures. Anti-aircraft cruisers joined the fleet, but better was RDF on some ships. It gave us much more advantage as the range and height of the enemy aircraft were known accurately and it gave more time to open fire. Extra guns were placed wherever possible, close-range weapons for use against low-flying aircraft like torpedo bombers of which the Italians had many. Several of these were placed around *Eagle*'s flight deck, in fact these twin Lewis guns were my night and harbour action station. It proved hair-raising sometimes during night raids. A pitch black night in Alexandria harbour with all hell let loose overhead. And there we were, heroes all, with just a tin helmet for protection against the *Regia Aeronautica*, or, more lethal, the rain of shrapnel from our own guns ashore coming back down! We opened fire through a seeming maze of other people's tracers which were tracking hostile low flying aircraft, if they existed. I think it was anyone's guess where all these rounds of ammo went but I doubt if they troubled the Italian airmen very much as they preferred high or medium bombing.

At sea we had some Sea Gladiator fighters and very active they were too. All the pilots were volunteers and were

magnificent. *Eagle* always seemed a prime target, unmistakable I suppose, and an easy choice to pick from high up.
Anyway we were bombed by enemy aircraft all round the
clock when we put to sea. I can recall one very near miss
which exploded close off our bows. Thick black smoke and
powdery soot emitted from the explosion and blackened
parts of our guns and the bridge area as well as all our
personnel closed up in these areas. But it did us no great
harm; in fact lots of the lads thought it hilarious and we all
hoped the Italians manufactured all their bombs like that
one!

The fleet was very active now all the time and extra
manning of warships to see to all the new equipment was
necessary. Replacement crew members were beginning to
arrive in Alexandria after long hazardous convoy journeys
around the Cape. *Eagle* received many new members which
were by now mostly HO (Hostilities Only) ratings, but very
determined lads and marvellous really. You found out why
later. One particular AB from London I later palled up with
was always hell-bent on going into action. I said to him
eventually, with the wisdom of a regular, 'You are *too* keen!'
He replied, 'Well, it's like this, before I left Blighty I lost my
wife and child in an air raid.' I never questioned his motives
again.

There were brief interludes of course when one could
relax and 'Jack' always knows how to make the most of them,
especially in wartime. In Alexandria it was warm enough for
hands over the side to bathe to be popular. We also had boat
sailing on which I was particularly keen myself. About once a
month I got the chance to be in the crew of the ship's whaler.
And usually the start of any day in harbour would be hands
to muster for a spell of PT (Physical Training) under the
supervision of the ship's PT Instructor (not the most popular
man in the ship!) and then double around the flight deck to
the music of the Royal Marines band. At times, if you were
one of the 4 inch or 6 inch guns' crew you would have to lift a
shell up and down above one's head to see how many times
one could do it. The shell weighed 100 lbs. In the evenings
too the ship's company would play Tombola (from which the
modern game Bingo is derived).

Sometimes too in harbour escorts from ships were asked
ashore for POW duties. The war seemed to be going very

*Sampans viewed through* Eagle's *porthole at Wei-Hai-Wei, summer 1939. (Copyright E. B. Mackenzie)*

*A direct overhead aerial view of HMS* Eagle *at anchor off Hong Kong in 1939 shows her deck layout to perfection. The large Union Jacks painted on her flight deck were warnings to Japanese bomber pilots en route to targets in Inland China. The* Eagle *and her seventeen Swordfish torpedo bomber aircraft represented Great Britain's sole naval air strength in the Far East against Japan's six large aircraft carriers crammed with modern monoplane fighters, dive- and torpedo bombers, the hundreds of long-range Navy bombers and the float planes of the Japanese fleet. Little wonder the Royal Navy was no deterrent in Pacific politics on the eve of the war. (Copyright Tom Sprake)*

'Smiley' and 'Cheeseye' rowing their sampan out to HMS Eagle at Wei-Hai-Wei, 1939. (Copyright E. B. Mackenzie)

A bad landing but not terminal. Swordfish aboard HMS Eagle, September 1939. (Copyright E. B. Mackenzie)

*Splendid aerial view of HMS* Eagle *at sea off the China Coast on 4th August, 1939. (E. Kennard)*

*Fairey Swordfish TSR aircraft of No. 824 Squadron, Fleet Air Arm, in close formation over 'Happy Valley',*
*Hong Kong, August 1939. (Copyright E. B. Mackenzie)*

*HMS* Eagle, *lowering a Swordfish on floats. This clear photo from an unusual angle shows the carriers boat booms extended, the restricted arcs of the three foremost 6-inch guns, the extensive bridge walk on her side bridge structure and the massiveness of her foremast, September 1939. (Copyright E. B. Mackenzie)*

*Convoy! February 1st 1940. HMS* Eagle *picks up a convoy of 30,000 Australian and New Zealand troops off Colombo. With the battleship HMS* Ramillies, *the heavy cruiser HMS* Sussex, *the light cruiser HMAS* Hobart *and the destroyer HMS* Westcott, *she escorted them safely across the Indian Ocean to Aden. The liners are* Empress of Canada, Empress of Japan, Orcades, Rangitata, Orion, Orford, Dunera, Athos, Strathaird, Otranto *and* Sobroski. *(Copyright E. B. Mackenzie)*

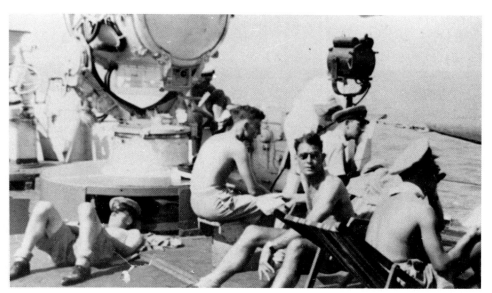

*The F.A.A. at sea! Relaxing between patrols somewhere in the Indian Ocean, March 1940. (Copyright E. B. Mackenzie)*

*A Swordfish pilot from the rear seat, this is 'Bulldog' Drummond at the controls over Sembawang Fleet Air Arm Station on Singapore Island in the spring of 1940. (Copyright E. B. Mackenzie)*

*The Quarter Deck of HMS Eagle at Aden. The shields of her three 6-inch guns can be seen in this unusual view. (Copyright E. B. Mackenzie)*

*HMS Eagle at Singapore on March 14th 1940. She is de-ammunitioning ship after a 250-lb bomb had exploded in the ship's handling room killing fourteen men and injuring a further nine. Damaged bombs can be seen on deck. The hazards of carrier operations and the vulnerability of such ships were graphically demonstrated by this incident. (Copyright E. B. Mackenzie)*

*HMS* Eagle *heading north through the Suez Canal 25th May 1940 to join the Mediterranean Fleet.
(Copyright E. B. Mackenzie)*

*The harbour at Port Said as seen from HMS* Eagle *on the 26th May 1940. The heavy concentration of
merchant shipping just prior the outbreak of war with Italy can be seen. (Copyright E. B. Mackenzie)*

*A Supermarine Walrus Amphibian ranged on the flight deck of HMS* Eagle *ahead of several Swordfish. (Copyright E. B. Mackenzie)*

*Seen from HMS* Eagle's *flight deck the battleship HMS* Warspite *just avoids a clutch of heavy bombs which explode harmlessly astern of her. Battle of Calabria, 9th July 1940. (Copyright E. B. Mackenzie)*

much Germany's way and the Atlantic convoy losses were serious. The French of course soon capitulated and we had all our guns trained on their ships at Alexandria, but it all ended quietly, unlike at Mers-el-Kebir and no blood was spilt thanks to the Commander-in-Chief. We then got on with the war proper.

# CHAPTER FOUR

# Lengthening Odds

Operations by *Eagle*'s air group from land bases continued from time to time. On the night of 22/23 September 813 Squadron carried out bombing attacks on Italian defence positions at Bardia in support of the British advance. On 28 September a large merchant ship was hit and severely damaged off Bomba. The Swordfish laid mines in Tobruk harbour on the night of 23/24 October. Aircraft from the ship attacked Tobruk once more on 24 October.

At 0730 morning of 25 October *Eagle* sailed once more with *Malaya*, *Coventry* and others to cover convoy AN5 in Operation MAQ2. The convoy coming from the Dardanelles was escorted by *Calcutta* and destroyers, while *Orion*, *Sydney* and destroyers were in support. *Eagle*'s group steered towards western Crete during the day but altered course after dark to arrive off the eastern tip of that island early on 26 October. From here the Swordfish were to attack Maltezana seaplane base at Rhodes.

The weather worsened during the day and the air attack was postponed until the early hours of Sunday. It was duly delivered and was a success with the Italians being surprised and little opposition being encountered in marked contrast to the last such raid. Meanwhile the 'First Eleven' had also been out and had conducted a bombardment of the Libyan coast in support of the army while the cruisers had been briefly engaged with the enemy.

From a position SE of Crete *Eagle* and *Malaya* left during the afternoon and returned to Alexandria at 1615 on 28 October. Italy had now invaded Greece and Churchill pledged Britain to send much-needed arms equipment and men to their aid. This distracted from the great British victories in the desert, and the transport convoys required to carry out such a policy became the main occupation for the Royal Navy in the eastern basin over the next few months.

The most immediate response was the sailing of the whole fleet at 1330 on the night of 28 October. *Eagle* and *Illustrious* for air protection, *Warspite Malaya, Ramillies, Valiant* for heavy metal, the cruisers *York, Orion, Gloucester* and *Sydney* with a score of destroyers as a screen.

They moved up at high speed along the usual route toward the western end of Crete, covering the movements of a convoy from Alexandria to Suda Bay. This was a great natural anchorage on the northern coast of Crete, but it had virtually no defences at all. A Mobile Naval Base Organisation was to be sent out from the UK to establish proper facilities and defences but took a long while to arrive. Nonetheless Suda Bay became a major (if very exposed) forward base for the fleet and was much used in the months ahead no matter what the risk. Cunningham intended to place his fleet to the west of Crete by dawn on Thursday 31 October, in the hope that the main Italian fleet would venture out in support of the invasion or make their own attacks on the tiny Greek Navy. Neither event took place.

*Eagle* and her companions therefore spent the next few days steaming along the coast of Greece well in sight of land (in fact the destroyer screen was only about a mile or so from the coast) but no sign of any Italian presence was to be found. Greek destroyers were seen by *Eagle*'s anti-submarine aircraft patrols and some of them carried out a bombardment of enemy positions in Albania. On 1 November the fleet reversed course, disappointed yet again, in two groups. On Saturday the enemy finally woke up to the presence of all these warships on their doorstep and heavy bombing attacks were directed at *Eagle* and the ships in company.

The cumulative effect of the shocks of many near-miss bombs from the various and many air attacks directed against *Eagle*'s frail old hull, coupled with high-speed steaming and continuous operations, now began to become apparent. An examination made on 5 November showed that her aviation fuel tanks were contaminated by leaks caused by these repeated concussions internally. It was signalled that the tanks would require a week to clean. This was a blow, for the major air strike against the Italian fleet at Taranto was being planned and she clearly would be unable to take part.

If she was now past her best with regard to main fleet work she could still be used as she was on her old job. It was signalled to London on 5 November that she did not require a further refit before resuming her duties on the trade routes. The arrival of the new carrier *Formidable* was expected to relieve her of her main fleet duties in the near future.

However, as the defective petrol system was going to put her in dockyard hands on 13 November, and the successful FAA attack was to be made on the Italian main fleet base of Taranto shortly before, five of her Swordfish aircraft and eight of her very experienced aircrew were embarked aboard *Illustrious* and played their full part in that historic victory.

This operation took place on the night of 11 November. Taranto was packed with Italian warships on the night of the attack. In the *Mar Grande* lay the brand-new battleships the 15 inch gunned *Littorio* and *Vittorio Veneto*, and the four older, but recently modernised battleships *Conte di Cavour*, *Giulio Cesare Andrea Doria* and *Caio Duilio* armed with 12.6 inch guns. These were the main targets of course, but there were ample other targets in port. Also in the outer harbour were the heavy cruisers, the 8 inch gunned ships *Fiume*, *Gorizia* and *Zara*.

The limited range of the torpedo-carrying aircraft was the biggest headache. The solution to this problem was to drop the third crew member to lighten the load and fit instead special long-range fuel tanks. With these measures the two carriers could launch some 180 miles from the target. There was some delay while these special tanks were got out to the Mediterranean from Britain and they arrived aboard *Illustrious*.

The next delay was the awaiting of the best weather and conditions of moon. A three-quarter moon was in effect on the actual night of the attack, giving the necessary visual aid to enable an accurate run and drop. The final date was fixed for the night of 11/12 November and was drawn up by Vice-Admiral Lyster and his team aboard *Illustrious* on 28 October, and amended on 6 November following the photo-reconnaissance flights by Maryland aircraft from Malta. It was codenamed Operation Judgement.

The number of torpedo-carrying aircraft was twelve, which were to attack in two waves, six per wave. Rear-Admiral Lyster and his force parted company with the C-in-C at 1800 on 11 November, and, by 2040, the first wave of Swordfish had taken off into the night with 170 miles of dangerous flying ahead of them to reach their target. This group was led by Lieutenant-Commander Williamson.

The second range was launched from *Illustrious* at 2134 but only eight of the nine got away on time, led by Lieutenant-Commander J.W. Hale, RN. One of the Swordfish, Lieutenant Clifford's L5F, damaged its wing fabric and had to be struck down on the lift to effect repairs. However, the crew were determined not to be left out of the attack and took off on their own to follow the others some 24 minutes later.

At 2315 the first flight of torpedo bombers pressed in through an inferno of fire, flitting in towards the anchored warships interlaced with angry streams of automatic weapon fire and the bursts of heavier cannon shells with a backdrop of searchlights questing for them from many different vantage points. The first flight of three (L4A, L4C and L4R) arrived together and approached from across San Pedro Island at 4,000 feet. They headed towards the centre of the *Mar Grande*. To do so they had to pass right through a tunnel of flak, heavy and light, hosing in towards them from the shore batteries on San Pedro, the cruisers and the destroyers as well as the battleships. They were clearly visible now and at point-blank range it is hardly surprising that the squadron leader's Swordfish was hit and shot down. Lieutenant-Commander Williamson's plane crashed almost immediately into the sea, close by the floating dock. Both he and Lieutenant 'Blood' Scarlett survived the crash and were quickly picked up by a boat sent from the dock. The remaining two Swordfish came clear unscathed.

They hit the southern end of the battleship line and the first aircraft, Lieutenant-Commander Williamson's L4A, selected, it later transpired, the *Cavour* as their target. His attack was clearly witnessed by observers aboard the destroyer *Fulmine* close by which was engaging her. L4R was seen at 2314 in the path of the moon diving at high speed with the engine cut out, some 1,000 yards from the destroyer which was firing steadily into the Swordfish.

The torpedo was dropped from a height of some 30 feet, narrowly missing the *Fulmine* herself and struck home on the battleship. A huge explosion lit up the harbour and sea as it detonated on her side. The other two pressed on, crossing the Tarantola shoal about two-thirds of its length from the shore at a height of 30 feet.

Their original target was the modern *Vittorio Veneto* but they could not pick her out; instead Sub-Lieutenant Sparke launched at the *Cavour*, from a distance of 700 yards, reporting an explosion near the ship a minute later. Sparke turned 180 degrees sharp to port and withdrew south of San Pedro, passing the stricken vessel close by her tilting bows. Sparke landed safely back aboard *Illustrious* at 0120 and Maculay at 0125. It would appear that in fact both torpedoes missed the target ship and ran on towards the *Doria*.

L4R also launched at the same time against the same target and not until their withdrawal did they actually notice the line of balloons at 1,000 feet outside the breakwater. Intense AA fire was encountered from the batteries both east and south of the harbour. At any event this vessel reported that two bombs had exploded ahead of her at 2315 and as no bombs were dropped at any time in this area, they were probably L4C and L4R's torpedoes detonating at the end of their runs.

The second flight now bore in from the north and Lieutenant-Commander J.W. Hale stooged around off the habour entrance for fifteen minutes waiting to make contact again. When he saw the flares going down he took his aircraft in at 1,000 feet over the breakwater being met with fierce fire from both shore and warships' positions. Nothing daunted, he dropped down over the *Mar Grande* and turned sharply to port at the end of the breakwater before launching his missile at 400 yards at 2315. He also had the satisfaction of seeing his torpedo striking home on the port quarter of the *Littorio* before he turned over San Pedro Island through a wall of flak from the guns and cruisers and won clear. He reached *Illustrious* safely at 0150.

The third torpedo-carrier was E4F, piloted by Lieutenant Maund, which arrived over the coast north of Cape Rondinella under the same heavy fire that his compatriots had faced. He cut engines and dropped to a launching position south-west of the Canal entrance, firing at the *Veneto* from about 1,300 yards' range. He then yanked the stick sharply to starboard and retreated over San Pedro through further intense flak. Unfortunately his missile missed the target and ran on to explode off the starboard quarter of the *Littorio* around 2315; its detonation was observed and reported by the *Duilio* at the time.

As they left, two of the battleships were sinking. The *Littorio* had been hit twice as we have seen. The first torpedo blew a hole 49 feet by 32 feet in the torpedo bulge abreast her No.1

secondary (6-inch) turret. The second struck her abreast her tiller flat on the port quarter, making a hole 23 feet and 5 feet. There was more to come. The *Cavour* was hit on the port bow under her No.1 main turret and a hole 40 feet by 27 feet appeared which flooded both No.1 and No.2 oil fuel tanks. As her list increased, the flooding spread to adjacent compartments. There seemed every prospect she would sink at her anchorage there and then.

All the first wave had withdrawn by 2335, but defensive fire never slackened as by this time the second wave of eight was on its way in.

Eight only, because although L5F had made goods its damage another aircraft, Lieutenant Morford's L5Q, lost its external overload tank on the way at 2205 and the loose strap began to cause damage to the plane as it banged against the flimsy fuselage. Reluctantly and heartbreakingly, the aircraft was forced to abort her mission.

Meanwhile, at midnight Lieutenant-Commander Hale had led in the torpedo-bombers from the north-west against an enemy that could not have been more ready for them. Four of them managed to launch their torpedoes, two attacked the *Littorio*, one attacked the *Veneto* and the last launched against the *Duilio*.

L5A, piloted by Hale, and L5K, piloted by Lieutenant Torrens-Spence, attacked simultaneously by diving over Cape Rondinella in the face of heavy AA fire from the San Pedro batteries and the battleships themselves. Hale dived from 5,000 feet over the mercantile anchorage and dropped against the *Littorio* at 700 yards' range, breaking away to starboard and exiting to the north of Tarantola shoal breakwater, hotly pursued by streams of flak from the destroyer flotilla. He survived and landed back aboard ship at 0200.

L5K's attack was almost identical, diving over the cape to about five cables' length from the canal entrance with battleships, cruisers and shore batteries enveloping him in a cone of fire. He also released at about 700 yards from *Littorio* then broke to the south. Unscathed, he returned to the fleet at 0215. One of these two missiles struck the battleship at 0001, exploding on her starboard bow. The actual point of impact was low down on her anti-torpedo bulge, just in front of the previous hit here. A hole 40 feet by 30 feet was blown in her. The second may have also hit, certainly a large dent was subsequently found in her starboard quarter. At all events one torpedo certainly was later found to have ended up into the mud beneath the battleship. It had failed to detonate but its striking cap was damaged as if by impact when later found there by the Italians.

The third aircraft of this leading flight, E4H, followed the other two in over Cape Rondinella and was never again seen by British eyes. The Italians later stated that an attack was made against the heavy cruiser *Gorizia* but the aircraft was instantly shot down, and both Lieutenant Bayly and Lieutenant Slaughter were killed.

Closely following the ill-fated E4H was L5H, piloted by Lieutenant Lea. She dived over the cape to a point some 2-1/2 cables from the south of the canal entrance. Her attack was made against the *Duilio*. It was a smashing success, the missile running straight and true and striking the target vessel on her starboard side, abreast her No.2 main turret, just below her No.1 5-inch secondary turret. The angle of impact was estimated to be 80 degrees at a depth of 29 feet and was extremely effective. A hole some 36 feet by 23 feet was blown between No.1 and No.2 magazines which were both flooded.

Lea didn't have time to admire his handiwork too much, because on turning hard to starboard he found his only exit was the narrow gap between the heavy cruisers *Zara* and *Fiume* and then north out over the San Pedro batteries. He could hardly have chosen a more hazardous route and was followed the whole way by fire from all arms of the enraged fleet's defences. He survived it all!

Also crossing over Cape Rondinella behind Hale came E5H piloted by Lieutenant Welham. They flew straight across the *Mar Picolo* and over the town of Taranto itself to get a good long look at their options, then they turned towards the middle of the outer harbour with a right turn, just avoiding the northernmost of the barrage balloons moored along the eastern shoreline. Heavy fire from light weapons met them as they dived to attack and the outer aileron rod was hit, which put the Swordfish out of control for a while. Happily Welham held her and took her back on a steady course towards the battleship line. At the close range of only 500 yards he launched against the port quarter of the *Veneto* but unhappily he missed. E5H then broke to starboard and escaped north of San Pedro through the same enormous volume of fire, receiving a second hit in the port wing as she did so. Despite these two strikes she reached the carrier at 0205 and landed back aboard safely.

On recovery of the final aircraft *Illustrious* turned to rejoin the main fleet and the flagship was in sight by 0700 12th November. Admiral Cunningham laconically signalled her: '*Illustrious* manoeuvre well executed.'

'Well executed' it certainly had been. For the loss of only two Swordfish, and the death of two officers and capture of two more, the main enemy naval base had been attacked and half his battle fleet incapacitated. It was in fact a major victory, nothing less. Nor was it solely an *Illustrious* victory. Five of the *Eagle*'s aircraft had taken part, one of which failed to return, and Lieutenant Grieve from that ship was present aboard L5B, so it was really a shared success. All the squadrons deserved the award of the premier battle honour of the Fleet Air Arm, TARANTO 1940.

This, the Fleet Air Arm's greatest victory, was won for it by the skill, bravery and dedication of just a handful of young pilots and observers. But if the men themselves were fledglings with hearts of lions, then their mounts, the unforgettable Fairey Swordfish, known to its crews with wry affection as 'The Stringbag', were far from the first flush of youth. That such an obsolescent machine could still be flying from modern aircraft carriers in 1940 seemed incredible to observers from the United States Navy with its sleek silver monoplanes. Indeed the Swordfish seemed a veritable flying throwback to the configuration of World War I aviation, creating legend after legend more than a generation later. It was a plank-winged biplane, its best operational speed was not much more than 90 knots which meant that its flimsy fabric-covered body clawed its way into battle a sitting duck for modern anti-aircraft weapons. At Calabria, for example, with a top speed of 90 mph, a headwind of 30 knots and the speed of the retreating Italian cruisers of 32 knots, the Swordfish had to overtake the enemy at a relative speed of 30 mph with every gun in the Italian fleet firing flat out at them as they stuttered into position.

The Fairey Swordfish performed miracles not only in the Mediterranean but anywhere it was deployed. It could dive-bomb amazingly well although not stressed for the task; its very slowness made it an ideal anti-submarine aircraft and minelayer. Fitted with underwing rockets Fairey Swordfish were still in action four years later at Normandy when they made attacks in support of the landings! They saw their successors and 'superiors', the Chesapeake, the Albacore, the ghastly Barracuda, come and go and still soldiered on ignoring the laughter and creating new records month after month.

Aboard *Eagle* her own two squadrons had, between 4 August 1939 and 4 August 1940, clocked up the following statistics: searched 1,851,586 square miles, consumed 166,732 gallons of aviation spirit and the pilots had totalled 8,000 flying hours. The aircraft had made 1,979 deck landings, scored at least 19 torpedo hits in action. Torpedoes had been prepared and adjusted for 'action' 632 times. Four Swordfish and one Sea Gladiator had been lost in action and seven Italian bombers were claimed shot down. Nor was this record exceptional for the Fleet Air Arm at this period of the war.

The Italian response to this famous victory was another night attack on the fleet at Alexandria on the night of 13 November, during which the destroyer *Decoy* was hit on her stern, eleven officers and men being killed. During another raid the Egyptian liner *Zan Zan* was also hit by a bomb but only suffered slight damage. Raids the next night laid a stick of bombs across the Naval HQ at Ras-el-Tin and Aboukir airfield was hit as was Dekheila. Three warships arrived on 14 November as replacements, the battleship *Barham* (to replace *Ramillies*) heavy cruiser *Berwick* (to take *Kent*'s place) and light cruiser *Glasgow* (to replace *Liverpool*).

Further troop convoys to Greece now took place escorted by the anti-aircraft cruisers *Calcutta* and *Coventry*, and destroyers. With the battleships *Barham* and *Valiant* and destroyers *Hyperion*, *Vendetta*, *Dainty*, *Diamond*, *Jervis*, *Greyhound*, *Gallant* and *Griffin*, *Eagle* sailed at 0230 on 16 November and proceeded to Suda Bay, Crete, to provide cover for these and the protecting cruiser squadron, *York*, *Berwick*, *Sydney*, *Orion* and *Glasgow*. also with troops aboard.

Early on Sunday 17 November, at 0055, there was an unexpected meeting with the 3rd Cruiser Squadron which had disembarked their troops and were returning. *Eagle* herself arrived at Suda Bay at 0945 that morning. Sea Gladiator fighters were to have been landed ashore to maintain fighter protection over the various troop ships, but these orders were subsequently cancelled as the ships were no longer loading at Bardia and the 'drome was too far away for a fighter patrol to operate over the ships. Extensive anti-submarine patrols were mounted by both British and Greek destroyers and the monitor *Terror* was also anchored in the Bay as a substitute for shore battery defences. *Eagle* sailed from Suda at 1705 that same day.

She left, as she had arrived, via the Kaso Strait and set course back to Alexandria. Next day while still off Crete, the newly-arrived *Barham* developed engine trouble and a destroyer had to steam close alongside her to carry out her condenser work, a skilful and ticklish operation. While they were away Alexandria suffered its heaviest air raid to date, and when they got back at 1400 on 19 November there were still fires in the civilian quarter.

Operation Collar followed between 25 and 29 November, another series of large-scale operations which involved many complex local convoy movements and offensive sorties and the passage of a convoy and reinforcements for Cunningham's fleet right through the Mediterranean from Gibraltar. This led to the Battle of Spartivento in the western basin but in the east *Eagle* was fully employed.

The 'Second Eleven', *Ramillies, Malaya, Eagle. Sydney, Orion, Ajax* and destroyers, *Hyperion, Ilex, Gallant, Dainty, Diamond, Defender Havock* and *Hasty* left Alexandria at 0530 on 23 November and steered to pass through the Kaso Strait at midnight to arrive at Suda Bay at dawn. At Suda a few bombs were dropped close to *Eagle*, but they sailed again at 1230 and took up a covering position some 200 miles east of Malta early on 25 November with the convoy some twenty miles off their starboard bow. Meanwhile the 'First Eleven', *Warspite, Valiant, Illustrious*, 3rd Cruiser Squadron and destroyers, left Alexandria that same morning. The whole complex series of operations was carried out according to plan.

*Eagle*'s main contribution was a bombing attack by eight Swordfish from the carrier on shipping in Tripoli harbour. The fires they started were visible from the ship at about 90 miles distance. One freighter was hit by three 500 lb bombs, warehouses were gutted and the 'Spanish Quay' was repeatedly hit. All the aircraft returned safely whereupon the squadron steered for Malta once more.

Over in western basin Admiral Somerville's Force 'H' caught the Italian fleet and chased them back to harbour but *Eagle* had a quiet return to Alexandria, which was reached at 2305 on 29 November. This proved to be the last easy passage of convoys through the Mediterranean for, stung by Italian inefficiency, Hitler sent down his dive bomber squadrons to deal with the Royal Navy and an armoured unit under Rommel to take care of the land side of things. Both arrived in the coming weeks and both proved an entirely different kettle of fish from the hapless Italians.

On 15 December it was notified that *Eagle* was to remain at Alexandria with the 19th Destroyer Flotilla for Operation MC2. Her days in the eastern Mediterranean were seemingly numbered, for on 31 December the decision was made that she was to form Hunting Group E1 with the light cruiser *Emerald* should Admiral Cunningham agree he could now spare her. Any hopes that he could were to be dashed by the Luftwaffe's crippling attack by dive bombers on *Illustrious* off Malta a few days later.

*Eagle* herself spent most of December in harbour but her two squadrons, 813 and 824, having been flown ashore, again operated in the front line of the Western Desert with great skill and daring. Christmas Day brought a message from the Commander-in-Chief himself, which is well worth quoting in full as a good guide to his character:

Few of us can spend this Christmas in the way to which we are accustomed in our own homes and with our own folk. So in wishing you a Happy Christmas the wish may seem a little empty but I feel that far away though we are from families our ties are perhaps closer than ever before because they, like us, are engaged in the very same delivery [sic] of facing up to the enemy and putting every incitement in beating him out of the ring. War, particularly at sea, has always been a matter of long and arduous periods of watching and waiting for those fleeting moments when it is possible to strike at the enemy, and this war is no exception. I am very much alive to the loyalty, determination and skill which have allowed the ships of the fleet and those of the local defence services so constantly to keep to the sea. The strain has become particularly heavy on the engine room departments whose job does not cease when the anchor is let go. To light craft and aircraft who have borne the brunt of the seagoing I trust that the safe arrival of convoy after convoy has brought some sense of satisfaction of work well done. To repair staffs and shore services in Egypt and dockyard at Malta we owe a particular debt of gratitude for all their hard and skilful work on behalf of the fleet. In the last six months I think we have established a considerable measure of control in a sea from out of which the enemy boasted we should be hunted and we have furthermore succeeded in giving the Italians some severe blows from which they are still suffering. These events have been backed up by the successes in the air and ashore. Thus we can look forward to 1941 in a spirit of hope that we may see great things and indeed we may be sure that this will be so as long as the present spirit continues to animate the Mediterranean Fleet. So I wish you a Happy Christmas and may the New Year bring us a victorious peace.

It came with the ship partly decorated and leave granted. One seaman recorded that: 'The ship's company has indeed spent a very delightful day.'

The *Eagle*'s Swordfish detachments in the desert added spotting for the fleet to their many duties during the attack on Bardia at the beginning of the New Year. 'Ginger' Tyler gives this account of his grandstand seat of the battleship bombardment:

A volunteer was called for to carry out a special job, and when I found that my aircraft was being used I offered my name. It turned out that we were to go up into the desert again and carry out a spotting mission for the bombardment of Bardia. On 2 January 1941, Swordfish P4208, carrying Lieutenant Leatham, Sub-Lieutenant Aitken from the *Warspite*, and myself took off from Dekheila and landed at Ma'aten Bagush, where we spent the night.

The next morning we left for Sidi Barani, and took off again for Bardia where we were to spot the fall of shot for *Barham* during a fleet bombardment of the port and military installations. Arriving over the target we soon spotted the gunnery positions and transport parks which were to be attacked.

Clearly, out to seaward, the battle fleet could be seen taking up their positions, whilst close inshore our old friend the monitor *Terror* and a number of destroyers could be seen.

Once in position, at the appointed time, the whole force opened up with all their guns and deluged the target with high explosive shells for about one and a half hours. To supplement this attack our army artillery surrounding the town poured in their own contribution. Within minutes Bardia and its installations were obliterated by bursting shells and we had great difficulty in pinpointing *Barham*'s fall of shot.

It had been expected that our presence would have been noted and that enemy fighters would have attempted to interfere with our spotting activities, but to our relief and surprise not a single enemy aircraft was seen during the whole of the operation. My time was occupied by passing spotting signals to *Barham* and of course manning my gun in case any intruders should appear.

By the time we were due to leave the area, Bardia was a scene of utter devastation. It must have been sheer bloody hell for the garrison down there and I felt very glad to be in the comparative safety of my aircraft away from the shambles below. Our mission completed, back to Sidi Barani we flew, refuelled and returned to Dekheila, happy to think that we had completed a very satisfactory day's work. On the following day Bardia surrendered and tens of thousands of prisoners were taken.

It was not until 6 January that *Eagle* put to sea again. A lot had happened in the meantime. The fleet had bombarded Valona in Albania, rubbing the Italians' noses in it. A whole enemy convoy was sunk in the Straits of Otranto, next door to their main fleet base at Taranto. Tripoli was bombarded. Thousands of Italian prisoners were streaming in from the desert.

The object of the trip to sea on 6 January was to conduct daylight deck landings, but one of the Sea Gladiators crashed while landing, though fortunately the pilot was unhurt.

*Eagle* again sailed on a major operation at 0200 on 11 January, leaving Alexandria in company with *Barham* and destroyers for Suda Bay to cover various troop convoys on 11 December. The 'First Eleven' was also at sea. Then the Germans arrived. Their presence was brought home forcibly to the fleet when Stuka dive bombers attacked and hit the *Illustrious* with heavy bombs, gutting the ship. She put into Malta, was hit again, and finally sailed back to Alexandria en route for extensive repairs in the USA.

Aboard *Eagle* the normal Sea Gladiator fighter complement

was supplemented by two Blackburn Skua dive bombers for this operation. But although the Germans had graphically demonstrated what dive bombers could do, the Navy preferred to use these monoplane aircraft as very slow fighters instead thus wasting their potential. Soon afterwards they were phased out altogether!

Operation MC6 was to have seen strikes made on Tobruk, Rhodes and shipping off the North African coast but this was later cancelled due to bad weather. During the afternoon of Sunday 12 January, bombing attacks were made against them, without effect. They arrived at Suda at 1915. *Eagle* and *Barham* refuelled at Suda Bay during the night. *Eagle* was carrying a large number of RAF personnel bound for Malta and these were transferred to the Australian cruiser *Perth* at Suda for the rest of their passage.

One observer aboard the carrier wrote poetically:

Tonight looks very romantic, a full moon, which seems to have increased in size and a cloudless sky. The mountains which surround this bay stand out against the light of the moon like huge ghosts, dwarfing the ships which are riding at anchor on this glassy 'lake'. The type of evening which I am describing of course makes things very easy for the Italian torpedo-carrying planes to attack. That is why the cruiser *Glasgow* received such a collection of hits, one forward, one aft. Our RDF (Radio Direction Finding, British cover name for radar) gear cannot work in this bay as the mountains are so high. Last night's raid was cancelled owing to bad weather over the target (Tobruk). Strong winds and sandstorms were reported.

Sailing from Suda at 0430 on 13 January they planned to carry out the air strike against Rhodes that same night and then search for Italian convoys but they were alerted that they were in the area that the Italian torpedo bombers were operating and special vigilance was required. The operational intentions were signalled to each ship from the Rear-Admiral aboard *Barham*. This night's signals were typical and a summary gives some idea of the complexity that each captain had to assimilate:

Intend to alter course at 1900 to 040 degrees. Intend to proceed at 18 knots at 1900. *Ilex* and *Wryneck* (escorting destroyers) proceed in execution of previous orders at 1900. Commence normal light zig-zag at 1930. Cease zig-zag at

2100. *Barham* exchange positions at 2100. *Eagle* take guide of
the Fleet at 2100. *Barham* and *Eagle* exchange positions at
2200. Admiral resume guide of the Fleet at 2200. Intend to
proceed at 16 knots at 2200, etc., etc., etc...

At this time a full gale was blowing and *Eagle* was rolling
enough to make even a daylight landing difficult, not to
mention a night landing. It was no big surprise therefore when
the operation was cancelled at 2230. On Tuesday the weather
moderated a little but strong winds and heavy sea still made
operations difficult. A few scouting aircraft were sent away at
1000 to search for the Italian convoy. One of the Swordfish
sent in a sighting report of two merchant ships and one
destroyer but this aircraft failed to return and was assumed
destroyed. A striking force of eight Swordfish armed with
torpedoes was flown off *Eagle* at 1330, but these returned at
1700 without having released any of their missiles. The weather
conditions were blamed for their failure to find the convoy. As
night came on, so the wind increased once more. Another
planned raid (against Benghazi) was therefore also cancelled.
*Eagle* was recorded as 'rolling and pitching like a cork'. In his
diary next morning one young seaman wrote:

> Last night was one of the roughest *Eagle* has experienced
> since joining the Mediterranean Station; even now it is
> blowing a gale. Visibility has been reduced to practically nil.
> We are now heading for Suda Bay and will remain there
> until this storm passes.

They arrived at this sanctuary at 1630 on 15 January. Next day
they put to sea at 1100 and steamed west. At 1700 Crete was on
their port quarter but the wind was still blowing considerably,
although the sea had calmed a bit, and a slight haze hung close
to the sea, causing yet another cancellation. They decided to
call it a day and course was set for Alexandria. Several bombing
raids were reported that evening after dusk by the light of the
rising moon but no damage was done to any ship.

As they neared Alexandria at 0200 next morning they were
told to stand off because the channels and harbour were still
full of unexploded bombs and suspected mines from the air
raids of the previous nights. *Eagle* and her companions were
therefore compelled to steam around Aboukir Bay until dawn.
The gale had renewed itself with fresh fury as they waited and
they were glad to be allowed in at 0730, although they found

conditions inside almost as bad as at sea. Of Cunningham's fleet, *Warspite*, *Valiant*, *Barham*, *Eagle*, *Orion* and *Ajax* were the only big ships in fully operational condition.

The newly completed *Formidable* was to be sent to take the place of *Illustrious*, but until she arrived *Eagle* was once more the only carrier in the eastern Mediterranean, and no longer in the 'Second Eleven'. However, seeing what Junkers Ju87 bombs had done to the armoured decks of *Illustrious*, there was no question of risking the old *Eagle* anywhere near their bases in Sicily or the central Mediterranean and her operations were confined to area defined as 'Stuka Sanctuaries' where the relatively short-range dive bombers could not reach. The fact that the Germans were fitting these deadly machines with long-range fuel tanks was not commented upon! As well as damaging the carrier, the Stukas had sunk the cruiser *Southampton* and damaged the *Perth*, and they quickly moved into the desert and sank the monitor *Terror* and several destroyers engaged in supply runs to Tobruk. At the same time the much weakened British army was first halted and then driven back towards the Egyptian border by Rommel's Panzer Army. Operations in the eastern basin became progressively more difficult as 1941 advanced.

With *Eagle* now bearing the sole responsibility for the fleet's air protection the number of fighters carried was increased at the expense of one of the squadrons of Swordfish, either 813 or 824 was now always disembarked in North Africa. Trials were held to see which were the most suitable fighter aircraft for her to operate. The Blackburn Skuas were not really fighters at all but were often used as such. They were soon abandoned. There were several Fairey Fulmars from *Illustrious*'s decimated squadrons reserves and these were initially embarked. In addition American-built Brewster Buffalo naval fighters had been obtained from the USA and these types were also tested for carrier operations. The new defensive measures designed to give the aircraft carriers of the fleet some measure of anti-aircraft protection against the German dive bombers also had to be practised and put into effect.

On 23 January *Eagle* put to sea, and Sea Gladiators and a Brewster Buffalo pretended to be Stukas in a series of mock 'dive bombing' attacks. *Illustrious*'s sixteen 4.5 inch guns and numerous multiple 2-pdrs had failed to stop the Stukas, so there was little chance that *Eagle*'s few single, unprotected 4 inch HA guns could do much to defend her. It was true that she had her armoured belt from her original battleship configuration but this was side armour not deck protection, which was what was required against dive bombing.

On 25 January *Eagle* re-entered the floating dock where she remained for five days. She re-emerged on 30 January and proceeded to sea for a new flying programme. The first Fairey Fulmar three-seater fighters now joined the ship while four Swordfish were flown off to Dekheila to make room for them. She returned to harbour at 1700.

Operation Result was mounted on 1 February and accordingly *Eagle* sailed at 0715 with the battle squadron. Seven Fulmars flew aboard, but three of them crashed on deck while they were embarking. Altogether her mixed complement amounted to thirteen fighters for this operation. That same morning the fleet practised putting up an umbrella barrage over *Eagle* to see if the dive bombers could be kept at a safe distance. As well as this operation, the fleet again gave protection to convoy movements. It headed north-west during Sunday, 2 February, but an enemy reconnaissance aircraft was sighted early on. Three Fulmars were scrambled to intercept this machine.

Next day the fleet changed course to the south-east and Crete was again visible off the port bow by 0730. The usual submarine alerts and depth charge attacks had punctuated their voyage westward and they also passed a number of floating mines, dangerously close to the *Eagle*'s side. At 1300 the destroyer *Jaguar* took the time to practise putting up her own protective umbrella over *Eagle* this day; each carrier in future would be allocated specific cruisers and destroyers whose main task in the event of a major dive bomber assault would be to protect the carrier.

The whole fleet returned to Alexandria the following day, arriving at 1915. There followed another long period of inactivity for the ship but once again her Swordfish kept her name alive in combat ashore. One squadron went up to Benghazi, while the other stood by to re-embark, along with 14 fighters, when next required at sea.

The damage to *Illustrious* and the delay in the arrival of *Formidable* due to the mining of the Suez Canal, meant that the flag of Acting Rear Admiral D.W. Boyd, Senior Officer, Aircraft Carriers, was formally hoisted aboard *Eagle* in

Alexandria harbour at 0800 on 18 February and re-transferred to *Illustrious* at 0800 on 19 February.

On the 19th also, *Eagle* sailed at 1210 with nine Fulmars, five Sea Gladiators and six Swordfish embarked. Opportunity was taken to conduct deck trials of the Brewster Buffalo while they were still near the coast. One Swordfish crashed over the starboard side of the flight deck having collided with the for'ard pom-pom but the crew were picked up by the escorting destroyer unharmed. The first trial of the Buffalo was a flop. The machine failed to make a landing aboard at all; the slowest it could approach the carrier was at well over 100 knots which made landing impossible. They joined up with the rest of the fleet that evening and steered once more for Cretan waters.

This sortie was for Operation MC8, the escorting of the naval auxiliaries *Breconshire* and *Clan Macauley* with vital supplies. Accordingly *Eagle* operated in company with the battleships *Barham* and *Valiant*, as Force 'A'. They were to rendezvous with the two auxiliaries two days later about 180 miles north of Benghazi and provide them with heavy cover for the most dangerous stretch of the journey. Again the destroyers practised the placing of the anti-Stuka umbrella over the carrier. The Sea Gladiators were to be kept permanently on patrol overhead as an early form of CAP (Combat Air Patrol) was tried out, and this commenced at 0325 on 21 February for as long as the fleet was in Stuka range.

Rendezvous was made with the convoy at 0800 that day and later three German Heinkel He 111 bombers made a low-level attack on the merchant ships. They were surprised by the Fulmars which happened to be airborne and close by. They chased the Germans and destroyed one and silenced the rear gunner of a second. All the Fulmars landed back on safely but one had a few bullet holes in her tail, although it was still flyable. The returning convoy from Malta and the fleet now steered eastward and *Eagle* kept up a maximum flying programme to ensure fighters overhead all the time. This seemed to deter the enemy for it was not until dusk that any determined efforts were made to attack them again. Even so the closest any enemy bomber penetrated was six miles. The radars in ships like *Valiant* were most effective for their time and passed to *Eagle* details of the number of aircraft, their height, range, estimated speeds, etc., usually picking them up at about 28 miles distant from the fleet. This gave the ship's guns' crews ample time to close up to action stations and prepare a long-range barrage and for the fighters held in readiness on deck to be scrambled away to intercept.

On 22 February the destroyers *Dainty* and *Hasty* changed escort duties with *Stuart* and *Vampire* and the fleet changed course to the north-east toward the Dodecanese Islands for another Swordfish attack on the bases there. Once more bad weather aborted this operation before the aircraft were launched. *Dainty* and *Hasty* meanwhile proceeded to Tobruk where the Stukas caught them and sank the former. The rest of the fleet arrived back at Alexandria at 1915.

Another attempt to land the Buffalo was tried on 3 March, with the destroyer *Jaguar* acting as 'crash boat' in case of mishaps. They sailed at 0730 and found the sea extremely rough. Nonetheless the Buffalo was safely brought down aboard without mishap this day and *Eagle* returned to harbour. However the general feeling was that this stubby little machine, although designed as a naval aircraft, was probably more suited to operating from shore bases. This they subsequently did both in Crete and Singapore, although they were outnumbered in the first battle and totally outclassed in the latter. They never served operationally at sea with the Royal Navy.

On 6 March an eyewitness reported that:

> All the cruisers and about thirty large merchant ships were loaded with troops, guns, tanks, supplies, etc. for Greece. The harbour is one mass of shipping and about the busiest it has been for years.

All those men and valuable equipment had been taken from the desert armies. In little more than a month all had been lost in a vain attempt to stem the Panzers and the pitiful remnants had to be evacuated without their equipment and at enormous loss to the fleet. It was proved to be a totally futile waste of lives, equipment and effort, brought on by Churchill's refusal to face reality.

The reason for their inactivity had been the blocking with magnetic mines of the Suez Canal by the Luftwaffe. The Canal was totally blocked to shipping for long periods and among the ships held up had been their relief, *Formidable*. Word reached them on 8 March that the carrier had succeeded in getting through at last along with over 100 merchant ships. Her arrival would mean *Eagle*'s departure and she did indeed arrive at

Alexandria next day along with the anti-aircraft cruiser *Carlisle*, whose captain was *Eagle*'s former commander. The damaged *Illustrious* left for Suez at 1600 the same day and *Eagle* was to have followed her but her sailing was again cancelled at the last moment and so they swung round the buoy again for many more weeks.

Her two valiant Swordfish squadrons meanwhile preceded her south, seventeen of these aircraft being despatched to the Port Sudan area on 25 March. Here they were to form a specialised anti-shipping unit to strike at the concentration of Italian warships based at the port of Massawa, Eritrea, which was now being 'pinched out' by British forces. We will return to their exploits soon.

It was not until 1745 on 9 April 1941, with news of the great victory at Cape Matapan reaching them, that *Eagle* said her final farewell to Cunningham's great and famous fleet and set course for Suez. For her it was the end of a magnificent period when she had been in the forefront of the naval war. A new era was dawning as she made her way east escorted by the destroyers *Encounter* and *Decoy*.

For some this was their last view of the floating home for the previous eighteen months for there were transfers from her crew to ships that were staying in the Mediterranean and were short-handed. One such was young stoker Collins. He recalls how much his time aboard the old carrier had prepared him for the demands made upon him and his companions during the battles that followed, like Crete:

I recall one incident earlier when my duty was Middle Watch in the Boiler Rooms. There was an emergency and a call for maximum speed. I was called to the engine room. The warrant officer told me to shake all the Chief ERAs and ERAs (Engine Room Artificers) and tell them to report to 'D' Boiler Room where we had three boilers opened up for cleaning and the auxiliary machinery all stripped down! Our captain had called for 'Full Speed' and was unable to get it. So everyone was in a panic.

After shaking everyone I went down to 'D' boiler room as ordered. I was standing on the upper grating looking down and laughing silently to myself when the warrant officer re-appeared and demanded to know what the joke was. I said, 'They all look like ants down there all scurrying around carrying bits and pieces.' Luckily he had a sense of humour and agreed with me, and then he gave me a right telling-off. What amused me most was on shaking the chiefs and the ERAs, they all said that the boiler rooms were not their part of the ship, it was quite a shock to some of them.

Once, while we were in dock at Alexandria, I was locked in one of the main circulating valves. We were in the floating dock at the time and my job was to grease the slides inside the valve chest. The valves were being shut and orders were passed by word of mouth from the engine room to the valve position by a team of stokers. The valves were not supposed to be fully shut but things did not go according to plan and I was locked inside the valve box. It was a very frightening experience for me, considering we were getting air raids at times. I thought that my time had come. However, after what seemed like an eternity, the valve began to open and as soon as it was open enough I was out and away like a jack-in-the-box (which is exactly what I had been!) and that was my first and last valve exercise I intended to be involved in under those conditions. I duly told the chief who was in charge that he could do the rest himself and I would stay outside. No more valves were done!

On 3 April I got a draft chit for the destroyer HMS *Griffin*. I was called to the engineering commander's office and told my draft chit could be changed and I could stay aboard. But I replied that my name was on that chit so I must go. He then told me it was a hard life on destroyers and I said, 'I don't think it can be harder than this ship.' Anyway he wished me all the best and off I went. In fact I was sorry in some ways to leave so many of my mates, but that's service life. On joining *Griffin* I enjoyed my job very much. We had lots of work to do but it was a more relaxed life and I accepted the responsibility that went with the extra work. I used to say to the chief that it was a holiday camp compared to *Eagle*.

Anyway my final word on *Eagle* is that she was the best training ship I could have had. Looking back I was proud to serve on her with all the work and graft I realised that I had learnt so much on board. When I left her I thought I knew very little about her but after being in the *Griffin* all my training stood me in good stead and I feel sure I could have gone back and flashed her up and got her ready for sea. So, all-in-all, with all her ups and downs, she was a good ship.

For the many veterans who remained aboard *Eagle* as she sailed away from Alexandria for the last time, a whole series of new adventures now lay in wait in the broader southern oceans.

# CHAPTER FIVE

# Red Sea Interlude

It will be remembered that the Suez Canal had still remained blocked by the wreck of the *Agnios Georgios* on 10 March and further dredging was being carried out night and day to provide a navigable passage around this hazard, so *Eagle* could still not proceed south. The Suez Canal Company notified the Admiralty on 12 March that they required 15 working days from and including 13 March to widen the channel past this wreck. The First Sea Lord of the Admiralty, Admiral Sir Dudley Pound, sent a signal on 23 March requesting an urgent date when *Eagle* could be sailed south.

If the ship could not proceed south to the Red Sea then, as we have seen, her aircraft could and they were accordingly placed at the disposal of the Commander-in-Chief East Indies under whom the Red Sea littoral came. The wiping out of the last remaining Italian naval force in Eritrea was being planned and *Eagle*'s Swordfish were destined to play a major part in this. Seventeen of the TSR aircraft from the disembarked squadrons therefore moved down to the coast flying to Port Sudan, arriving there in the afternoon of 25 March.

On 24 March a signal was received stating that *Eagle* must re-embark her aircraft from Port Sudan as soon as possible owing to the urgency of her deployment on the Indian Ocean and Cape of Good Hope trade routes where the German raiders were now operating freely and with some successes against our merchant ships.

A new estimate of the completion of the widening of the Suez Canal was achieved on 27 March which gave the earliest date as 8 April, but this was subject to modification.

The re-widening of the Suez Canal to enable *Eagle* to pass was reported on 3 April to be put back to 12 April. If this date was kept she was to join the South Atlantic Station as soon as she had completed her passage and the C-in-C East Indies was requested to signal his proposals for her quickest transfer to Cape Town to comply with this deployment. On 16 April these proposals were signalled including a boiler clean.

While their parent ship stuck at the northern end of the canal and 'Their Lordships' fumed at home, the Fairey Swordfish were proving themselves once more in combat with a series of deadly dive bombing attacks that kept *Eagle*'s name in the forefront of the conflict.

The Italian colony of Eritrea on the east coast of Africa with its naval base of Massawa on the Red Sea, should have been a potential knife threatening the vital British sea routes from round the Cape, India, Australia and the UK up to the Suez. But although the Italians had a cruiser, *Eritrea*, three auxiliary cruisers, *Ramb I*, *Ramb II*, and *Ramb IV*, nine destroyers, *Giovanni Acerbi*, *Cesare Battisti*, *Leone*, *Daniele Manin*, *Pantera*, *Francesco Nullo*, *Vincenzo Giordano Orsini*, *Nazario Sauro* and *Tigre*, eight submarines, four escort vessels and five MTBs based there their menace was more potential than real and their efforts did little or nothing to curb Britain's daily operations. Nonetheless the threat could never be totally ignored and a few cruisers and a half-flotilla of destroyers had to be kept on the station to guard against sudden bold sorties by the Italian ships and keep their submarines in check. This was done with efficiency and by January 1941 only four of the submarines remained. They sailed for Bordeaux in France leaving behind at Massawa just one flotilla of the surviving eight destroyers and a few auxiliary ships.

By the beginning of April 1941, the British were advancing on all fronts in east Africa and the collapse of the Italian 'empire' in Somaliland, Abyssinia and Eritrea was clearly only a matter of time. The naval forces under the C-in-C East Indies, Vice-Admiral Ralph Leatham, were augmented by the carrier *Hermes* and a few extra cruisers, *Shropshire*, *Cape Town* and *Ceres*, for the final bombardments and *Formidable* added her strike forces to the quota of attacks while on her way to the Mediterranean.

Admiral Bonetti was placed in command of Massawa's defences and the first British probes at the enemy defence positions prompted a mass evacuation by all the ships capable of putting to sea. The port's surrender was imminent when three of the destroyers, *Leone*, *Pantera* and *Tigre* sortied with the vainglorious announcement of attacking British shipping at

Suez. Unfortunately for them, they got no further than one of the islets just outside the entrance to their main base where *Leone* ran aground and was abandoned. Her two companions turned their guns on her instead of the British who were fifty hours' steaming to the north and then returned to port.

Time was now running out. Faced with the choice of scuttling in harbour or making a 'death or glory' raid Captain Gasparini decided to attack the softer target of British shipping at Port Sudan. Embarked aboard *Battisti*, and with *Manin*, *Pantera*, *Sauro* and *Tigre* under his command, he accordingly set sail on 2 April.

Once the British got word of the sailing of this flotilla Operation Atmosphere was planned, in which the FAA aircraft were to intercept the enemy once the RAF had located them. Both air forces were then to attack the destroyers until the three British 'K' class destroyers based at Port Sudan could come up and engage them. As it turned out, the navy had to do most of the job themselves. The reason why and the way in which *Eagle*'s young aircrew carried out their task are deserving of detailed attention. The torpedo bomber role of the Swordfish has been well documented but this Red Sea operation showed how well they could operate in the dive bombing role against large, fast destroyers. The failure of the RAF to contribute effectively to the operation also emphasises just how impotent their forms of attack were against shipping at sea and post-war accounts of 'contributions from the RAF' bear little relationship to their achievements.

Commander Charles Lindsey Keighley-Peach, DSO, RN, was in command of the striking force as SFAAO (D) (Senior Fleet Air Arm Officer (Disembarked), Port Sudan, and it was he who initiated Operation Atmosphere. Once it was considered probable that, prior to the surrender of Massaw, five or six of the serviceable Italian destroyers there would try to break out of harbour and either attempt to interfere with shipping in the vicinity of Suez or bombard Port Sudan. Consequently sixteen Fairey Swordfish were held in constant readiness at Port Sudan airfield, armed with 250 lb bombs, mainly GP (general purpose) bombs but a few with SAP (semi-armour piercing) which were considered inappropriate for thin-skinned and unarmoured warships like destroyers. Nonetheless that was all that was available owing to shortages of bombs at Port Sudan.

Bristol Blenheim aircraft of No.203 Squadron, RAF based at

Aden made the first sighting report at 1630 on 2 April. Their afternoon reconnaissance stated that, at 1430, they had sighted three large enemy destroyers which had left Massawa steering 000 degrees and two others were steering 090 degrees at 20 knots. The delay in reporting these sailings meant that there was no chance of mounting a strike that afternoon due to the distance from Port Sudan to Massawa. Keighley-Peach therefore decided to intercept the enemy destroyers at dawn the next morning and plans were laid accordingly.

In order to locate the enemy reasonably early and so formulate the attack before they had proceeded too far north a diverging 'step-aside' plan was evolved utilising six of the Swordfish to cover the area of their expected progress, crediting the enemy vessels with a speed of between 20 and 30 knots, between the east and west coasts of the Red Sea. These Swordfish, the 'First Search' were (Aircraft – pilot; observer; TAG) as follows:

E5A: Lt (A) Welham; S/Lt(A) Paine; Ldg Airman Ferrigan.
E5C: S/Lt (A) Suthers; Mid (A) Samuel Stanley Laurie; Ldg Airman Charles Philip Hector Baldwin.
E4F: Lt (E) Sedgwick; Lieut Lyle; PO Airman Bowman.
E4G: S/Lt (A) Child; S/Lt (A) Dawe; Ldg Airman Ford.
E4M: S/Lt (A) James Leslie Cullen; Mid (A) Edward Elliott Barringer; PO Airman Charles Frederick Beeton.
E4L: S/Lt (A) Morris; Mid (A) Harsant; Ldg Airman Tyler.

In addition Keighley-Peach searched the approaches to Port Sudan in E5G with Warrant Observer Wallington aboard. All these search aircraft were to take off at 0430 (local time) on 3 April with the intention that by first light half an hour later they could be a certain distance out in the area where the enemy might be expected to be, should they be steering a course to avoid reefs on approaching Port Sudan to bombard or be hugging the coast on a direct line to attack shipping at Suez.

There were no British ships in the vicinity so it was also decided to carry out the usual dawn reconnaissance patrols to cover the approaches to Port Sudan and to mount additional patrols to the south-east. And so it fell out. The weather on Thursday, 3 April, was cumulus cloud cover 8-9/10ths, from

800 up to 1500 feet and visibility was variable, being about two miles initially but opening up to eight miles; a 5-10 knot wind veered east from north-east.

At 0430 as planned six Swordfish (5A, 5C, 4F, 4G, 4M and 4L) took off for the dawn search, taking their departure from Port Sudan and all were armed with six 250 lb GP or SAP bombs apiece. They were ordered to make enemy sighting reports via 254 Wing's W/T station ashore but, because of the wasted hours and the need for the earliest possible launch of the main striking force, they were also to send in their sightings by self-evident code and naval aircraft code only. All machines had their Syko coding machines aboard but these were not used for enemy reports. Also, all the search aircraft had standing orders to turn to intercept, report and bomb the enemy on receipt of a first sighting report.

At 0510 aircraft 4M made an alarm report '2DR 170' (two destroyers, steering 170 degrees) but the ground station failed to pick it up. A minute later the same aircraft 4M reported two enemy destroyers in position 081 Port Sudan 28 miles, steering 170. This aircraft made an amplifying report and continued to shadow the enemy ships.

At 0525, the course of the Italian destroyers was reported as 230 degrees, speed 24 knots, and three and five minutes later aircraft 4M made yet further alarm reports of two destroyers and continued to shadow them closely.

Despite this diligence the first sighting report was not received by the FAA operations room until 0540. At once all flying crews were mustered and all maintenance personnel (some seventeen NCOs and men) were sent to the airfield to crank start the first striking force's aircraft. All these aircraft were sitting with bombs already loaded from the previous night. One shortage was aircrew. Although there were enough pilots to man each aircraft there were only three observers for the whole force, and no TAGs at all. One observer, Lieutenant (O) C.L.F. Webb, RN, had been lent to the RAF's 254 Wing to provide them with a knowledgeable observer for maritime operations for their Vickers Wellesley medium bombers. Another was detailed to lead the Swordfish striking force while the OC 824 Squadron remained in the operations room to deal with developments until the return of Commander (F). The final composition of the 'First Striking Force' was thus:

E5F: Mid (A) Lawrence (six 250 lb A/S bombs)

E5K: Lieut (A) Murray (six 250 lb GP bombs)

E5L: S/Lt (A) Camidge (six 250 lb GP bombs)

E5M: S/Lt (A) Turney (six 250 lb GP bombs)

E4C: Lieut Leatham; S/Lt (A) Stoven-Bradford; Ldg
Airman Ferrigan (three 250 lb GP and three 250 lb SAP
bombs)

E4H: Mid (A) Sergeant (six 250 lb GP bombs)

E4K: S/Lt (A) Timbs (six 250 lb SAP bombs)

Extra 250 lb GP bombs were promised by the Wing Commander of 254 Wing for re-loading the Swordfish for a second attack and fortunately these were supplied in good time.

Swordfish 5A made an enemy report at 0540 indicating the presence of four destroyers now, which had turned on to a northerly course. From then on a continuous flow of accurate reports flowed from the various aircraft in contact with the enemy into the operations room ashore so tracking of the force was never in much doubt.

What had happened to the Italian flotilla overnight? As usual they were unfortunate. The commander's ship, *Battisti*, suffered from engine problems, then a breakdown and her speed was reduced. She signalled the rest of her flotilla to continue on without her and made her own way slowly to the Arabian coast which she reached the next day. There her crew scuttled her. Thus only four ships remained in company on the morning of 3 April.

In compliance with her standing orders 5A attacked the rear destroyer from up-sun at 0545. The stick of bombs was avoided by this vessel by alteration of course and the bombs fell thirty yards clear of the target ship on her starboard side.

Back at Port Sudan at 0605 Swordfish 5G had taken off on a routine reconnaissance flight of the approaches to Port Sudan, having taken in part only of an enemy sighting report before she left the ground. The first attack had already shaken the Italians' resolve and at 0620 they were reported to have altered course to 040 degrees and were increasing speed!

Swordfish 4F now made her contribution, attacking the leading destroyer at 0635, but all her bombs overshot the target. Five minutes later 5G attacked the same vessel, the leading ship of the enemy line. This time one of the bombs scored a near miss. Return fire from the destroyers was described as 'intense but inaccurate', and the volume of this steadily fell off as the day wore on. None of the Swordfish was unduly troubled by it at any time. As well as their main armament of four 4.7 inch guns, each of the enemy ships had two 40 mm and two 13.2 mm AA guns and light machine guns with which to fight back. The four destroyers continued northward on conclusion of these first three attacks.

Five minutes later the first striking force took off from Port Sudan. This consisted of Swordfish 5F, 5K, 5M, 5L, 4C, 4H and 4K. The TAG of 5A, which had just landed at Port Sudan, did a quick dash from one machine to another and took off aboard 4C. He found the W/T set inoperational but managed to get it working by the time the Italian squadron came into view.

One other Swordfish, 4L, had landed at 0700 with a faulty engine and nine minutes later 5C piloted by Lieutenant (A) Welham with Sub-Lieutenant (A) Paine and Leading Airman Tyler, was ordered by W/T to continue shadowing the enemy until 0800 in addition to 4M which had first sighted the enemy and was still sticking like glue to them.

The First Striking Force had taken their departure from Port Sudan and steered 085 degrees to intercept the enemy ships and gained an altitude of 4,500 feet but, owing to the low cloud and poor visibility, they found it necessary to descend to 1,500 feet before continuing.

Reports from the shadowing aircraft were not received at this time because the W/T set was out of action so the following courses were steered to locate the Italian destroyers:

*True Course* 020 – six mins.
233 – six and a half mins.
065 – seventeen mins.
000 – twenty-four.

They then sighted the E4M which passed the bearing of the enemy. Soon after the destroyers were in sight in position 050 Port Sudan 50 miles and proceeding in a north-easterly direction. The striking force immediately turned away and began to climb. On their reaching an altitude of 5,000 feet they took up position in line astern and made their approach from above the cloud layer and from up-sun.

In the interim the attacks had re-commenced. Swordfish 5C failed to intercept the enemy initially, but made a landfall to get her bearings and then made a second search. She was successful on the second try and attacked the rear destroyer at 0715. The whole stick of bombs fell some 100 yards astern of the target.

Five minutes after this abortive attack the shadowing Swordfish 4M sighted the first striking force approaching and signalled to them by Aldis lamp, but they failed to see her. She was to be relieved by Swordfish E5A (which had no bomb load herself) which had taken off at 0740. This aircraft was ordered to report the enemy position, course and speed every twenty minutes. The last enemy report received up to then had been timed at 0715. But at 0817 another enemy report received from the striking force Leader E4C, and course was altered on this report, E5A herself sighting the Italians at 0824. Thereafter this Swordfish made continuous reports until 1020, by which time the second striking force was attacking.

It was now the turn of 4M (Sub-Lieutenant (A) Cullen, finally to have a go at the destroyers he had followed so patiently and at 0758 he dive-bombed the rear destroyer from 4,000 feet to release at 1,000 feet. Only the third destroyer fired at him during his dive, in echelon only. His aim-off was three-quarters of a length. The explosion from her bombs were seen on the target's port quarter and at the same time the first striking force began their attacks which continued until 0825.

The main striking force now began their attack. The Italian destroyers were proceeding at high speed in open order, the leading three in starboard quarter line and the fourth following some distance astern. The first and third destroyers were seen to be larger than the other two. E4C commenced the attack by diving the third ship in line which turned away to port. E4H Midshipman (A) Sergeant, followed down at 0815 and selected the same target. The dive was made from 5,400 feet to 1,000 feet from up-sun. Aim-off was one to one-and-a-half lengths and Sergeant was rewarded with a spectacular strike, scoring direct hits with his entire salvo of bombs. His victim, the destroyer *Sauro*, sank in about thirty seconds!

E5K (Lieutenant (A) Murray) at 0758 and E5L (Sub-Lieutenant (A) Camidge at 0815, attacked the second ship, both released at 1,000 feet. Aim-off for Murray was one-and-a-half to two lengths but Camidge had not enough deflection laid off and aim-off was only half-a-length. No AA fire was observed. Coming in over the ship's starboard bow , Murray's stick scored near misses along the port while Camidge approached from across her stern and his salvo dropped in a line at right angle to the ship's wake, E5M (Sub-Lieutenant Turney), also attacked this ship but his bombs failed to release and he returned at 0825 to attack the rear destroyer, scoring near misses down the port after side. E5F (Midshipman (A) Lawrence) attacked the first ship in the line from up-sun diving from 5,000 feet down to 1,000 feet for release. His approach was against the starboard bow and his aim-off was one-and-a-half lengths. He was carrying anti-submarine bombs and was not after direct hits but trying to achieve the underwater 'hammer' effect to blow her bows in below the water line. His aim was excellent and all six exploded in a line tight across her stem, straddling the bows.

E5K (Lieutenant (A) Murray) attacked the rear destroyer, again in a dive from 5,000 feet to 1,000 feet; the first of his stick dropped 20 yards over the port quarter.

On conclusion of their dives each of the Swordfish of this wave returned independently to Port Sudan where they landed safely between 0900 and 0945. Both 4M and 4G (which failed to find the enemy) also landed at this period. Owing to the weather conditions it was considered best to send them out as a team rather than as individuals so while their aircraft was refuelled and re-armed, the crews were sent to breakfast before resuming their war!

The next to make her run in this sequence was E4F (Lieutenant (E) Sidgwick), at 1015 who approached from up-sun at 4,000 feet down to 1,000 feet. Sidgwick's approach took him across the bows of his target, the leading ship, which executed a very sharp 30 degree turn towards him. E4F responded by herself turning sharply back into the destroyer's port bows and released with a one-length aim-off as he crossed the target, his stick of bombs exploding beyond the vessel's starboard side.

The surviving destroyers were now some 55 miles from Port Sudan and, at 0850, the second striking force was despatched. The make-up of this force was as follows:

E5B: S/Lt (A) Morris
E5C: S/Lt (A) Suthers; Mid (A) Laurie; Ldg Air Baldwin
E5G: Lt (A) Cheesman; Wt Obs Wallington
E5M: Mid (A) Hughes; Mid (A) Harsant
E4F: Lt (E) Sidgwick; Lt Lyle; PO Air Bowman.

All these aircraft were armed with six 250 lb GP bombs. The weather was now deteriorating with 8-9/10ths cumulus clouds from 1,200 to 2,000 feet and visibility was patchy varying from two to nine miles. There was a north-easterly ten-knot wind.

Again, owing to this poor visibility, these Swordfish were instructed to spread in loose formation in line abreast to cover a front of about eight miles to ensure they did not miss the enemy ships in the murk. No.254 Wing was requested to re-transmit the enemy reports from 5A which was shadowing to the leader of the second striking force to make certain of a correct interception.

The second striking force therefore formed up in loose 'V' formation covering an eight mile front at a height of 900 feet with a TAS (True Air Speed) of 87 knots. They took their departure from the Port Sudan Light at 0851. They took a running fix from the Sanganeb Reef Light and, at 0945, altered course on receipt of a sighting report from E5A which had been re-transmitted by No.254 Wing W/T and been picked up by E4F ten minutes earlier.

Within eleven minutes they had two of the surviving Italian destroyers in sight bearing 020 degrees and a range of eight miles, all the aircraft gaining visual contact at the same moment. The third destroyer was not visible and so it was decided to concentrate on the two initial contacts rather than waste time searching for her as well. Thus, at 0956, two destroyers were sighted by the second strike force leader bearing 020 at eight miles range. All the Swordfish sighted these ships individually and climbed through the cloud cover.

As they deployed, the leading destroyer altered course to 340 degrees while the second maintained her north-easterly course. The first aircraft to attack was 5C who climbed to 3,000 feet and carried out the attack from up-sun, diving through a small cloud and releasing his bombs from a height of 1,000 feet. His victim was the second destroyer, *Daniele Manin*. There was only slight anti-aircraft fire to put him off and his aim-off was one length. The attack was from the ship's starboad bow as she made a hard turn to port away from him. He was rewarded with two direct hits, both bombs hitting their target, the *Daniele Manin*, between her funnels. Another a near miss just off her starboard bow stove it in with the underwater concussion. The ship quickly caught fire abaft the bridge, and oil fuel was observed gushing out of the hole blown in her starboard bow.

The stricken vessels lost way, turned to starboard and was seen to be on fire forward and emitting a large amount of black smoke. By 1020 she had come to a stop and lay dead in the water. The crew lost no time in abandoning ship.

Ten minutes later both E5G and E5M attacked the leading destroyer, but no hits were observed. At 1015 E4F also attacked this ship, again without result. She continued to make off at high speed to the north-east and made no attempt to go to the aid of her sinking sister. She, *Manin*, was last seen at 1113, E4F sighting her off the port bow at about four miles' range. She was still stopped, listing to starboard and down by the bows. She was surrounded by numerous rafts and floats.

All aircraft landed safely ashore between 1130 and 1145. The strike force leader, however, took over shadowing duties from 5A which returned to base but she was in turn forced to abandon her watch at 1115. The last reported position of the two surviving destroyers was that they were in position 033 Port Sudan 154, MLA (Mean Line of Advance) 070 degrees and retreating at an impressive 34 knots.

Ashore the re-armed Swordfish had been readied for action as a third striking force, but it was considered that the enemy's high speed would place them out of effective operational range. It was therefore decided that the RAF's Wellesley and Blenheim medium bombers, with their greater range, should take over the hunt.

It was assumed that the two surviving destroyers were making for the neutral port of Djeddah in Saudi Arabia, and so permission had to be obtained through diplomatic circles before this strike could be sent off. Confirmation of their own attacks was received at 1113 when the drifting hulk of the *Manin* was sighted by 4F on her return track. She was stopped, listed to starboard, with her upper decks awash and down by the bows. She was surrounded by numerous rafts and ships' boats.

Both No.14 Squadron (Bristol Blenheims) and No.223 Squadron (Vickers Wellesleys) were available to No.254 Wing, RAF, and they were sent out at intervals as separate striking forces. With them went Lieutenant Webb. The Wellesley of 223 Squadron carrying the naval observer took off at 0615 on 3 April and was ordered to locate and attack the Italian destroyers whose speed and position were given as 085 Port Sudan at 0525 steering 230 degrees at 24 knots. They carried out a square search around this location for an hour without seeing anything at all of their quarry or receiving any further positioning reports. Lieutenant Webb therefore decided to return to base for more information.

They landed and were given more up-to-date information. The enemy flotilla was now described as being 060 some 27 miles from Port Sudan, course 034 degrees at a speed of 20 knots. The Wellesley took off again at 0740 and conducted another square search relative to the reported MLA of the enemy ships, but after two hours they had drawn another blank. On their final leg they sighted Marsa Salak at eight miles' range, bearing 275 degrees. Obtaining a fix from this Webb discovered to his dismay that he was 34 miles from his estimated position. It seemed obvious to him that these RAF aircraft were fitted with totally inaccurate compasses and ASIs (Air Speed Indicators) and that these had caused this huge error. Lieutenant Webb listed the circumstances which made accurate navigation and therefore the sea search and interception of the enemy almost impossible as:

1. Compasses and other navigating instruments were not sufficiently adjusted for this type of work. This may have been peculiar to the first aircraft in which I flew.

2. Only one observer's compass was in the aircraft and I was told it was never used or swung. It could not be shipped to obtain bearings as the compass mounting was removed and an additional Lewis gun shipped on each side. There was no hand bearing compass in the aircraft.

3. W/T reception was frequently interfered with by the use of R/T for squadron inter-communication.

4. Other aircraft's enemy reports were not received direct. As the Wing HQ station was very busy indeed, the answer to requests for this information took a considerable time to get through.

5. Windfinding over the sea was very difficult as the drift sight was wooded by the tail wheel and sternpost, consequently sea markers could only be seen for a few seconds. Drift by bombsight could not be obtained owing to the weather conditions (absence of wind lines on the sea surface). Coral reefs were utilised for this purpose with some success.

6. The observer's seat was situated directly above the mainplane giving a very poor field of vision.

On their return to Port Sudan, the aircraft were refuelled and again the five bombers took off at 1215. By now Webb had learnt that two of the four destroyers had been sunk by his FAA companions and that the surviving pair were believed to be heading flat out for the sanctuary of neutral Djeddah in Saudi Arabia and that by the time the Wellesleys reached them they would be almost there. Webb's instructions were only to carry out an advancing line search in a south-westerly direction starting in position 21 degrees 28 minutes North, 38 degrees 50 minutes East. He had no confidence in the aircraft's compass so he decided to proceed to the coast five miles north-west of Djeddah and obtain his own fix before commencing the search. It was 1328 when Webb sighted Ras al Aswad and six minutes later spotted two destroyers in position 187 Ras al Aswad, six miles distant. They approached at a height of 3,000 feet and Webb was able to identify both vessels as Leone Class destroyers. He could also see that they were in deep water drifting stern to the shore and flanked by coral reefs. Their crews were in the position of abandoning both ships and he estimated that this must have been in progress for about half-an-hour previously. He reported their position by W/T to HQ and told base that both ships were being abandoned but were not sinking. The reply was 'Bomb with accuracy'.

The five bombers circled for another half-an-hour to give the Italian crews ample time to get clear and then proceeded with their orders. Despite the fact that the two vessels were stationary, undefended sitting ducks and mere target practice,the RAF failed to come'even close to hitting them from their deliberate attacks. Two of the bombers released their bombs in high level attacks and two others carried out shallow bombing runs. There was no opposition. The fifth aircraft developed serious engine trouble and had to force land before dropping her bombs. The four Wellesleys that did attack approached from different directions and dropped single bombs throughout. Lieutenant Webb watched each painstaking attack and reported 'all fell wide of the targets, the *nearest* being about 20 yards away'.

On conclusion of these abortive attacks, the officer commanding the squadron, Flight Lieutenant Wild, RAF, decided to land alongside the fifth aircraft which had been seen to come down some four miles south of the point to which the Italian sailors were scrambling ashore. The idea was to rescue the aircrew to save them from internment or being the subject of an incident with the Italian seamen. The chosen landing spot did not look good but there appeared to be none better in the vicinity.

Accordingly, at 1445, the Wellesley carrying Lieutenant Webb landed, but as it began to taxi back before taking off again it ran into a soft patch of sand and stood on its nose, damaging the airscrew. This now left two aircrew stranded instead of one. One of the remaining bombers was then instructed to patrol over the disembarked Italians to discourage them from seeking revenge on the helpless aircrew. The other two aircraft found a good landing ground on a hard sandy island about seven miles walk round the shores of the bay to the southward. The party of airmen and Lieutenant Webb then removed food, water, CBs, navigating instruments, parachutes and two Lewis guns from their own aircraft. At 1545, the remaining airborne bomber also landed. Five minutes later both stranded Wellesleys went up in balls of smoke and flame after a few bursts of Lewis gunfire were directed into the wing fuel tanks.

The Blenheims of 14 Squadron meantime arrived on the scene at 1625 and they were soon conducting their own attacks against the still drifting destroyers. The aircrew heard an explosion soon afterward. About a quarter of an hour later the superstructure of a 'K' class destroyer (actually the destroyer HMS *Kingston*) was visible above the sand banks, gunfire was heard and two more violent explosions marked the final ending of the *Pantera* and *Tigre*. An hour or so later the rescued crews embarked and all the bombers took off. As they did so the two ships came in direct view of the Wellesleys as they circled them. Lieutenant Webb described them thus:

' ... one was seen to be on her beam ends in shallow water and the other in deeper water, had her bows blown off and was on fire amidships.'

Thus it is quite clear that both destroyers were actually sent to the bottom as a result of naval gunfire from the *Kingston*, and *not* scuttled as has been incorrectly stated in reference book after reference book, including both British and Italian official histories.

Some interesting observations and conclusions were reached from this impressive little action. In his own report Commander Keighley-Peach concluded that:

It is submitted that this operation has proved quite definitely that low dive bombing is the best method of attacking fast destroyers or similar ships, from the air.

Steaming at 34 knots, these ships, under full helm, spin round remarkably quickly, and it is considered that the most efficient way of hitting them is to attack in sections of three aircraft; one diving from either beam and one from astern, at intervals of a few seconds. This ensures that whichever way she turns, one aircraft should be presented with a fairly steady target. It requires a nicety of judgment.

In this connection it is worthy of mention that the handling of *Tigre*, the leading destroyer, was exemplary. He frequently reversed his course under full helm, thereby avoiding sticks of bombs which subsequently fell on either side of him.

As to the bombs themselves, 250 lb GP Tail-fused with 1' delay, the commander stated:

For bombing of destroyers and similar types constructed with thin plating – and with personnel in exposed positions above deck, the GP bomb is the most efficient.

The effect of a stick falling on the *N. Sauro* was almost instantaneous and ship blew up and sank in 35 seconds. In addition, both *Pantera* and *Tigre* had a large number of dead and wounded on board prior to abandoning ship; the result of a number of near misses.

All the Swordfish pilots were well aware of the fact that anti-aircraft opposition was likely to be small and that therefore a low height of bomb release was justifiable under those circumstances. 'It was the first time that a fast moving target had been attacked with bombs,' wrote Keighley-Peach. It was noticed that the avoiding action taken by the *Tigre* Class destroyers was much quicker and more effective than that taken by the *Sauro* Class. From his observations the commander also stated that:

The most effective form of avoiding action by the destroyers appears to be a turn directly towards the attacking aircraft. In addition to 'combing' the stick of bombs, there is a tendency for all the bombs to fall over the target. In both cases, where the destroyer was hit, avoiding action consisted of a turn away from the aircraft. The 'aim-off' ahead of the target, though difficult to assess, appears to be between one and one and a half lengths for a 30 knot target.

The conclusions of Commander Keighley-Peach agreed almost exactly with observations made by German dive bomber pilots off Norway, Dunkirk and the French ports which this author has studied. His comments on casualties caused to thin-skinned ships by near miss bombs also confirmed to observations made by the Australian destroyers operating in the Mediterranean Fleet at this time. Despite this, the opinions expressed on this report by Their Lordships back at Whitehall varied considerably.

Lacking much enthusiasm in support of the views expressed was the DNAD (Director of the Naval Air Division). He wrote on 15 May 1942 that:

> The bomb recommended for use against destroyers is the 250 lb SAP bomb fused TDO.025 (To detonate 25 seconds after impact). It is considered the suggestion that the GP bomb should be used in preference is based on insufficient evidence. One destroyer was sunk outright using GP bombs but it apparently received a salvo of six although it is not quite clear how this was possible if the stick spacing was correct. In such an event it is considered not surprising that the ship did sink.
>
> In the case of the other destroyer two hits and one near miss were achieved which resulted in the vessel sinking. Here the GP bomb scored success although the fusing of TD1 was much greater than would be recommended. But, this does not prove that two hits with SAP bombs, which are much more robust, would not have also sunk the ship. In this respect it may be said that it would be most extraordinary if the near miss was responsible for any damage. As the bombs were fused 1 second delay they would detonate about 60 ft deep.

DNAD therefore was adamant in the view that in order to ensure penetration of the bomb to the vitals of ships such as destroyers, escort vessels etc., the SAP bomb should be regarded as the most suitable. The GP series would in his view cause considerable damage provided it did not break up but this could not be assured. He did, however, concur with the commander's remarks about aim-off and tactics.

DTSD (Director of Training and Staff Duties Division) noted that:

> The survival of *Tigre* and *Pantera* till they were abandoned off Jidda [*sic*] shows the value of high speed and drastic use of rudder to avoid being hit by bombs. Their avoiding action is remarked on ... as being more rapid and effective than that of the other destroyers.

With this opinion, and that of the commander's, the Director of Gunnery and Anti-Aircraft Warfare was in violent disagreement.

> With regard to 'avoiding action', the impression gained from this report and DTSD's remarks, is that the use of helm and high speed will materially decrease the chance of being hit. This is not true for dive bombing.

In his opinion:

> ... the bombing was no more accurate at ships on a steady course than it was when they were under helm. On two occasions when hits were scored, the ships were altering course. Although alterations of course at suitable moments do tend slightly to decrease the accuracy of aim of a dive bomber, they are also very liable to decrease the effectiveness of gunfire and, in consequence, may often be *dis*-advantageous.

Whatever the views of the various senior officers there was no disputing that this action as a whole was a smart piece of dive bombing by the young Fleet Air Arm pilots from *Eagle*'s striking force and, after an incredible amount of deliberation by the Honours and Awards Committee, Keighley-Peach himself was awarded the BEM for this action. Sub-Lieutenant (A) Suthers and Temporary Midshipman (A) Sergeant both received the DSO and there were Mentions in Despatches for Acting Sub-Lieutenant Cullen, Temporary Midshipmen Laurie and Barringer, Petty Officer Airman Beeton and Leading Airman Baldwin.

Nor was this the final part *Eagle*'s aircraft played in the termination of all Italian pretensions of power in East Africa. An air strike was mounted against the remaining warships in Massawa harbour on 8 April and they scored a hit on the destroyer *Giovanni Acerbi*, and which had to be sunk soon after.

Also scuttled was her sister ship *Vincenzo Giordano Orsini*. This completed a nap hand for the British and when they entered the port a little later nothing of the Italian Navy remained afloat there.

Signals sent from the Commander-in-Chief, East Indies Station, to Admiral Cunningham at Alexandria at this time reflected both the work of *Eagle*'s aircraft and the ship's future deployment:

ST1722Z/1.4 from CinC E.I: – *Eagle*'s Swordfish have sunk Italian destroyer *Pantera* off Massawa 1415/1.4

ST1122Z/3.4 from CinC E.I: – Owing to the good work of *Eagle*'s aircraft your need for the two destroyers is probably greater than mine. I am however keeping *Greyhound* and *Griffin* for the present.

ST0658Z/16.4 from CinC E.I: – *Eagle* accompanied by *Cornwall* to leave Aden as soon as possible after arrival and proceed to Mombasa with all despatch where *Eagle* will have 4/5 days to boiler clean.

After finishing off the two enemy destroyers HMS *Kingston* removed the ensign from one of them, *Pantera*, and presented it to *Eagle*. This ensign was hung in the after end of the hangar, another trophy to accompany the sacred Ikon which had been presented to the ship at Crete earlier. The work of the Swordfish continued. 'Ginger' Tyler recalls events in the Red Sea thus:

Some days later I was in a reconnaissance Swordfish, flying from Teclai in Eritrea. Arriving at the Dachlach Islands we found the lagoon full of Italian shipping, probably evacuated from Massawa. They were moored close together, and some had been scuttled and were sitting upright on the seabed. Suddenly we noticed a launch coming away from one of the ships which was already settling in the water. Obviously this was the scuttling crew, and immediately we dived to put a stop to their activities. As we went down the pilot gave them a long burst from his Browning, and as he pulled out I added my quota from the rear gun. Three runs was enough, and the launch disappeared under the shark-infested waters of the lagoon. Not a pretty sight.

At little over a thousand feet it was always possible to see sharks swimming in the sea below. Flying in a single-engined machine this was not a happy sight. Occasionally we would dive and machine-gun the sharks ...

One frightening incident put a stop to our machine-gunning activities. This was when my pilot dived and used his gun on a number of sharks, only to pull out of the dive very quickly when a series of ominous shudders shook the aircraft. Back to the carrier we headed, and on landing we found that a number of bullets had gone through the blades of the airscrew, owing to fault adjustment of the synchronising gear. Understandably the pilot vowed that he would never again shoot up a school of sharks. I fully concurred with his decision.

Flying over endless miles of ocean with only a single engine to keep us airborne, the thought of having to ditch was not a very cheerful prospect, especially if the ditching had to take place out of sight of the ship. The dinghy, stowed in the upper mainplane was supposed to inflate automatically on hitting the water, but so far this had not happened with any of the lost aircraft.

Consequently, whenever my aircraft was being over-hauled, I made it my business to assist the rigger, my first priority to make sure as far as possible that the dinghy and its automatic and manual releases were in good working order. Happily I was never to test the efficiency of the dinghy, but for my work on the aircraft I was saddled with the nickname of 'Rigger Mortis'!

The stately progress of HMS *Eagle* from Alexandria to the Red Sea itself to pick up her squadrons after their splendid exploits was rather pedestrian. She passed straight through Port Said at 0900 on 10 April and entered the Suez Canal, while her destroyer escort returned to Alexandria. At 1600 the same day she was squeezing carefully by the stern of a merchant ship that had been mined and whose bows had been towed away to a port for rebuilding.

Proceeding down the canal, *Eagle* dropped anchor in the Great Bitter Lake at 1800 that evening. Here she remained in the stifling heat from Thursday night until the morning of Tuesday, 15 April. During these three days' immobility strong winds had been blowing continuously, which made it impossible to steer the carrier past another wreck. This block was originally a large Greek vessel which had set off one of the accoustic mines assiduously sewn by the Luftwaffe while travelling toward Port Said. Hoppers and tugs had also met similar fates but they were more easily cleared; the Greek merchantman was more of a headache.

The Arabian side of the canal was dredged out which made it possible, with care, for large ships to pass the wreck. *Eagle* proved a difficult task for the canal owners' tugs to tackle when she came to the wreck; her high sides and block-like presence made manoeuvering in the gales that were still blowing like trying to shut a barn door with the handle of a broom. It took them an hour's delicate work before she was safely through.

They finally reached Port Suez at 1245 and commenced oiling. On Wednesday, 16 April, *Eagle* sailed from Port Said at 0945 and proceeded to Port Tewfick on the northern Sudanese coast, unescorted. She did not arrive at Port Sudan itself just down the coast for another three days, anchoring at 0700 on 18 April. The harbour there was very small compared with Alexandria. Here they found a few merchantmen in harbour along with the light cruiser *Cape Town*, the AMC *Lucia* and some A/S trawlers. *Lucia* left at 1800 for Massawa, now under British occupation but *Eagle* gave leave ashore from 1630 to 2230. One of the merchant ships in port was the neutral Brazilian vessel *Taubute* which had been indiscriminately bombed and machine-gunned by the Luftwaffe in the Mediterranean a few weeks previously.

Next day *Eagle* put to sea at 0510 and her 17 victorious Fairey Swordfish flew on board once more at 0930. Once the squadrons were re-embarked *Eagle* continued to make her way through the Red Sea, which was now totally free of the enemy. Indeed President Roosevelt of the United States had declared it safe for American shipping and no longer part of the war zone. Aden was reached at 0705 on 21 April and here they found their old companion the cruiser *Cornwall* who was to team up with them once more for raider hunting. After a short rest there both ships sailed at 1615.

By dawn on Tuesday they were proceeding at a steady nineteen knots through the Gulf of Aden, steering a course which took them close up to the coast of Africa on their way to Mombasa. This voyage was largely uneventful but was made memorable by a 4 inch AA gun shoot at a target towed by the *Cornwall*'s amphibian. The bursts of shells largely ignored the drogue and crept ever more close to the towing 'plane.

Eventually a particularly 'accurate' burst exploded just ahead of her which provoked the true and original famous signal from the indignant *Cornwall* which has been quoted and misquoted in dozens of books: 'We are towing target, not pushing it.'

Next day it was the turn of the 6 inch guns to show what they could do by carrying out a full calibre 'throw-off' shoot on *Cornwall* and later that same day *Cornwall* conducted her own 'throw-off' shoot by her eight 8 inch guns against *Eagle*. Here, by some misjudgement one of her salvoes of 8 inch bricks fell just 100 yards short of *Eagle*, amidships! More tragically one of the Swordfish out on patrol, failed to return. There were long faces aboard but later on a signal was received from a merchant vessel stating that she had safely recovered both aircraft and crew intact! The tramp herself was on her way to Aden but at least they knew the men were safe.

On Saturday, 26 April, the two ships arrived finally at Mombasa in Kenya at 1000. They moored alongside the cruisers *Glasgow* and *Colombo* and the destroyers *Kingston* and *Kandahar* arrived in from a patrol that same afternoon. Among the many merchant ships in harbour were both American and Japanese vessels.

The weather now was very different to what her crew had been used to in the Mediterranean. The rainy season was under way with torrential downpours. However it was recorded that this made the temperature aboard ship a little more bearable. On 28 April it was 94 degrees in the shade, very hot and stuffy.

All was now set for their important new role. There was much to do for many German raiders were already at sea and momentous decisions were already being taken to send out yet more, including the brand-new 45,000 ton battleship *Bismarck*. The urgency of the situation was reflected in yet another signal received on 25 April: 'ST1942Z/25.4 from CinC E.I. – *Eagle* and *Cornwall* are to leave Mombasa and proceed to Durban with all despatch.'

They were off on the hunt once more.

# CHAPTER SIX

# Rounding up the Raiders

*Eagle* was originally to have operated in company with the New Zealand light cruiser *Leander* in a new group. However, the pace of events dictated otherwise and her initial task was to search for the raider which attacked a merchant vessel at around 0102 GMT on 28 April. The latitude of the attack was not given in the SOS signal transmitted by the victim, the longitude was estimated to be about 63 degrees East. Her original orders (which had been to sail from Mombasa on the afternoon of 1 May in company with the cruiser *Cornwall* and proceed to Durban 'with all convenient despatch'), were cancelled.

Instead of that, *Eagle* sailed from Mombasa at 1050 on Tuesday, 29 April, and her squadrons flew aboard at 1230. Her abrupt departure was further prompted by the receipt, earlier that morning, of the distress signal whose origin was plotted as some 1,200 miles distant, roughly halfway between Mombasa and the Maldive Islands in the Indian Ocean. She was instructed to proceed at 15 knots with the light cruiser *Hawkins* towards position 002 degrees North, 60 degrees East to hunt for this raider. The carrier was to steam at her best speed toward this location in the hope of picking up the trail of the raider, but she could not do so immediately because the cruiser *Hawkins* had been earlier instructed to rendezvous with *Eagle* and this was not achieved at 1800. In the meantime the *Cornwall* was sent off hot-foot on her own, sailing from Mombasa at 1000.

Next day, 30 April, *Eagle*'s Swordfish patrols reported that they had sighted a ship and course was set to overtake her. This proved to be a false hare, and was in fact a neutral vessel, a Swedish merchantman. *Eagle* patrolled at 12 knots on west side of the search area up to Freetown, Sierra Leone and then began her return voyage to Mombasa, having found no trace of her quarry at all. An extensive search was conducted throughout that day and the next as the two British warships were now in the middle of the area known to be the raider's patch. Nine Swordfish were despatched at first light on 1 May, and continuous patrols carried on until last light, all to no avail.

The same routine continued on both 1 and 2 May, with the carrier steaming slowing east during the day, altering course to take advantage of the wind to fly on and off her aircraft as they ranged to-and-fro. After dark *Eagle* would reverse course and steam back slowly westward, gradually quartering a huge area of the empty sea in her patient hunting pattern. New demands came across the ether on 1 May. *Eagle* was 'Urgently Required' at Gibraltar and was to be recalled from her present operation and proceed in company with the battleship *Nelson* after calling at Durban. Next day it was confirmed that she was to proceed to Durban with the *Hawkins* after a fuelling stop a Mombasa.

On 3 May, as no further news was heard from their quarry, *Eagle* complied with these new signals and by noon they were well on their way to that hospitable South African port. They duly anchored there at 0830 on Sunday 4 May, and began oiling. Leave was granted from 1615 until 2300.

At 0610 the following day, 5 May, they were at sea once more in company with *Hawkins* and proceeded to the south-west towards Durban. Also that day it was learnt that their voyage was likely to take much longer than previous ones of a similar duration for their orders were not to stop to replenish and their speed, accordingly, had to be kept down to the most economical in fuel oil. Making between 18 and 21 knots the two ships made a leisurely passage southward and arrived at that South African port of such happy memories, at 1630 on the afternoon of Friday, 9 May. Here they found the majestic bulk of the battleship *Nelson* (32,500 tons, nine 16 inch guns). She was to act as their new partner in a fresh hunting group.

*Eagle* left Durban at 1300 the next day and joined *Nelson* outside at 1515. Both ships steamed south again, making for Cape Town. During the following days as they approached the Cape mountainous seas were encountered and both big ships rolled heavily. Cape Town harbour was therefore a welcome sight and the mist-enshrouded slopes of Table Mountain welcomed them in to some sort of sanctuary from the elements. Both ships anchored alongside each other and oiling commenced at high speed. Clearly something was in the wind.

One young sailor aboard the carrier was in reflective mood as he compared the buzzing brightness of Cape Town with what he was hearing and reading of much-bombed and blitzed London as the Luftwaffe continued its savage pounding of the capital night-after-night. The endurance of the Londoners was incredible, smaller provincial cities, Coventry, Liverpool, Plymouth had suffered two, sometimes three or four, nights of the blitz which was bad enough, but London 'took it' from September until March, an unmatched saga of pluck and dogged determination by a civilian population. This made an impression on all who heard about it even at a great distance. The young sailor wrote:

> Tonight, while listening to the news from London, my thoughts were with the people and comparing them with those here in South Africa. The contrast at present is very great. England, darkened, completely blacked out, ever on the alert for 'invaders'; what a wonderful change it would be for the people to have a day in the life of a South African. For example: when steaming into port it was a truly awe-inspiring sight. As far as the eye could see there was a sea of lights dancing and twinkling, spreading up the huge slopes to the very foot of Table Mountain which forms the perfect background to Cape Town itself.

It was also a raiders' and U-boat's delight, for all shipping was silhouetted against this display. U-boat captains found similar conditions off the American east coast later in the war and wreaked havoc thanks to the lights ashore. None of this serious effect concerned the observer that night however. He continued:

> In the background, the heart of the city lay, red, green, blue and numerous other neon signs were flashing on and off as if beckoning to our massive floating steel man'o'war as she slid gently but swiftly into habour. The dockside illuminations silhouetted the cranes, warehouses and other ships which were secured alongside. Streets, houses, shops with their bright decorations and cars seemed to be emphasising the amount of light which helped build up this dazzling picture. This, like many other South African ports, is what these people are enjoying. They have never experienced black-outs and perhaps never will. How utterly impossible it must be for them to realise what life is like and living

conditions are like back home in the war zone. Even as I write, this ship is battened down, blacked out, ever on the alert, silently slipping through the night like a grey ghost. England is much the same, only instead of the stillness and quiet bombs are thundering down and the roar of gunfire is constantly heard.

Even in the lee of the harbour the seas continued to run high. Just how rough it was is illustrated by the fact that the next morning a motor-boat from *Nelson* was returning to the battleship when it capsized. Two of the crew were drowned and five others were seriously injured in this tragedy. Another accident delayed her departure until 1800 that evening. When leaving harbour she rolled so badly in the terrible seas that were running that her anchor cable was pitched across her fo'c'sle.

Twenty-seven of her ratings were swept away by the enormous links. Two were knocked clean overboard and devoured by sharks, ten others later had to be sent ashore with broken legs while the rest were still having treatment aboard the ship's sickbay.

*Eagle* was to join South Atlantic Command for administration purposes only, but this was to remain temporary for she was to continue to act under the direct orders of the Admiralty in London as and how they needed her. We now know that the unravelling of the enemy codes had to be kept secret, even at very high level, but by despatching the *Eagle* and other warships to where they knew from plotting the enemy supply ships were, and by carrying out air searches to locate them and bring them to book, the enemy would remain convinced that it was lucky hunches or chance encounters that resulted in the rounding-up of his clandestine supply chain, and not through the breaking of his secret signal codes. And so it turned out.

One of the vital 'Winston's Specials', the WS convoys that passed round the Cape of Good Hope from the UK to the Mediterranean, was due at this time. These were always given strong protection as they were usually the most valuable of ships with troops and vital war materials destined for the Middle East embarked. The current convoy, WS8A, had the battleship *Nelson* and the brand new 6 inch cruiser *Mauritius* as escort and *Eagle* was to add her care to this already formidable force when their paths crossed on 17 May. Later the cruiser would escort *Eagle* into Freetown, Sierra Leone, on the West African coast.

On 13 May the two big ships sailed at 0650 from Cape Town on the next leg of their journey up the South Atlantic. Fuelling difficulties were anticipated for two such large vessels, and after three days at sea it was found that *Eagle*'s old engines were still using oil at an uneconomical rate. The plans were changed and a fuelling stop at St Helena was therefore arranged so that both heavy ships would be instantly available for new operations during their passage north. The two big ships therefore changed course and headed for lonely St Helena island where the ships would oil while anchored off that island. The only way this could be done was by the stirrup pump method from a fleet oiler secured astern.

From the latter years of World War I and right through the inter-war decades, experiments in oiling ships at sea from tankers while both were underway had been carried out. Almost exclusively this involved the tanker taking up position ahead of the warship and passing the oil lines into her. This was a very slow and time-consuming method. Both the American and German navies had developed ways of alongside fuelling, whereby with the oiler streaming pipes on both sides of her she could get several lines in each ship and carry out the job far more quickly and efficiently. The Royal Navy was only now beginning to adopt such methods but, at that stage of the war, had no large, fast tankers especially built for this method. So almost always the smaller oilers of the Royal Fleet Auxiliary Leaf Class rather than the larger and better equipped Ranger Class had to be employed instead.

It was while on *Eagle*'s passage to St Helena that the German raider *Atlantis* sank the British freighter *Rabaul* (5,618 tons). A few days later, on the night of 17/18 May, the raider herself was drifting with most of her crew asleep when she had a very nasty fright indeed, according to the German writer Muggenthaler. He was to write that soon after midnight on 18 May two ships were seen approaching through the darkness in line astern and heading straight towards the raider herself. The alarm was raised and her engines were started silently. The bow-waves and bows-on silhouettes of the approaching vessels were by now 'clearly distinguishable', he states.[1] 'They were warships, British, the unmistakable battleship *Nelson* and carrier *Eagle*,

[1] *German Raiders of World War II*, Robert Hale, 1978.

both plowing along at fourteen knots heading north.'

Both these ships passed *Atlantis* at a mere 7,000 yards' range. By this time the raider had, according to Muggenthaler, got her engines working, turned away to present her stern and thus escaped detection. Apart from wondering how a bows-on view of two ships in line-astern at night could instantly be recognised as *Nelson* and *Eagle* (if line astern, how could they see the rear ship?) one wonders why the Germans could see in the dark and not the far larger look-out complement of the two British vessels. Also as *Atlantis* was equipped with four single 21 inch torpedo tubes, one wonders why she did not use them. She had the advantage of absolute surprise, close-range against an unprepared enemy. Two torpedo hits on each of these two major vessels would have disabled them if not sunk them and she could have then called up U-boats to finish the job. What a prize and coup for the Fatherland. Instead, if the story is correct, she chose to creep away and save herself for the destruction of further rusty old tramp steamers instead! A strange decision indeed.

One incidental observation on this 'close encounter' is given by TAG Tyler:

> By now we had installed in the aircraft the newly-arrived ASV radar sets and during the searches we had been able to put them to good use. During one squadron exercise we had been able to detect the ships at a distance of about forty miles, approach above cloud cover and successfully carry out a dummy torpedo attack. With this equipment we hoped to be successful in our search for raiders known to be at large in the South Atlantic.
>
> As the ship's installation was not yet complete, I suggested to my observer that an aircraft could be left on deck at night, and the ASV could be used in an effort to detect any ships which might come into range during the hours of darkness. No action was taken on my suggestion, possibly a costly error, because after the war I read an account of how an enemy raider, on passage to the south, had sighted *Nelson* and *Eagle* in the moonlight at very close range, but had stealthily altered course and escaped. The lookouts on our two ships must have been singularly inattentive on that night, and we lost a valuable catch.

*Eagle* and *Nelson* eventually arrived off Port James, St Helena at

1515 on Sunday, 18 May. While there they received a signal that the *Shropshire* had been blown up off Cape Town. Many of the naval personnel assumed that this was the heavy cruiser of that name and that sabotage was suspected in a similar manner to the loss of the *Bulwark* and *Natal* in World War I. However it later transpired that the vessel concerned was the ss *Shropshire*, a merchant ship, which was anchored in Durban harbour on 9 May.

Port James itself had no harbour; the sea reached to the very foot of the huge cliffs which made the replenishing of ships very difficult. A couple of armed merchant cruisers lay at anchor off the port which was completely exposed to any marauding U-boat. It was therefore something of a relief to get underway again, when both heavy ships sailed at 2330 that same night.

While at sea next day both *Nelson* and *Eagle* carried out HA target practice during the afternoon and entered what was known to be an area with much German submarine activity. It was very welcomed when it was announced that two destroyers were on their way to join them and act as their screen but neither was expected until 21 May. *Eagle* herself was back in what was described as the 'Mediterranean Routine', in other words full alert and readiness at all times. Exactly as promised, at 1300 next day, the destroyers *Duncan* and *Highlander* joined company. They continued their voyage.

Both ships were due at the outer end of the searched channel into Freetown at 0800 on 23 May. On 22 May, however, they received warnings of movements of an unidentified enemy unit in their general area.

The ether was full of raider reports at this time; one enemy surface ship was reported about 700 miles west of Freetown and the group was heading in that direction to carry out a more detailed search. Unfortunately the short endurance of the fleet destroyers of the 'A' to 'I' classes meant that both ships had to be detached to return to Freetown for refuelling the next evening and for the next two days they were again without anti-submarine protection save for their ever-vigilant Swordfish.

On Friday, 23 May, they had no sightings on their quarry whatsoever and were heading towards Freetown themselves. Word was received of the sinking of the Egyptian liner *Zan-Zan* which they had last met in the Red Sea. She had been on her way to New York with a very valuable cargo which included X-Ray machines and equipment. A German raider was known to be in that area but they could not cover the whole South Atlantic on their own.

Early on Saturday morning two more destroyers, *Boreas* and *Velox*, joined them, and later still *Duncan* and *Highlander*, having refuelled, also returned giving them quite a respectable screen for the final stages into Freetown itself. It was just as well for a merchant ship was reported torpedoed in that very area the day before one of *Eagle*'s Swordfish located the survivors in two boats. One of the destroyers was accordingly detached to rescue them. At 1830 that day *Eagle* herself was passing through masses of floating wreckage from the torpedoed ship. She had by then steamed more than 11,000 miles since leaving the Mediterranean. Later the same day came the shocking news of the blowing up of the *Hood* by the *Bismarck* far, far to the north. Should the monster battleship ever shake off her pursuers and head for southern waters *Nelson* and *Eagle* were well-placed as 'long-stops' to intercept her. However, there were many battleships and carriers much closer to her and seeking revenge, including *Nelson*'s sister ship *Rodney* who in fact was later to be in at the kill.

Both *Eagle* and *Nelson* were therefore instructed to proceed towards a position 009 degrees North, 02 degrees 5 minutes west. This movement was made on the assumption the enemy might be a warship. Further cruisers were sent out to cover the area and be on hand available to co-operate in the interception on 23 May. All this took place in the aftermath of the *Bismarck* episode when all the German supply ships stationed in the Atlantic were identified, located and rounded up.

The two big ships and their escorts arrived without mishap at Freetown at 1045 on 25 May and refuelling began immediately. An observer aboard wrote that:

This harbour, like all African ports, is full with merchant ships of every shape and size. At present there are well over fifty large merchantmen here as well as smaller craft. His Majesty's ships *Vindictive*, *Albatross*, light cruiser *Curacoa* and AMC *Edinburgh Castle* (flagship), submarine chasers and other small naval craft are also stationed here. As malaria is prevalent in this region leave is only granted up to sunset and black-out regulations are in force here.

On 26 May *Nelson* left Freetown harbour early in the morning on her way to Gibraltar to take the place of Force 'H' as most of Admiral Somerville's heavy ships were far out in the Atlantic taking part in the *Bismarck* chase and the west gateway of the Mediterranean was open to both the Italian and Vichy fleets. In the event they both failed to take advantage of this 'stretch' of British naval forces.

Aboard *Eagle* the most important event was the departure of Captain A.R.M. Bridge, their skipper during their Mediterranean assignment and since. He was relieved by Captain E.G.H. Rushbrooke. The usual captain's farewell speech was not delivered by Captain Bridge. One writer aboard the carrier thought that this was due to earlier trouble on board the ship.

Next day the brand-new battleship *Anson* arrived at Freetown being described as 'a new 14 inch battleship'. This comment in a seaman's diary of the time is a victory for the work of the 'ship's disguises' committee for the vessel was, in reality, the old battleship *Centurion*, which had been converted into a radio-controlled target ship as long ago as 1930. She had been taken into Plymouth dockyard at the start of the war where she was converted into what has been called 'a credible imitation of the new battleship *Anson*' and she was on her way round the Cape in a 20,000 mile trip to Bombay. She later served in the Mediterranean as a floating anti-aircraft ship in lieu of a real battleship on some Malta convoys.

The work of provisioning *Eagle* to her full capacity continued unabated during this time and it was not until 1730 on 29 May that she sailed from Freetown escorted by *Velox*.

Again they were on the hunt for the enemy. It was not a German warship but an enemy oiler that was their quarry. Its position was put at within 30 miles of 25 degrees North, 34 degrees, 40 minutes West in a signal of 28 May. It was thought she was lurking there in readiness to refuel the German 8 inch cruiser *Prinz Eugen* which had originally accompanied *Bismarck* on her sortie, and, regretfully, had escaped her bigger cousin's just fate. On 29 May the light cruiser *Dunedin* (4,850 tons, six 6 inch guns) was therefore sailed to assist *Eagle* in her search.

All day Friday they headed north-west where a German supply ship had been reported. A long hunt was envisaged and refuelling at sea was expected, but on Saturday, 31 May, the

*Dunedin* joined them. The carrier herself went to 'Action Stations' at 0200 on 1 June following a brilliant flash of light from *Velox*. It turned out to be a false alarm, the destroyer's 'de-gaussing gear' (an anti-magnetic mine cable) had short-circuited! As usual *Velox* had to return to harbour due to lack of fuel.

Later *Eagle* was reporting that low endurance and enemy submarine activity off Freetown weakened her ability to use Bathurst and that to do so she required further local escorts for her protection. *Dunedin* parted company at 1915 on 5 June. The 8 inch cruiser *London* was on hand at this time but she was despatched on 2 June and ordered to proceed at 25 knots to the south-west after another hot sighting.

That following Monday morning *London* was believed to be about sixteen miles off their port bow but was never sighted. One of the Swordfish flew low over a merchant ship during the morning. The ship opened fire with machine-guns and hit the aircraft in the tail. The pilot and crew were not injured by this reception and the aircraft resumed its original flight. Next day they learned that *London* would not be meeting them but *Dunedin* re-joined them during the morning.

Now began a patient period of searching of the kind with which the crew of the carrier were now only too familiar. The following day found them in position 24 degrees 09 minutes North, 34 degrees 07 minutes West on a course of 290 degrees at thirteen knots. One of her crew worked out they were approximately 1,700 miles from Bermuda, 2,200 miles from either Land's End or New York, 1,600 miles from Freetown and 1,700 miles from Trinidad. What was obvious that here, in mid-Atlantic, there was an awful lot of water to be scoured to find a very small vessel. They also had to refuel themselves and had a rendezvous with their own oiler on 5 June.

At 0700 they stopped engines in a calculated risk and the RFA *Bishopdale* secured her stern to *Eagle*'s starboard side aft the bridge structure. Hawsers made her fast athwart the carrier thus and the oiler's own engines were kept at slow ahead so that the ships did not roll together and touch. In this position the oiler was in effect slowly towing the carrier sideways. Numerous sharks could be made out in the clear water circling the ships in anticipation. Further out *Dunedin* also patrolled in a large circle around the two stationary vessels on watch. It was a tense and hair-raising experience and all felt like sitting ducks just awaiting a chance U-boat captain to come along and have all his dreams come true. The lack of underway fuelling capacity on the Royal Navy was forcing them to take such chances. The sad and lonely fate of the *Dunedin* in these same lonely waters a few months later showed just how dangerous.

The job was not finally completed until the evening and then all three ships steered in a westerly direction throughout the night and the cruiser took her turn to refuel the following day. Meanwhile word came in that *London* and her accompanying destroyer *Brilliant* who were also operating against enemy supply ships had intercepted the tankers *Esso Hamburg* (9,849 tons) and *Egerland* (9,789 tons) and that their erstwhile companion the battleship *Nelson* along with the cruiser *Neptune* had a similar success with the German *Gonzenheim* (4,000 tons), while the tanker *Gedania* (8,923 tons) was first sighted by aircraft from the carrier *Victorious* and then intercepted and surrendered to the *Marsdale* at the same time. Other such prizes were known to be in *Eagle*'s area and the search continued. They figured that anything the *Victorious* could do, the far-more experienced *Eagle* could do better. And so it proved!

It was now Friday, 6 June and all this time the patient Swordfish had been carrying out their lonely patrols. Then, at about 0815 that morning all their patience was rewarded. One of the aircraft sighted and challenged a merchant ship. She gave her name as a Norwegian vessel but shortly afterwards increased speed and made a sharp alteration of course.

When the Swordfish got back to the *Eagle* they checked on the vessel's name and discovered that the Norwegian ship bore no resemblance at all to their contact. At once a striking force was flown off the carrier to investigate further and, if necessary, to bomb her if she could not prove her identity satisfactorily. Each of the aircraft was armed with a 500 lb bomb for the job.

At 1300 word came in that the aircraft flown off had failed to find her and had been forced to jettison their bombs owing to the great distance they had already covered searching for her. A fresh striking force was prepared and flown off and later that evening, around 1800, they tracked her down. The suspect had meantime given herself away completely by sending out radio messages first in English and then in German. The Swordfish carried out an attack and hit her with a single bomb amidships.

Her cargo proved to be oil stowed in drums and her crew were reported abandoning the vessel and taking to the boats. Her poop was by now under water and she was burning fiercely, some 160 miles from *Eagle*. Their victim turned out to be the German blockade-runner *Elbe* (9,179 tons) on her way back to the Fatherland from East Asia.

That evening, well pleased with this result but eager to save life if they could, *Eagle* steamed a course south-east by east up to 2200 and then turned north-west by north to the position where survivors of the *Elbe* would probably be found. By dawn the following day and search planes were up early, they found no trace of the German seamen, even though the British ships passed through about 200 empty floating oil drums at around 0930.

They could tarry no longer as other quarry were about and they headed south-east by south once more. Another hiccup was now found in that the *Bishopdale* had not supplied them with the right grade of aviation spirit for their Swordfish and this compelled them to head once more for Freetown to embark enough of such aviation fuel to keep her search planes airborne. While on their way there early on the Sunday, they again changed course sharply as another tanker, hopefully carrying the correct grade, was sighted by the Swordfish.

It was also fortunate that the weather they were encountering at this time was uniformly good or else the task would have been very difficult indeed. On occasions clouds would blow up but mainly the hot tropical sun beat down all day, rising at 0540 and setting at 2150, these times altering as they moved east and west in their search patterns. But on the evening of the Sunday the wind began to freshen.

Next day, in position 24 degrees 05 minutes North, 32 degrees West the oiler was sighted and went alongside *Dunedin* and she completed oiling by midday. the oiler then went alongside the carrier and aviation petrol and fuel oil were pumped aboard until darkness fell. They then steered 185-195 degrees at a steady 15/16 knots throughout the next two days purposefully. On 12 June they were instructed to remain patrolling where they were until further notice and that *Bishopdale* would again fuel them in a few days to keep them on station. The 'Ultra' intercepts of the German Enigma coding machine were of course top secret and remained so until long after the war, but even the meanest intelligence aboard the carrier could tell that they were receiving 'very good information from somewhere.'

One innovation at this time was the fitting of depth charges to the after part of *Eagle*'s flight deck, one on each side. These were not fired off as from a destroyer's throwers, but were simply rolled over the nets and were set to explode at a depth of 150 feet. The Swordfish on A/S patrol carried modified 'semi-streamlined' depth charges as the standard ones were large and cumbersome, making flying difficult and resulting in awkward landings.

They oiled again on 13 June and the word was widespread that an enemy vessel was somewhere in their immediate vicinity. *Bishopdale* cast off at 1800 and twenty minutes later a striking force of four Swordfish was in the air armed with 250 lb bombs. In the interim *Dunedin* took her opportunity to oil. She completed at dusk but there was still no sign of the enemy ship.

They steamed south at sixteen knots during the next day and that following night their quarry was reported. The *Eagle*'s diligent and patient air searches were now fully rewarded. At 0800 on 15 June a hundred per cent 'clearing search' of the patrol area was flown off and they returned at 1145. At 1015 a continuous line patrol was commenced across the northern end of the search area. Should any vessel be reported by this patrol Force 'F' was in the best position then to intercept her by daylight. Thus it came about when, at 1215 in position 18 degrees 37 minutes North, 37 degrees 29 minutes West, *Eagle* received an alarm report of one merchant vessel from Swordfish E5B, which was the first aircraft on this line patrol. A few minutes later an amplifying report gave her course as 160 degrees and described her as a tanker. The Swordfish crew comprised the pilot, Temporary Midshipman (A) William L. Hughes, observer temporary Sub-Lieutenant (A) Philip A. Denington and TAG, Leading Airman Norman C. Wills.

On closing the tanker 5B signalled the vessel to stop and, as no notice was taken, machine-gun fire was opened ahead of the ship. This warning was promptly returned by accurate machine-gun fire from the vessel itself, which scored several hits on both fuselage and main-planes of the Swordfish. 5B wasted no more time on warnings; tipping over she carried out a dive bombing attack on the tanker and scored two direct hits with both her 250 lb SAP bombs, straffing with her machine-guns as she did so.

Their target commenced to circle leaving behind her a thick

oily wake and, at 1350, shortage of fuel forced 5B to return to the carrier. Her place was taken twenty minutes later by E5K. Her crew comprised the pilot, Sub-Lieutenant (A) Charles R. Camidge, RN, Observer, Temporary Sub-Lieutenant (A) William H. Lett and TAG, Leading Airman Frank A. Dean. They found the tanker, which was in fact the German supply ship *Lothringen*, the former Dutch *Papendrechte* (11,000 tons) five weeks out of La Pallice, and commanded by Captain Max Friedrichsen. She was brand-new having been building at Rotterdam when the Germans invaded and was taken over and completed as a supply ship for them. She was steaming erratically, apparently damaged and leaking oil. She had two white flags flying at the foremast and a white sheet was being waved from the bridge. The Swordfish crew could also see that she was attempting to lower a power boat. To deter her abandonment and scuttling, they opened fire on this boat with machine-guns and it was promptly dropped into the water with only one man in it. 5B then circled the ship and machine-gunned all the other ship's boats which had the desired effect of keeping the crew on board. Repeated requests for her nationality were finally rewarded when she signalled back by lamp, 'German'. Three more Swordfish joined in the circling of the vessel but they all had to return to *Eagle* at 1608.

The race was now on to get to her before she could be sent to the bottom by her crew. At 1335 *Dunedin* had been ordered to proceed to the position of the tanker. She had one boiler blocked off awaiting repair and the best speed was therefore only 24 knots. However, most unusually for a German ship, although there subsequently proved to be a number of naval personnel on board and six time-fused scuttling charges were found to be in place, no steps were taken to scuttle her, even when the British cruiser appeared on the scene. This was therefore one of the very few occasions when a ship surrendered to aircraft, although there were others.

*Dunedin* sighted the tanker hull-down at 1705 with three Swordfish overhead. She had already been reassured that the ship was not yet sinking and as the cruiser closed from astern at 1725 her crew was piped to action stations. Five minutes later *Dunedin* hoisted the signal WBA International at both yardarms. (This meant – 'Stop. Do not lower boats. Do not use radio. Do not scuttle. If you disobey, I open fire'). She also ordered the Swordfish to keep a good watch for enemy U-boats which might be lurking in the vicinity awaiting their opportunity to slam torpedoes into the stopped cruiser. To the cruiser's captain it all seemed suspiciously like a lure or a trap. As they closed they could see the crew throwing packages overboard, no doubt confidential signal books, logs and the like.

*Dunedin's* cutter being hoisted on her port side, she approached the tanker in a loop from across her stern, reducing to eighteen knots and around her starboard side, where she dropped two depth charges as a precaution against U-boats, and then across her bows taking up position off her port bow facing towards her. The explosion of the depth charges upset the already panic-stricken civilians aboard the *Lothringen* and signals started flashing from her in haste. The tanker was lying stopped with a marked list to port with the sea around her covered in oil fuel. At 1752 and boarding and anti-scuttling teams were sent across under Lieutenant-Commander R.M.H. Sowdon and Engineering Officer Lieutenant-Commander (E) A.W. Hughes. Both teams proved most efficient. The German wounded were transferred to the cruiser's sick bay for care.

The German chief officer and chief engineer co-operated by pointing out to the British the six scuttling charges, none of which had been set, it transpired, and these were duly removed. The pumps were got working and the damaged tanks pumped out. By 2000 the British party had the *Lothringen* ready to proceed. As a considerable bonus Telegraphist Percy Jackson of the boarding party made a second search of the wireless room and, fallen down behind a wrecked W/T set, he found the W/T cypher log in plain language, cyphered versions of W/T signals sent by the ship and a list of confidential books held. It seemed as though the German operator, while destroying the set with a sledge-hammer, had dislodged these books which had previously been placed on top of it. The operator himself was said to have been 'deeply chagrined' when he learned of their discovery!

After the cruiser had arrived, an anti-submarine patrol was organised by the carrier to protect both captured and captor but they could only remain in the area until 1820. By 2040 *Eagle* herself arrived on the scene and found that *Dunedin's* skipper, Captain R.S. Lovatt, RN, had things well in hand. The German ship's engines and steering were reported to be intact and he proposed to put a prize crew aboard her and send her in to Bermuda, a course of action with which Captain Rushbrooke of the *Eagle* fully concurred. Accordingly a crew under Lieutenant R. Beveridge was put aboard while the German chief officer, three other officers and 19 ratings were also retained aboard to help work the ship. These were all mercantile men and very reluctant warriors. The German naval party was of a different stamp and they showed much resentment at the tame way the ship had been so easily given up to the British.

The prize was got under way at 2350 on a course for Bermuda and *Dunedin* remained in company with her until 0150 the next morning when she was well on her way without any difficulties. Force 'F' therefore left her and turned eastward.

Following this spectacular coup *Eagle* was ordered to return to Freetown and they steamed steadily east at 16/17 knots through the next few days. It was then that the weather, hitherto so kind to them, began to worsen considerably; it grew chilly in the extreme, and heavily overcast.

New plans were being hatched ashore. On 17 June the destroyer *Brilliant* was sailed from Freetown to rendezvous with *Eagle* and *Dunedin* and it was intended that these three were to form a hunting group with the heavy cruiser *London* under the command of C-in-C, South Atlantic.

By Wednesday, 18 June, the wind had risen and was blowing from dead ahead, but the cloud banks broke up a bit as a result and no longer obscured the sun all day. The first sign of approaching landfall was when the destroyer *Brilliant* met them in the afternoon of 19 June and on Friday they passed a large convoy. They had to wait outside the harbour while large mechant ships left and did not finally anchor at Freetown until 1630, when they immediately began oiling from the *Cedardale*. After the loneliness of their mid-Atlantic patrolling the port was a bustle with ships of all types. The old seaplane carrier *Albatross* had sailed for the Cape for a refit. The heavy cruiser *Shropshire* was in harbour but she too sailed for a refit, in the UK for a few days later. Experiments were conducted with a Swordfish amphibian which was flown on and off the ship while they were in harbour. They also found the 'rainy season' in full swing with sharp torrential downpours throughout the day while the rain fell steadily for eight hours at a time.

It was another time to take stock and it was worked out that since they left the Mediterranean Fleet at Alexandria *Eagle* had steamed 20,514 miles which was only 1,086 miles less than the distance around the world. During their last long period at sea alone they had steamed 7,854 miles at an average speed of 15.9 knots. Her Swordfish had searched 612,096 square miles which brought the area covered by these aircraft since the outbreak of war to a staggering 3,168,706 square miles of ocean covered. They had consumed 286,028 gallons of aviation fuel in doing it.

They remained at Freetown two weeks. Further instructions followed on 5 July when a signal spelt out that *Eagle* was to work with *London* out of Freetown and with *Dunedin* and the AMC (Armed Merchant Cruiser) *Alcantara*, was to form Force 'Z', with *Eagle* being senior officer of the force. Various methods were promulgated on how best to identify various merchant vessels by the ship's aircraft.

They had actually sailed for St Helena at 0915 on 4 July, escorted initially by the destroyers *Velox* and *Vansittart* and expected to meet the *Alcantara* on the Sunday. The two destroyers left them early that day and the AMC was sighted in the afternoon. They were now in the area of the SE Trades which blew with a force of 4-5. Once south of 12 degrees they backed to easterly and the temperature gradually dropped as they proceeded southward. Both ships arrived off St Helena on 8 July and found *Dunedin* already at anchor.

Force 'Z' formally got underway when all three ships sailed at 0600 from St Helena to carry out new raider hunting operations. It was common knowledge aboard that a German merchant ship was in the area, in addition to a raider or raiders which were working with her. The ships carried out night encounter exercises on 12 and 13 July with star shells and searchlights being employed and they patrolled patiently for the following week with no sign of the enemy or any change to mark one lonely day from the next.

As a postscript to their earlier success it was announced on 12 July that part of a safety clip from a bomb dropped by one of *Eagle*'s aircraft on the German vessel *Lothringen* was found in one of the ships oil tanks, which suggested that the bomb did not explode. A report on this matter was sent in as it could have been very serious.

By 18 July nothing had been found, the AMC continued to

patrol but *Dunedin* and *Eagle* were ordered to return to St Helena to refuel. The patrolling Swordfish did locate one mysterious vessel on their way back and she was duly challenged from the air but gave the correct code signals in reply. Even so, *Dunedin*, at that time detached, came across the same ship. Her challenge was more probing and it was discovered that the ship belonged to the Vichy French. A prize crew was put aboard her and she was sent into Freetown. She was reported to have been 'heavily laden, and overrun with rats!'

Later the two warships joined forces again and a 6 inch throw-off shoot was conducted by *Eagle* against *Dunedin*, which resulted in a very close call indeed for their companion. 'Tug' Whymark remembers how they were conducted, what was involved and a little incident that took place this day of which he had some knowledge!

When *Eagle* was off the African coast in April 1941 a 6 inch armament 'controlled' practice throw-off shoot was carried out with practice shells. Our accompanying cruiser, *Dunedin*, acted as the target vessel. I was closed up at my action station, that was a trainer on No.2 starboard 6 inch gun. All the other 6 inch guns crews were closed up at the same time in readiness.

Our communications number, on orders from our gunlayer petty officer, 'Kate' Lewis, reported to the controller 'Starboard 2 gun closed up' and immediately we received back from control both the bearing and the range, the first of which was my responsibility as gun trainer. My job was most important in such a throw-off exercise as it was essential that the fall of shot should be strictly ahead of the moving target, especially as in this case it was not a target but a real live cruiser!

The necessary adjustments and alterations as received had to be set by me on the trainer bearing dial. In my case the dial pointer would be set so that the projectiles would fall at a pre-ordained distance ahead of the *Dunedin*. The trainer's gunsight would therefore be ON the target itself but the gun barrels are offset, hence the expression 'throw-off' shoot.

To make these adjustments on the trainer's dial there was a protective cap covering the adjustment mechanism which was released by a screw and thread movement, but my dial cap was severely jammed, for many reasons I suppose: months at sea, weather, hardly any practice shoots, who knows? Our captain of the gun was getting anxious and the rest of the crew had reported to him as being 'ready'. Control were also waiting and 'Kate' Lewis was becoming concerned, because once the cover was clear the adjustments would be applied in a matter of seconds.

Suddenly the cover came free. I called to the gunlayer. 'I think I have done it, Kate.' Whether he misundersood and thought that not only had I got the adjustment cover free but had also set up the necessary safety degrees on the dial completely I don't know. In fact I'd freed the protective cap only.

Simultaneously the 'Starboard 2 Open Fire' bell rang. The gunlayer closed the gun's intercepter and gun fired! Looking through my gunsight the *Dunedin* was in full view, the projectile fell dead amidships, but, thank heaven, short by several yards.

Starboard 2 gun was immediately ordered from Control to 'cease firing' for the rest of the throw-off shoot. Later there was a full enquiry by the senior gunlayer's staff, I assume with a satisfactory conclusion with the mistakes ironed out amicably. As I have mentioned before we were a happy crew under the circumstances especially while we were out in the tropics.

Night deck landing exercises were also conducted from 0300 on 22 July and all the pilots made good landings. The two ships duly arrived back at St Helena on 23 July and *Eagle* refuelled from the oiler *Nyholm*. While she was here the badly damaged cruiser *Dido* called in. She was one of the many ships of Mediterranean Fleet that had been crippled by German dive bombers in the Battle of Crete that May and was on her way back to carry out extensive repairs.

Both ships were then sent to operate in area J.35, and were due to return to St Helena on 3 August. This was done and they duly sailed at 1300 on 24 July. They patrolled in that specific area without any sightings, thus both were reported as available to provide cover to convoy WS10X if required, refuelling at St Helena on their way to join it.

*Eagle*'s next instructions were to carry out a patrol with *Dunedin* in an area west-south-west of St Helena returning there by 3 August. This was done and proved totally uneventful. Another refuelling at the island on 3 August and then they were ordered to return to Freetown. They took aboard 43 labourers from the island to take passage there and were ordered to carry out further searches for Vichy French ships during the journey. Again nothing marred the boredom of their voyage and they dropped anchor on 10 August.

They remained at Freetown while they carried out a much-needed boiler clean until 26 August which enabled her crew to enjoy some shore leave at this fetid port in the steamy climate of West Africa. Eyewitnesses gave these description of life in that forgotten part of the world suddenly elevated to a strange importance by the needs of the war:

> The harbour, as may well be imagined, is always full of merchant ships, some proceeding to England, others proceeding to different parts of the world. Freetown at present can be described as a junction for the mechant navy. It is here that ships on passage to and from England are sorted out into their respective standards, i.e. speed, destination etc., and made ready for convoy. Escort vessels, numbering at least thirty, and comprising mainly destroyers and corvettes, undertake the duties of covering ships as far as the UK. At present there are about sixty large merchant ships waiting to be convoyed.
>
> A few days ago the cruiser *Edinburgh* and destroyers of the 'J' class arrived with a convoy numbering sixteen ships from England. The ships were all large liners (*Andes* being one), full of troops, presumably for either Alexandria or Singapore. These have now left and are proceeding south. There is one Free French submarine-chaser here that is co-operating with our ships and Mr Sopwith's private yacht has been converted into an escort vessel and arrived here yesterday.
>
> This evening, at 1620, an air raid alarm sounded off, one bomber was flying extremely low over the assembled ships. The bomber belonged to the Vichy Government and is believed to have been passing information to the Germans. It was shot down a few miles away by fighters. No bombs were reported.

Later the same observer gave a good account of how the tropical conditions added to the normal hazards of war, even in harbour:

*Seen from one of her own returning Swordfish aircraft HMS* Eagle *turns to port as another line of Italian bombs throws up a picket fence of explosions taller than masthead height in her path. Eastern Mediterranean, July 1940. (Copyright E. Kennard)*

Eagle *had no fighters of her own but hastily embarked three Gloster Sea Gladiators at Alexandria. These three machines were flown by Swordfish pilots and constituted the Fleet's only aerial defence against the hundreds of Italian bombers sent against them. Nor was any ship equipped with radar at this stage of the war in the Mediterranean. Here the 'Commander Flying', Keighley-Peach takes off from the* Eagle *to attack yet another enemy squadron. Between them the three Gladiators shot down a shadower and hit two or three bombers. Keighley-Peach himself was hit in the thigh by return fire from the faster enemy bombers. Battle of Calabria, 9th July 1940. (Copyright E. B. Mackenzie)*

*A Gloster Gladiator from HMS* Eagle *passes over the battleship HMS* Barham. *(Copyright E. B. Mackenzie)*

'One of the very few', *Gloster Gladiator fighter aboard HMS* Eagle *in the Eastern Mediterranean July 1941. (Copyright A. W. Leyster)*

*More mishaps. A Gloster Gladiator is dumped overboard from HMS* Eagle *after a pile-up. Note the RAF officer in the group. (Copyright E. B. Mackenzie)*

*The Battle Fleet in line ahead in the Eastern Mediterranean, July 1940.* Malaya *(closest to camera),* Warspite *and* Ramillies. *Seen from HMS* Eagle. *(Copyright E. B. Mackenzie)*

*Battle of Calabria, 9th July 1940. Lieutenant E. B. Mackenzie's 'bedroom' aboard HMS* Eagle *laid out as a dressing station during the combat period. (Copyright E. B. Mackenzie)*

*July, 1940, prelude to the Battle of Calabria. Looking like the modern equivalent of a medieval 'Man-at-Arms' this is the war equipment of Sick Berth Attendant Pattinson aboard HMS* Eagle *ready to give medical help to any injured crew members. He was not called on for his services this time. (Copyright E. B. Mackenzie)*

*Lifebelts 'will be worn'. In the almost ceaseless Italian air attacks subsequent to the Battle of Calabria the*
Eagle *was a popular target. Here a group of officers await the next attack as the fleet returns to Alexandria.*
*(Copyright E. B. Mackenzie)*

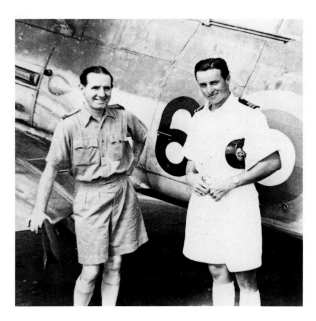

*Surgeon Lieutenant 'Mack' Mackenzie*
*with 'Henry' and 'his' Gladiator*
*aboard HMS* Eagle *off Greece,*
*31st October 1940. (Copyright*
*E. B. Mackenzie)*

*HMS* Eagle. *One of the first operational Fairey Fulmar fighter aircraft aboard the carrier is prepared for operations in the Eastern Mediterranean, Spring, 1941. (Copyright 'Tug' Whymark)*

*A good clear aerial photograph showing HMS* Eagle *in her war paint in the Eastern Mediterranean, autumn 1940. (Copyright E. B. Mackenzie)*

*HMS* Eagle *patrolling to the west of Crete in 1941. 'A' and 'B' 4-inch HA anti-aircraft guns seen from the ship's bridge. (Copyright 'Tug' Whymark)*

*A rare bird in the Eastern Mediterranean. A Blackburn SKUA dive-bomber of the Fleet Air Arm landing aboard HMS* Eagle *in the spring of 1941. (Copyright E. B. Mackenzie)*

*With HMS* Illustrious *out of action for more than a year after being hit six times by German Junkers Ju.87 Stuka dive-bombers off Malta – HMS* Eagle *resumed her lonely role as the Mediterranean Fleet's only aircraft-carrier. Here the Fleet's Rear-Admiral, Aircraft Carriers, L. St. G. Lyster, CVO, DSO, RN, flies aboard HMS* Eagle *to fly his flag aboard her until the delayed arrival of HMS* Formidable *fresh out from the UK but stuck in the Red Sea due to the aerial mine laying of the Suez Canal by the Luftwaffe. (Copyright E. B. Mackenzie)*

The weather at Freetown continues to be very stormy, the sky being overcast the better part of twenty-four hours. The harbour becomes almost impossible to navigate by small craft in safety. The tide changes every four hours, setting up a very strong current, which travels at about seven-and-a-half knots on the ebb. The sloop *Bridgewater*, lying one hundred yards away off *Eagle*'s beam lost eight men in the harbour at 1800 today. A liberty boat, returning to the ship, sank. The survivors were fortunate enough to make for other naval craft as they drifted with the tide. Darkness had already set in making rescue difficult and almost impossible. Ships lying near trained their searchlights on the scene. Later on in the evening I was searching with the motor boat from *Eagle* for these survivors and we picked up twelve, after which the task had to be abandoned as the night was so rough and visibility only a few yards in spite of our powerful searchlights.

*Eagle* also lost one man today (Tuesday, 26 August). He was employed in rigging the 'centre line bridge'. The guard rails he was tightening suddenly fell apart, causing him to fall thirty feet to the flight-deck below.

On 21 August a signal was received informing them that *Eagle* was to be temporarily withdrawn from the South Atlantic station and sailed as soon as practicable for the United Kingdom.

A batch of fresh blood for the carrier's crew, some officers and 8 ratings, arrived aboard the *Dunnottar Castle* from home on 22 August. The C-in-C, South Atlantic asked if he could retain the carrier until 28 August to provide convoy protection and this the Admiralty granted. *Eagle* was then to sail from Freetown with two destroyers as far as 021 degrees North, 019 degrees West to sail to Gibraltar and was due to arrive on 30 or 31 August, provided an escort could be scraped up for her. On 28 June she was ordered from Freetown in company with the light cruiser *Newcastle* towards Gibraltar after a suspected sighting of a German Hipper Class cruiser at large in the mid-Atlantic area. On 29 August she sailed at 0815 with the heavy cruiser *Dorsetshire* in company as Force 'F'. Her return to the UK was postponed indefinitely in view of the seriousness of this new information.

They sailed to provide maximum cover for groups of various southbound merchant ships which might prove highly

vulnerable to a German heavy cruiser raider. With *Dorsetshire*
(*Newcastle* was detached from Force 'F' to act independently but
in co-ordination) they patrolled on the assumption that the
raider was proceeding to the South Atlantic area from the
North Atlantic. The heavy cruiser remained in company and
refuelling was arranged to take place from the fleet oiler
*Echodale* to enable them to stay out at sea during this crucial
period. This proved easier said than done.

They initially sighted the tanker at noon on 4 September but
high seas and a strong wind made oiling impossible to
contemplate that day. The next day saw *Echodale* coming
alongside the carrier and during the afternoon several attempts
were made to secure her, without success. Six hawsers snapped
during these attempts. Fresh attempts were made during the
night with the same result. An escorting corvette kept up a
continual anti-submarine patrol while these efforts were in
progress and the *Dorsetshire* kept some ten miles distant also
circling. The swell continued to be high. On 6 September the
tanker was temporarily secured during the night but the hoses
could not be got across and she cast off again at 0800. Another
attempt was made with the *Echodale* securing ahead of the
carrier's bows. Another 14 hawsers had snapped during these
operations.

At 1300 the oiler was secured ahead of *Eagle*; at 1800 the
oiling hose was run across and three-quarters of an hour later
the petrol hose was also got inboard. Both ships now moved
slowly ahead at 4-5 knots and it was estimated that by this
method the replenishment would take 20 hours to complete.
On the Sunday morning the two wire hawsers, one carrying the
petrol hose and the other the oil hose, parted under the terrific
strain. The petrol hose wire, running over the flight deck to the
tanks, caught two ratings as it parted and whipped. One
received facial injuries, the other had arm, leg and abdominal
injuries.

The ahead method was abandoned and the astern method
proposed in its place. Another attempt was made at 1630 but
once more the hawsers parted. They steamed in a large circle
during the night and at 0830 *Echodale* again came alongside
and secured ahead. The hoses were passed into the carrier by
1000 and oiling re-commenced. At 0300 next morning the oiler
broke away once more but as only about 500 tons of oil were
still required all further efforts were abandoned and *Dorsetshire*

took her turn. Seven officers and 15 men were transferred to the tanker and the corvette that day for their return to Freetown, which indicated to *Eagle*'s crew that either they were in for a long patrol or were going to another station.

Once *Dorsetshire* had replenished, the two ships headed southward down the centre of the South Atlantic following slender leads as they came in from the Admiralty. Their ultimate destination was again to be St Helena which they were due to reach after a week's patrolling. The days followed one another with little or no incident and no sign of the enemy. Night deck landings were carried out from 0400 on 15 September. One Swordfish was slightly damaged, when her hook caught the ramp instead of the arrestor wires. In addition the lieutenant-commander, experimenting with special large 'bats' with lights attached to enable the pilots carrying out such landings in the dark, was struck by one aircraft landing on and suffered severe facial injuries as a result. The Walrus amphibian from the cruiser also carried out trial deck landings aboard *Eagle* and there were practice torpedo bomber attacks carried out against *Dorsetshire* and dive bombing attacks on *Eagle*.

They reached St Helena on 17 September and oiled from the *Darkdale* and utilised their own motorboats fitted with depth charges to conduct anti-submarine patrols. During the night the oiler smashed the fenders and twisted the jump nets around the flight deck in the heavy swell. She also carried away the ladder leading to the flight deck on the starboard side of the ship. Another accident was damage to the Walrus when a large length of wire became entangled while she was being lowered into the sea from the *Eagle*.

They sailed from St Helena that evening and sailed south with *Dorsetshire*. Their orders, as Force 'F', were to patrol in position K35A and B on 'Raider Search' duties. This location, codenamed 'Zeal' was in fact a waiting position off St Helena where they were to remain for a week. Just how dangerous even these distant waters were to unescorted heavy ships was shown by the fact that reports of U-boat concentrations in neighbourhood of 3 degrees North, to 8 degrees South and 30 degrees West meant extra airborne patrols and precautions for their own safety had to be flown.

On 20 September there was a serious incident when a fire broke out aboard the carrier. The exact events were as follows.

At 1725 an aluminium sea marker exploded under the port mainplane of one of the Swordfish in the hangar. The air mechanic was dismantling the marker from the aircraft when it fell to the deck and ignited. White-hot aluminium was immediately sprayed over him and a fire soon started. The rating was burnt horribly from head to foot and he died at 0930 the next day. The fire alarms sounded off and the hangar sprays came on automatically. The fire itself was soon under control, the damage being almost exclusively confined to the aircraft. As almost her entire outfit of Swordfish were in the hangar at this time nearly all received a good wetting with sea water which rendered them US for a period. Despite some accounts these were later repaired by the ships own facilities. However this temporarily left only four Swordfish completely serviceable and reduced the carrier's operational effectiveness and usefulness. It did *not*, however, prevent her continuing operations, as has sometimes been claimed.

The ill-fated Walrus from *Dorsetshire* came to grief for the last time the following day. She attempted to land on the carrier during a violent rainstorm. Visibility was extremely poor and the pilot was unable to judge his distance correctly. He touched down half-way along the flight deck and as the deck itself was considerably wet and greasy the tyres were unable to grip and slow the plane down before she reached the end of the deck. Consequently the Walrus disappeared over the stern into the ocean and sank. Fortunately her crew managed to escape with some difficulty and were picked up by one of the *Eagle*'s motor boats. All ended up in sickbay suffering from shock while the pilot himself had lacerations.

The patrols continued and two days later they felt the need of these aircraft for they were sent to search to the south to check out a suspicious ship and also to find a calm fuelling area south-east of Trinidad. It was now that the old *Eagle* again began suffering engine defects which brought this patrol to a premature end. One of the evaporator coils in the boiler rooms had been leaking, making the feed water for the ship salty, and this grew steadily worse. The carrier's speed had to be greatly reduced as a consequence, because such contaminated water crystallised on the tubes and prevented condensation of steam when travelling at high speeds.

With *Dorsetshire* on 25 September *Eagle* was patrolling once more and arrived back at St Helena to refuel at 1200 on the

26th of the month. Once more the question of *Eagle*'s return to the UK came up for docking. She was ordered to proceed to Freetown, arriving with the cruiser a.m. on 3 October. She was then to sail for Gibraltar and home by 5 October. Arrangements were made for repair to her aircraft at Wynberg. Accordingly she sailed from St Helena for the last time at 0900 on 28 September. Her ultimate destination was the Cammell Laird shipyard, Liverpool, where she was to be taken in hand for a refit. On her arrival at Freetown with *Dorsetshire* on 3 October, Force 'F' ceased to exist and another chapter in *Eagle*'s war career came to a conclusion.

# CHAPTER SEVEN

# Home and Away

Force 'F' duly disbanded on 4 October. The destroyer *Croome* was assigned by FOICNA (Flag Officer in charge, North Atlantic Station (Gibraltar) ) to sail the destroyer *Croome* to meet *Eagle* and escort her safely in to the Rock. Both were then to sail for the UK with the carrier *Argus*.

Another job assigned to her (no warship was ever wasted no matter what her instructions) was to keep on the alert to intercept the enemy vessel *Germania*, which was known to be ready to sail from neutral Teneriffe. She was to be intercepted if it were practicable to do so.

It was finally arranged that *Eagle* would sail from Freetown escorted by the Free French sloop *Commander Duboc* and that her aircraft were to conduct searches for the merchant ship *Silverbelle* which had been torpedoed on 22 September. Unfortunately events so arranged themselves that this search was not carried out. TAG Tyler remembers:

> Two destroyers escorted *Eagle* to sea, and they were to be relieved by two others in the Bathurst area, but somehow the reliefs did not make contact. *Eagle* was under orders not to disclose her position by using her radio, and I was sent off to a position a hundred miles astern of the ship, to try and get in contact with Freetown by radio.
>
> Fortunately I succeeded in getting in contact and passed my message. As a result our escort made contact and we proceeded merrily on our way. Working out the plot later on, my navigator informed me that the distance to Freetown when we passed the message had been 700 miles, quite an achievement with the radio equipment we carried.

*Eagle* had sailed from Freetown with *Dunedin* two corvettes and the French sloop at 1810 on Saturday, 4 October, two days later there was an alert when the French ship sighted a U-boat but no attacks developed. All her companions had left her by the time the Canary Islands were in view early on 9 October but a fresh part of her escort on that day was the destroyer *Wild Swan*, which herself refuelled at Las Palmas and sailed to join *Eagle* at 1800Z (Zonal time). Their ETA Gibraltar was 0700A 11 October with *Croome* and other escorts while her probable date for sailing home was given as 18 October in company with *Argus*.

The Rock was finally reached at 0900 on 11 October and here they found the usual Force 'H' crowd just returned from a Malta convoy operation, *Ark Royal, Argus, Rodney, Nelson*, the latter in dry-dock with a torpedo hole in her bows, and the usual mass of cruisers, destroyers and lesser craft. Their stay at Gibraltar was somewhat longer than anticipated due to an upsurge in U-boat activity around the Straits at that time. A corvette was torpedoed and sunk there on 13 October. Thus they remained secured alongside there until 21 October. The only happening was a rather meagre 'inspection' by the Duke of Gloucester. Dick Greenwood remembers it well:

> One sunny day while at Gibraltar we were lying at our berth alongside the jetty under the huge tripod crane located there, not doing very much of anything in particular and waiting to go home. Suddenly, with no warning, over the ship's tannoy system came the order, 'Everybody not on watch, get into your Number One's' (a rating's best uniform, reserved for parades and going ashore looking for girls) 'and fall in on the flight deck in your divisions.' It turned out that the Duke of Gloucester was paying us a visit (whether we liked it or not!). So we all fell in on the flight-deck spick-and-span. All branches were immaculately dressed, standing at ease, with the Royal Marine band at the ready.
>
> Then, 'Ship's Company, *Atten-Shun*!' followed by 'Three cheers for the Duke of Gloucester. Hip, Hip, Hooray,' repeated three times ringing round the Rock. But where was the Duke? We kept glancing this way and that out of the corners of our eyes and wondering if he had come up the forward or the after lift to the flight deck. Nothing. Then came, 'Ship's Company, Ship's Company – *Fall Out*'. We asked our divisional officer, where was the Duke? He smiled and replied, 'He just flew overhead in a 'plane!'

Force 'H' busied themselves about their duties day by day but

*Eagle* and *Argus* remained immobile.

The question of providing adequate fighter protection for the two vulnerable and aged carriers was discussed and they finally slipped from the detached mole at the Rock on 21 October with *Argus* and the destroyers *Foresight*, *Forester*, *Zulu* and *Sikh*. A Catalina flying-boat also kept them company until dusk and the destroyers *Vidette* and *Lamerton* provided extra protection between 0915 and 1140 that day. With two Sea Hurricanes embarked aboard on 11 October it was arranged that *Eagle* would provide the fighter cover while *Argus* maintained the A/S patrols. The intention was to commence her urgently required refit at Liverpool on 1 November and to complete by 15 November. There was some discussion about her returning to the South Atlantic again after the refit which eventually came to naught. For the passage back to the UK *Eagle* also embarked two former Vichy French Dewoitine D250C fighter aircraft which had defected from North Africa and landed at the Rock on 16 October with a spare passenger.

The news reached *Eagle* that between 30 and 40 U-boats were concentrated in their area so when, at 1348 in position 35 degrees 58 minutes North, 7 degrees West, an unexplained underwater explosion was heard, there was not much surprise. As Captain Rushbrooke commented at the time, this may well have been a torpedo fired by the submarine which made a transmission that was picked up by the Admiralty. The next two days were uneventful and on Friday, 24 October, they met the battleship *Malaya* and destroyers *Havelock*, *Harvester*, and *Lightning* on their way to join Force 'H'. *Eagle* exchanged two of her escorting destroyers, *Sikh* and *Zulu*, for *Harvester* and *Havelock* as they passed. At this time the winds had reached gale force from the south-east and the seas were typical of those experienced in the Bay of Biscay, and they remained rough with the ships rolling heavily. All flying had to be cancelled. The temperature plummeted ten degrees since they had left Gibraltar and continued on down relentlessly. The ship was now known to be bound for Greenock, to be staying there a few days and then making for dock in the Mersey.

On 25 October *Eagle*'s ETA off Greenock on the Clyde was given as 1000 the following day (with *Argus*) and arrangements were made to fly her aircraft ashore. The nine Swordfish of 813 Squadron and the two Sea Hurricanes flew off to Machrihanish and Belfast respectively at 0815 on 26 October, and at 0900 the nine Swordfish of 825 Squadron also flew off to Machrihanish.

A long refit meant leave which, after two years away from home for most of the crew, and four years for the ship, were longed for. However, on 22 October, the Admiralty emphasised that *Eagle* was to be prepared for sea at the earliest possible moment owing to heavy demand for aircraft carriers. The leave of the ship's company was therefore to be curtailed while arrangements for her arrival on the Mersey were finalised.

They finally arrived off Tail 'o the Bank at 1135 escorted by the Polish destroyer *Burza*. Here they found a host of merchant ships and their old friend the battleship *Royal Sovereign*. Other ships which arrived were the cruisers *Cardiff* and *Trinidad*. The temperature in the ship was now 58 degrees compared with 84 degrees which had been normal for them. It was announced that the ship was to re-commission. Leave was therefore to be granted according to the time men had been aboard, up to 18 months got 14 days leave, up to 24 months got 21 days' leave and more than that 28 days, and for many of her ship's company this was the last they were to see of the old *Eagle*. There were to be many of course joining her for the first time, while others continued as usual.

After a short stay in the Clyde the carrier sailed again on 30 October, passing the boom at 1800 with the Polish destroyer *Burza* as escort to Liverpool. On 1 November she was towed into dry-dock. Even before she reached the Mersey, signals were received which postponed her refit completion, first to 1 December, and then back to 30 December.

The actual refit by the well-known shipbuilding and repair firm of Cammell Laird of Birkenhead was quite extensive. Her greatest need was for a complete re-boilering, but this proved out of the question. Even as *Eagle* lay in dock the *Ark Royal* was finally lost, while *Illustrious* and *Formidable*, smashed up at Crete were in American dockyards and the brand-new *Indomitable* ran aground at Bermuda. This at a time when Japan entered the war against us and her ten large carriers ran amok in the Pacific Ocean. So her lack of speed remained an irritating factor for the rest of her career, and she was never good for more than about 20 knots. The amount of fuel oil storage was cut to make room for extra aviation fuel stowage which increased the number of aircraft she could carry, but her radius of action suffered accordingly, coming down to 2,780 nautical miles at 17.5 knots.

If nothing could be done with her aged propulsion plant at this time some worthwhile improvements to her defensive capability were put in hand. This included the fitting of Type 290 combined Air/Sea Warning radar at the head of the mainmast, a Type 285 fire control radar was also added to the Control Top and the high angle director for the 4inch guns was moved there also to give a better coverage. The Type 72 homing beacon commented upon earlier was on a pole mast above the Top.

As expected the anti-aircraft armament, which had been pitiful even in 1939, was to be upgraded to meet modern warfare conditions, and especially those of the Mediterranean zone. The useless 0.5 inch machine guns were removed and replaced by twelve far more valuable 20 mm Oerlikon automatic cannon around her flight deck on two single tubs and two doubles in sponsons on either beam. Strangely the old single 4 inch guns were retained as they had a good high elevation of almost 90 degrees, but their crews were given some splinter protection by the addition of protective zarebas around them. Her 6 inch armament was also retained in full. Although this was thought by many to be just so much dead weight and useless one veteran recalled that:

> *Eagle* on a number of occasions used her 6 inch in low-level barrage fire against attacks by torpedo bombers coming in just above the waves. A splash barrage could be quite a deterrent if laid down accurately in their path.

All this took a great deal of time and while she was refitting the war situation grew steadily worse by the day. The need to get her back into action was therefore all the more pressing. Meanwhile her crew, new and old, were adjusting to the new situation according to their lights. One thing that had not improved was her accommodation. Even larger numbers of specialists were required to work all the new equipment but no extra space was provided for them. Most of the older ships in the Royal Navy faced the same problems. Douglas Clare recalls just what conditions were like aboard *Eagle* in the tropics before her return to England.

> The old *Eagle* was always short of fresh water, and in the South Atlantic it reached chronic proportions. If you didn't

have a bucket, or didn't fix with your oppo to get you some water at the appointed time it came on when you were on watch then you just had to go without. Buckets of water were stashed away everywhere, but speaking for myself I don't remember one instance of someone 'stealing' my half bucket, that sort of thing simply wasn't done.

Flour was quite often infested with weevils. Nothing unusual to be able to pick them out of your bread. Each mess usually made their own tea in large tea kettles, probably held a gallon or so. Thick, brown drink, well dowsed with sugar and tinned milk. Milk cans usually opened by punching two holes at opposite sides of the can, and if any left for future use you had to make sure the holes were sealed or the ever-present hordes of cockroaches would soon find their way in. The messdecks were infested with rats (four-legged ones!). All sorts of methods were instituted to eliminate them, even wire nooses similar to those used to snare rabbits. I know the above sounds as if *Eagle* wasn't too clean, but of course the messes were scrubbed daily and everything as spotless as it could be, but there was no getting rid of weevils, cockroaches and rats. I can't remember ever giving much thought to them, it was an accepted fact of life at sea in those days, particularly for such an old ship.

Like most ships during the war there were nowhere near enough billets to sling hammocks, and mess table, mess decks, flag decks at night were all used to bed down. You just unrolled your bedding and fell asleep. Messes had very little ventilation and were extremely hot and sweaty, no individual mess refrigerators or anything like that, with drinking water inevitably warm. Again we are talking now of fifty years ago and little, if anything, was thought of such things as they are today. In those days ships were built to fight and not for comfort.

Doug Clare was leaving *Eagle*: Les Goodenough was seeing her for the first time:

My initial memory of her at Gladstone Dock where I joined her was of chipping and painting the ship's side in January 1942 while she was undergoing her partial refit. As she was my first ship I had not done this before and it was quite nerve-racking letting yourself down with a drop of over 100 ft to the dry-dock below. For one young rating working alongside me it was his first and last over the side as he lost his nerve and was hauled inboard by his lifeline. It was while on such an exercise that I looked down and saw my brother who was about to come aboard; he was a leading cook, a long-serviceman. When my mess heard of this I was always the one detailed to scrounge extra loaves of bread or duff (pudding) or scran (food in general) so our mess never went short.

While in Gladstone Docks in Liverpool we had runs ashore and most of us stayed at the YMCA hostel near Lime Street Station for the night, only cost one shilling with an early call the next morning. We then caught the old tram back to Gladstone. The first public house was the 'Caradoc', and more black-market 'fiddles' took place there than at any other place I know.

A similar experience was related by Stoker J. Milne:

I joined *Eagle* as a young (18) Engine-Room rating in October 1941. She was having a refit at Gladstone Dock, Liverpool, and I must say when I first saw her and the condition she was in I did wonder why I had joined the Royal Navy. I had the choice of the RN or the Royal Tank Corps which I had volunteered for some months previously and my papers had arrived at the same time. I chose the RN, as it happened and on a bleak winter's day, a cold, dark afternoon, as I clambered aboard with hammock and kitbag and case I did wonder if I had done the right thing! The ship was dirty, cold pipes, engineering equipment everywhere, decks almost black – yes a few of us, all young 18-year-olds, were a little worried that awful winter's afternoon.

However, after some weeks with runs ashore in Liverpool and of course the entitlement of the rum ration, we became more confident. The batch I joined the ship with were all new entrants with only a few months' training so I suppose we could be excused for being a little worried at first sight of a large ship. As the weeks passed also, *Eagle* became more and more of a lady. Boiler rooms and engines bright and shining, decks whiter, paintwork renewed. The ship came alive in proportion to the dwindling numbers of careless dockyard maties as they left and the Navy took over. Eventually we all (well, the ratings and petty officers of the engine room staff that I knew) came to love her and when she steamed out of Liverpool dock after Christmas for working-up trials it was a great feeling, especially for us new sailors, or 'sprogs' as the old hands called us.

Ken Pierce was also one of those sprogs:

The draft consisted of mainly second class stokers, of which I was one, and OD (Ordinary) seamen (all of us HOs – 'Hostilities only'). The Regulating Chief Stoker, Arthur Bond, and the Chief Buffer nearly had a fit when they saw what they had to contend with. These men were of the old school and with respect to them, they soon shook us down to a good, efficient and disciplined crew.

Finally Cyril Williams on the same initial reaction and his later conversion:

I joined *Eagle* in January 1942, as an Air Mechanic 'O' with the Sea Hurricane fighter squadron. She was my first ship and somewhat of a disappointment. It was getting dark as we climbed on board this big, black dirty-looking monster. There were no hammock-slinging positions and I had to lash a ladder to the deck bolts then slung my hammock ladder to the bulkhead. In the morning we were at sea with water everywhere and I eventually caught up with my shoes which had floated some way down the hangar. Did I come out with a mouthful of the choice words I had picked up since joining the Navy! In time though I came to love the ship, the Service and my shipmates.

On Christmas Day 1941, it was announced that she was to sail back to the Clyde when ready for sea and undertake 14 days' working up. The New Year arrived, but still the dockyard fell steadily behind schedule. On 2 January it was anticipated that *Eagle* would finally be ready to sail for Clyde a week later. But it was not until 9 January, escorted by the destroyers *Skate* and *Blyscawica* (Polish), that *Eagle* finally sailed from Liverpool. The latter destroyer was assigned to the carrier as her attendant escort during her working-up period on the Clyde, from 15 to 27 January.

As well as the ship herself her aircraft complement underwent changes at this period. Initially she was equipped as before with two squadrons of Fairey Swordfish TSR, from Numbers 813 (Lieutenant-Commander A.V. Lyle had relieved Lieutenant-Commander D.H. Elles) and 824 (Royal Marine

Captain F.W. Brown had relieved Lieutenant-Commander A.J. Debenham, DSC) Squadrons. Yes, despite three years of war these obsolete machines still formed her main striking force! The only concessions to modern air warfare were that these machines were now radar-equipped, but apart from a few other modifications they were still the same painfully slow old biplanes with which the Navy had entered the war. She shipped a total of eighteen of these antiques. She was supposed to take *Ark Royal*'s place with Force 'H'; her twelve knots lack of speed was added to by the fact that she could only carry four modern fighter aircraft, four Sea Hurricane 1Bs with fixed, not folding, wings. She therefore could not strike these down on her lifts and they had to stay topside parked out of the landing area behind the bridge.

Trials followed the completion of the dockyard work, during which time the new equipment and the new personnel in the old ship had to shake down and work together as a team. This was not always an easy thing to achieve as those involved recorded. Les Goodenough:

> Our working-up trials on the Clyde at Greenock went quite smoothly. Down the Clyde we sailed, past the Isle of Arran, marvellous scenery and wonderful people in Greenock, especially the Church of Scotland personnel at the hall where we used to go for meals.
>
> Every ship on the Clyde had to take turns at 'Duty Ship' and when it was our turn our guns crew slept in the gun shelter on duck boards wrapped up in duffel coats. They were all frozen to the marrow and continually sipped cups of 'Ki' (cocoa). It was on one such night, foggy with four or five inches of snow on the flight deck, that AB Frame walked over the side of the flight deck. Although the ships boats were sent away for a search in the icy, black and swirling waters, no trace of him was to be found. His body was later washed ashore. As usual practice in the RN the rating's clothes were sold off to raise money for the next-of-kin. 'Sale of Effects' it was termed and very emotional it was when high bidding was done for a shipmate's uniform.

Tug Whymark recalls:

> It seemed to us that the loss of *Ark Royal* accelerated and cut short our docking. At any rate all haste was made to complete whatever stage of repair and maintenance *Eagle* was in at that

time, and no doubt a lot of necessary things never did get done. New crew and replacements were hastily drafted in. We were hurriedly prepared for leaving dry-dock and for sea trials and working-up at Greenock. As I was one of the original commission still retained, my duties changed and included boat crew, my action station being gunlayer on the starboard 2, 6 inch gun or Gun Trainer. These were my primary positions but of course all the guns crews had to have knowledge of each position at the gun.

While at Greenock the ship's complement was topped up as there were some absentees. The weather was freezing snow, sleet and heavy seas were rolling inboard.

Once fully ready for combat again *Eagle*, still under the command of Captain Rushbrooke, with Commander B.J. de St Croix and Commander Flying W.G.C. Stokes, was sailed from the Clyde with the destroyer *Duncan* to help escort convoy WS16 which was in two parts. Both warships were then to sail to Gibraltar. During the working-up period they came under the command of C-in-C, Western Approaches. *Eagle* sailed on 16 February and joined the convoy. Here they found the carrier *Formidable* also sailing south, with the Indian Ocean her ultimate destination. The Japanese were running riot in South-East Asia at this time, and with Hong Kong, Malaya and Singapore fallen, and with Burma on the verge of defeat British power in India and that part of the globe seemed very fragile. Nor was the war in the Atlantic proceeding very well, and *Eagle* herself was attacked by a U-boat while proceeding down to Gibraltar, tracks being sighted in position 32 degrees, 10 minutes N, 80 degrees, 25 minutes West.

Les Goodenough:

The weather in the Bay proved as nasty as ever. My first trip to Gibraltar to join Force 'H' through the Bay was unbelievable. To see our flight-deck, normally sixty to eighty feet above sea-level, hitting the waves! My first bout of sea-sickness naturally followed almost immediately and I must have looked as green as I felt. My defence station was on the multiple 2-pdr (the famous pom-pom or 'Chicago Piano'), a marvellously aggressive weapon. My action station was loader to the after starboard Oerlikon. AB Tassell was No.1 AA3. While sailing to Gibraltar we took aboard our Swordfish but due to the rough sea and possibly also new pilots, a heavy toll was taken of these 'planes; many had faulty landings and finished up over the side, pilots being rescued.

Eventually we left the convoy we were escorting and turned for Gibraltar.

Also in company was the battleship *Malaya*, the flagship of Force 'H', and both heavy ships and their escorts arrived at Gibraltar at 1830 on 23 February.

The prospect of war in the Mediterranean in 1942 with the Axis approaching the peak of their power and strength in that area, was no sincecure for any warship not fully up to the mark. Force 'H' at this period was much reduced owing to losses and other commitments. The famous team of *Renown*, *Ark Royal*, *Sheffield* and the 8th Destroyer Flotilla had by this period been replaced by *Malaya*, *Eagle*, *Hermione* and the 13th Flotilla. The light cruiser *Hermione* and the big 'L' class destroyers were modern ships, but the two heavy ships were both older and slower than their predecessors. The main duties remained as before, the escorting of vital convoys through to Malta and the supplying of an endless stream of RAF fighter aircraft which were flown off the carriers to that island to replace the enormous wastage caused by the Axis 'Spring blitz' on that island.

They were soon off eastward into the Mediterranean, sailing at 0320 on 27 February, to carry out their first mission, Operation Spotter a flying-off of Supermarine Spitfire fighter aircraft as reinforcements for hard-pressed Malta then undergoing very severe attacks. Force 'H' comprised *Malaya*, *Eagle*, *Argus* and *Hermione* with the destroyers *Laforey*, *Lightning*, *Blankney*, *Croome*, *Duncan*, *Active*, *Anthony*, *Whitehall* and *Wishart*. Unfortunately this operation had to be postponed at 2134 the same evening when it was found that the Spitfires hastily embarked on the Clyde were suffering difficulties with their long-range fuel tanks. There were many defects, a disgraceful reflection on British organisation at home and which could have jeopardised the lives of all the brave young pilots. Leaking fuel tanks on so vulnerable a vessel as an aircraft-carrier could also have jeopardised the whole ship. *Eagle*, with the rest of Force 'H' returned to Gibraltar on 28 February, where an enquiry was made into the problem. Like all such enquiries it achieved little or nothing; it was not to produce very much improvement from the RAF embarkation authorities at home as we shall see.

While they waited for the faults to be rectified and further Spitfires to be brought out, *Eagle*'s complement of aircraft was increased so desperate was the plight of the island at this time.

On 6 March Vice Admiral Sir Neville Syfret again took his whole force to sea for the second attempt to carry out Operation Spotter. *Eagle*'s companions were *Malaya*, *Argus*, *Hermione* and destroyers *Laforey*, *Lightning*, *Blankney*, *Exmoor*, *Croome*, *Active*, *Anthony*, *Whitehall* and *Wishart*. They were sighted and reported by the Italian submarine *Brin* on the very day they put to sea but, despite this, 15 Spitfires were flown off and guided to Malta by seven Bristol Blenheim bombers from the Rock. Their return to harbour was not without incident. Gordon Drake was one of the radar ratings aboard *Eagle* at this period. He told me:

> Our radar proved itself in the middle watch one night on the first trip with Spitfires. Many in the Navy still believed in range-finder ranges only but this night I was on the set and we picked up two hostile aircraft closing the fleet. These aircraft came up the port side of the destroyer screen at approximately 20,000 yards and then appeared dead ahead. We plotted them as they went out of range only to return minutes later down the starboard side of the screen.
>
> Prepared ranges were passed to the bridge but the fleet kept silent. When it became obvious that the intruders had spotted us and their rate of closing increased rapidly indicating an attack run, it was 'Open fire' with our radar ranges. They closed to within about 8,000 yards but quickly took evasive action when the barrage hit them and both split up, their ranges rapidly increasing as they passed us and went out over the stern of the fleet.
>
> The following morning the Captain and many senior officers visited the 285 Gunnery set, which was situated in one of the highest points of the ship on top of the tripod just below the range-finder. It was obvious that for most of them this had been their first experience of what radar could do, and from that point on it was always radar ranges that were used, except for independent firing below 3,000 yards.

The whole force returned safely at 1840 on 8 March.

This operation, brief though it was, exposed some further defects in *Eagle*'s old engines, which, it will be recalled, had not been replaced. However the temporary repairs carried out proved unsatisfactory. The Admiral Superintendent at Gibraltar criticised the fact that only one short operation trip was possible before further repairs became essential. *Eagle*, an old lady, was definitely feeling her age now. Increasingly, although nursed and tended with skill and dedication by her engine room staff, she needed vital repairs more and more frequently. She had to be docked for these to be done and this period of inactivity lasted until 13 March.

A week later, on 20 March, *Eagle, Malaya, Argus, Hermione* with the destroyers *Laforey, Blankney, Exmoor, Croome, Duncan, Active, Anthony, Whitehall* and *Wishart,* sailed east yet again for Operation Picket. The attempt again had to be abandoned prematurely and they returned to Gibraltar on 23 March.

The same ships sailed to carry out Operation Picket-2 on 27 March and this time sixteen Spitfires were successfully flown off to Malta, Force 'H' returning three days later to the Rock. On their way they found that of the aircraft embarked, one Fairey Albacore TSR and one Spitfire were unserviceable. However, several Spitfires, along with two Bristol Beaufort twin-engined fighters, were successfully flown off *Eagle*'s decks to Malta.

Following her return from 'Picket-2' on 30 March *Eagle* was once more taken in hand by Gibraltar dockyard for urgent repairs to her steering gear. It was expected that she would remain docked until the end of April. While still in dock there were urgent discussions on using her and her aircraft to stop the giant Vichy French battleship *Richelieu* (35,000 tons, eight 15 inch guns) returning to the main French base at Toulon from the West African port of Dakar. She had been repairing damage suffered there by British attacks in September 1940 and it was feared that Admiral Darlan wished her now to reinforce his main fleet in the south of France as Britain's position looked very shaky in view of continued Axis advances in Russia, North Africa and the Far East. Also while she was in dock her place on the Malta 'Spitfire run' was briefly taken by the US carrier *Wasp* which made a sortie, Operation 'Calendar', between 14 and 26 April when 46 out of 48 Spitfires flown off reached Malta, only to be destroyed on the ground within 48 hours.

By the end of April *Eagle* was ready to play her part in sustaining the gallant George Cross island's struggle for survival once more. On 30 April she sailed in company with the anti-aircraft cruiser *Charybdis* for exercises, returning later the same day. She was now temporarily a part of Force 'W' and the battle-cruiser *Renown* had returned to Gibraltar once again to take up her role as that squadron's flagship. It was signalled on 4 May that the force itself was only to remain 'in being' when employed on actual operations, thus avoiding the ambiguity of the old Force 'H' which had led to problems of command decisions earlier in the war and the dismissal of Admiral North.

More fighter reinforcement operations were at planning stage. Operation Bowery was next while those Spitfires not flown off in the abortive Operation Picket were to be ferried out after that.

Accordingly, on the night of 7/8 May *Eagle* sailed from Gibraltar in company with *Renown*, *Wasp*, AA cruiser *Charybdis* and destroyers *Partridge*, *Ithuriel*, *Intrepid*, *Echo*, *Antelope*, *Wishart*, *Wrestler*, *Vidette*. *Lang* (US), *Sterrett (US)*, *Georgetown* and *Salisbury*, the latter two ancient ex-American 'four-stacker' vessels, to carry out Operation Bowery. The Spitfire fighter aircraft were successfully flown off on 9 May from the two carriers and 61 out of 63 reached the island. The force returned to Gibraltar safely after which the *Wasp* sailed back to Scapa Flow.

The *Wasp* received a huge blaze of publicity from Churchill and the media for these two missions, and it was well deserved. *Eagle* and *Argus*, our own carriers, were totally ignored by both but kept diligently plugging away just the same and doing a good job. It is also instructive to note that, two months after *Eagle* had experienced the dangers and tribulations of careless and sloppy work by the RAF embarkation authorities, there had been no improvements. On the first mission by *Wasp*, an official report found that, 'ninety per cent of their long-range tanks were defective, ninety-five per cent of their guns were dirty and unsynchronized; seventy per cent of their radios were inoperative and that on the whole, there was a very great deal wrong with them.' On the second run the Americans were forced to stop the actual loading of Spitfires aboard *Wasp* for the same reasons. The Flag Officer in Charge, Glasgow, pointed out why in a pithy memo to the Admiralty:

> The reason for this order was that on the previous trip, it was found that, on filling the jettisonable tanks, ninety per cent of them leaked, and flooded the hangar ... The fact that the

planes were provided on both occasions with tanks which had not been tested and had not been rendered serviceable is unsatisfactory, and has unfortunately created a very bad impression.

But the fault lay entirely with the RAF. Things were better when the aircraft were shipped out from home in aircraft transport ships crated and then re-assembled on the dock alongside. Tug Whymark recalls that:

*Eagle* was kept busy ferrying Spitfires out to Malta. These were shipped to Gibraltar, uncrated, assembled ashore and from there loaded aboard ship by the sheerlegs. The RAF technical staff and the pilots were victualled on board the same as the ship's crew. They were also issued with a rum ration like us, and it was a bonus for us matelots who had an airman victualled in the same mess because many of them didn't like Navy issue rum and gave their tots to us!

*Eagle* and her escorts would ferry the Spitfires to within flying distance of Malta and they would take off, but there was no return for them. They only had the pilot's personal kit, maximum fuel and no armament. Any problem after they had taken off and it meant ditching in the ocean. After a few such trips the Axis provided snooper 'planes which picked up the unarmed Spitfires on fly-off and followed them back to home in their own fighters from Sicily to intercept them.

Dick Greenwood remembers how the Spitfires came aboard:

We used to secure alongside the jetty where the huge tripod crane was positioned. Its main usage was for lifting boilers out of refitting warships, but we used to lie there while the RAF personnel assembled the Malta Spitfires from crates. As each 'plane was complete so it was hoisted onto our flight deck until we had enough for the Malta run.

Les Owen has vivid memories of the young Spitfire pilots also:

These Spitfires had a spare fuel tank fitted under their body which was jettisoned when empty. After their long trip over the sea, these brave young pilots hardly had time to refuel before going into action to defend Malta. As my brother-in-law was stationed at Malta with the army, I wrote to him and the RAF boys delivered the letters. Before taking off the pilots would fill every inch of their 'planes with food and cigarettes.

Oliver Barritt remembers one Spitfire mishap because of its gruesome outcome:

> The French pilot had his head cut off when trying to land back his Spitfire. He appeared to be standing up in his seat trying to look over the top of his open cockpit. I don't know why – perhaps he could see better that way or wanted to be able to jump clear quickly. Whatever the reason one of the crash barrier wire cables caught and decapitated him. I'll never forget it because I picked his head up! In an earlier incident, while conducting night landing trials off Lamlash there were several crashes. One aircraft came in and hit a landing light. While it was being checked another came in and landed on top of the first one. By some miracle nobody was injured although the propeller of the second aircraft almost cut the first 'plane in half just behind the pilot's cockpit. Our surgeon commander, known as '*The* O'Rourke' was kept busy later when the Spitfires were flown off by their very young-looking RAF pilots. Brave laddies indeed. Some didn't make it because of their weight and extra fuel tanks, even though they were fitted with special pitch props to get them off the deck quickly. Our Sea Hurricanes, painfully slow in the air, were much better at taking off. Initially we only carried four of our own fighters. They all had names, I can remember 'Impatient Virgin' and 'No Orchids for Miss Blandish' as two of them. One of our pilots, Lieutenant King-Joyce I think he was, a real ace, was killed after the war as a test pilot.

The next operation planned for was Operation L.B. and once that had been carried out then all the 32 further Spitfires brought out aboard the aircraft transport *Empire Conrad* were to be flown off from the *Eagle* to Malta in Operation Style.

Operation L.B. got underway on 17 May when *Eagle* sailed with *Argus*, *Charybdis* and destroyers *Partridge Ithuriel*, *Antelope*, *Wishart*, *Wrestler* and *Westcott*, while *Vidette* delayed by engine trouble, also joined at 0700 on 18 May.

Submarine contacts were frequent, *Charybdis* dropping three depth charges on what appeared to be the swirl and wash of a diving submarine just before midnight on 17 May, and both she and *Partridge* sighted torpedo tracks at 0830 next morning, causing an emergency turn to be made by the whole force. The destroyer carried out a hunt with one of the Swordfish and made attacks on a firm contact. No results were seen. At 1007 *Westcott* reported sighting a submarine which was later considered a doubtful report, but a later sighting report from an enemy submarine confirmed the enemy's undoubted presence in that area.

At 1100 the first flight of Spitfires was ranged and the Albacore flight was struck down after a final engine test on the flight deck. *Vidette* dropped depth charges after another submarine contact at 1110 resulting in yet another emergency turn.

In the middle of their flying-off preparations Captain Rushbrooke received a report at 1147 while *Eagle* was in position 37 degrees 20 minutes North, 1 degree, 51 minutes East, that one of the anti-submarine Catalina amphibians (7XMF) had been attacked by Vichy-French fighter aircraft and had been forced to ditch some twenty miles to the north-east of Algiers and that both the pilots were hurt. The French were not merely content with this cowardly act. A further report was received at 1151 that these same two fighters were attacking the ditched aircraft again. The destroyer *Ithuriel* was instructed at 1205 to proceed to the rescue of the Catalina's crew and then to rejoin the main force, 'if circumstances permitted'. Plans were made aboard the *Argus* to despatch FAA fighters to cover the destroyer from any further Vichy aggression and two Fulmars were flown off from her at 1228. Sure enough, at 1412 a signal came in from *Ithuriel* reporting that she was being strafed by Vichy aircraft and five minutes later gunfire was heard to the southward. At 1440 one of the Fulmars landed back aboard *Argus* and reported that he had shot down one French Dewoitine aircraft at 1435 while it was about to attack the other Fulmar.

Another signal came in from *Ithuriel* at 1528 which stated that the crew of the Catalina, two of whom were wounded, one seriously, had been saved and that yet further French fighters were attacking her and had destroyed the other Fulmar. The destroyer managed to save the pilot but the observer was lost. *Ithuriel* despatched the still-floating wreck of the seaplane with gunfire, then hastened to re-join the fleet. Another pair of Fulmars was duly despatched to cover the withdrawal and they returned at 1715 without further incident. A relief Catalina arrived, embarked one of the injured pilots and took him back to Gibraltar, while *Ithuriel* steered to rejoin the squadron.

Meanwhile the *Eagle* had been getting her Spitfires away. At 1300 the *Vidette*'s engines again started causing trouble and she was sent back to Gibraltar. Twenty minutes later the first attempt to fly off the Spitfires was made while in position 37 degrees, 28 minutes North, 2 degrees, 25 minutes East. The wind, which had been light easterly during the forenoon, was steadily dropping and was then only five knots. This was insufficient for a Spitfire launch. Not until 1440 did the wind freshen to seven knots and the first launch got underway. By 1515 the second flight was flown off with wind speed over the deck at 30 knots so these aircraft took off easily and without incident. Both flights formed up and took departure within ten minutes of their first machine taking off.

From 1757 a shadower was picked up visually and he continued in contact until 2010. The radio guardship *Charybdis* failed to report this aircraft, perhaps because it was flying too low for detection. Two Sea Hurricanes were flown off at 1900 to cover the Albacore flight and half-an-hour later six of these torpedo bomber biplanes were flown off for Malta. The force then turned back eastward. Within half-an-hour one of the Albacores was seen returning and she requested permission to land on. While turning to the wind to comply a second Albacore was seen and both were landed back aboard. Course was then resumed towards Gibraltar but, at 2026, the remaining four Albacores were seen returning and at 2030 both they and the A/S patrol of Swordfish were landed on. All the Albacores were found to have serious engine defects. Once more they turned back eastward but with the approach of dusk came a new threat, *Charybdis* radar began picking up incoming flights of 'bandits'. They could only be Italian torpedo bombers and all hands were immediately closed up at action stations. It was twilight but rapidly growing dark with a light haze over the sea, ideal torpedo bomber conditions. The force was at 23 knots reducing to 19 knots with visibility half a mile to a mile down moon and one to two miles up moon.

Almost at once an aircraft was sighted close off the port quarter of *Eagle* and the splash of its torpedo was observed as it was dropped. The helm was put hard to starboard and the engines rung down to maximum revolutions and the torpedo missed astern as the aircraft turned away. At this point *Charybdis* was leading *Eagle* and *Argus* in line ahead. The action then became general. Between 2130 and 2203 the carrier was flung around like a toy as Captain Rushbrooke tried to avoid further torpedo bomber attacks as they came in. Course was altered 30 degrees to 50 degrees either way by W/T signals, the average time between alterations being about three minutes. The mean course steered was directly toward the moon, which was not giving a very strong light but was still silhouetting the ships when they were not end-on to it.

Some three separate attacks were counted, although only two aircraft were seen. These attacks, the most determined torpedo-bomber assaults that *Eagle* ever faced up to, were each made by two Savoia Marchetti SM79 torpedo bombers, a total of six machines and were steadfastly and bravely pressed home.

After the first attack *Charybdis*, with her numerous anti-aircraft guns both heavy and light, was ordered to take station astern of *Argus* and her barrage fire proved most effective during the following two attacks. *Eagle* herself contributed a 6 inch barrage and the close-range weapons joined in on the rare occasions that targets could be briefly made-out in the night.

The next attack developed while *Charybdis* was turning to starboard to comply with her new positioning and again the aircraft approached from the port side but was left astern of both carriers by their turn-away. The track of the torpedo passed between them and ahead of the returning cruiser.

*Charybdis* had just taken up her new position astern of the carriers when another torpedo bomber came in from the starboard quarter and turned away under heavy fire. Either the same aircraft or another then made a co-ordinated attack from the same position, astern on the starboard quarter, to draw fire while another aircraft approached *Eagle* from the port side dead amidships and was met by the 6 inch barrage which turned her away.

The next aircraft came in from the same direction and may possibly have been the same 'plane returning. Again it was met by full broadside fire from *Eagle* and turned away down-moon. No further attacks materialised.

Providentially, no damage or casualties were taken by the British force, but it had been a close call. One torpedo track was seen to pass close up and parallel to *Eagle*'s starboard side and was only avoided by 'a fortunate alteration of course', helm having been put over when the aircraft was sighted and she was engaged by the port close-range weapons. *Eagle* fired off 38

rounds from her 6 inch Mk XVII, 12 rounds from her 4 inch
Mk V, 40 rounds from her 2-pdr Mk VIII pom-pom and 240
rounds from her 20 mm Oerlikons at ranges from 3,000 yards
down to 300 yards. One large yellow flash was seen on the water
during the 6 inch barrage. As none of the destroyers on the
screen was hit it was thought that this flash could only have been
caused by an aircraft and that therefore one of the attackers
might well have been destroyed.

During the second and third attacks a series of three or four
loud underwater explosions were head and felt. Captain
Rushbrooke gave most of the credit for their survival to the
radar warnings they got from *Charybdis*. 'The general warning
this gave to the armament enabled blind procedure to be fully
effective and thwarted each attack before it had time to
develop', he wrote. When Their Lordships came to study this
attack later they added their own comments. The Director of
Gunnery and AA Warfare commented:

> The attack appears to have been made by six SM79s
> approaching in pairs from down moon. It is not clear from
> the accounts how many torpedoes were released. No hits
> however were scored. In the second and third approaches
> the aircraft were turned away at 6,000 yards. *Argus*, with no
> RDF, fired no 4 inch guns. *Eagle* fired blind barrages with 6
> inch and 4 inch guns. *Charybdis* fired blind, using predicted
> fuses for 4.5 inch guns, in the second and third attacks. This
> latter form of firing appears to have been an effective
> deterrent. *Charybdis* modified Type 285 was equal to the
> Type 281 for picking up targets at low heights and its
> performance is encouraging.

The Director of the Signal Department added:

> The results obtained by Type 285 MI are slightly above
> expectation, but further experience may prove them to be
> normal. (*Charybdis* reported detecting Italian torpedo aircraft
> at 100 feet at 30,000 yards.) The performance of Type 281
> was normal for aircraft below 500 feet.

They came through this ordeal and as the last contacts faded
from the radar scopes resumed course at midnight to 255
degrees. Nor was this the end of the matter for the force was
also later trailed by four Italian submarines. Anti-submarine
flying operations the next morning were therefore intense. At
0630 *Argus* transferred three Swordfish to *Eagle* and flew off

inner patrol. Two hours later two of these were flown off in turn. At 0949 a low flying aircraft was taken under long-range 4.7 inch fire by *Ithuriel* and *Argus* flew off two Fulmars to chase her off.

At 1111 one of the Swordfish, 4K, was forced to ditch ahead of the screen and the crew were rescued by *Westcott*. As the destroyer's whaler was returning with the crew on board the Swordfish's depth-charges exploded but luckily the boat was far enough away to escape damage. The explosion brought in the 'snooper' to investigate and this nosy enemy was engaged by both *Westcott* and *Charybdis*, without effect.

Soon after the force entered an area of thick fog and had to reduce speed to 15 knots for the next hour but, by 0528 next morning, *Eagle* had secured to No.43 berth back at Gibraltar yet again none the worse for wear.

Four days later, on 24 May, they formally re-constituted Force 'H' with *Malaya* etc. to operate as such 'when circumstances permitted'. Meanwhile the irony of using the Navy's Fairey Fulmar and Hawker Sea Hurricane fighters in protecting warships carrying the latest marks of Supermarine Spitfires was causing much wry and bitter comment. The undesirability of continuing to use such obsolete machines for such a vital duty was stressed to Their Lordships, but they could do little to help as the RAF had made sure that they had no navalised Spitfires of their own to allocate.

Further exercises off Gibraltar in company with *Charybdis* took place from 0718 on 1 June. Vickers Wellington bombers, which would be conducting a bombing attack on Cagliari in Sardinia prior to *Eagle's* next sortie, would report on whether or not the Italian cruiser squadron based there had left port to attack the convoys, a threat confirmed by the disastrous outcome of Operation Harpoon later that month, but the latest flying-off mission was unmolested.

On 3 June *Eagle* flew off 31 Spitfires for Malta during Operation Style. Force 'H' on this occasion comprised only *Eagle* and *Charybdis*, with destroyers *Ithuriel*, *Antelope*, *Wishart*, *Wrestler* and *Westcott*. The fighters took off in the approximate position 37 degrees 47 minutes North, 2 degrees 46 minutes East. One Spitfire crashed on take-off. However the pilot was rescued and returned to the *Eagle* by one of the destroyers. Of the rest tragically only 27 arrived at Malta, because the last two flights were attacked *en route* by German Me110 twin-engined fighters from Pantellaria.

Operation Salient followed, again *Eagle* sailing from the Rock in company with the AA cruisers *Charybdis* and *Cairo* and destroyers of 'The Old Firm', *Partridge, Ithuriel, Antelope, Wishart, Wrestler* and *Westcott*, on 8 June. The following day 32 Spitfires were flown off, all arriving safely at Malta that afternoon. A Consolidated Catalina flying boat was reported that day as having taken the surrender of the Italian submarine *Veniero*, an all-but unique event. The destroyer *Partridge* was despatched from *Eagle*'s escort in position 36 degrees 45 minutes North, 000 degrees 29 minutes East, to assist in bringing back this prize. The carrier herself returned to Gibraltar with *Charybdis* and her other consorts on 10 June.

It was to be their last easy operation.

# CHAPTER EIGHT

# To Save an Island

Malta was now in desperate straits. There were Axis plans to invade the island from the air as they had done Crete the year before. Certainly no patch of ground had undergone such an intense aerial bombardment as had that gallant island and the award of the George Cross by His Majesty King George VI, although sourly spurned by a later generation of Maltese politicians, was an honour bravely won and honourably earned.

At 0350 on 12 June *Eagle* sailed yet again with *Malaya* and *Argus*, cruisers *Kenya*, *Liverpool*, *Charybdis* and *Cairo*, fast minelayer *Welshman*, and the destroyers *Marne*, *Matchless*, *Partridge*, *Onslow*, *Blankney*, *Middleon*, *Badsworth*, *Kujawiak* (Polish), *Ithuriel*, *Icarus*, *Escapade*, *Antelope*, *Wishart*, *Wrestler*, *Westcott* and *Vidette* to cover a six ship convoy to Malta, Operation Harpoon.

This was a risky venture with the Axis at the peak of their strength and it was not a success. This was no reflection on the work of the *Eagle* and her aircrew however. Because of the expected scale of the air threat she embarked twelve extra Sea Hurricane fighters of No.801 Squadron as well as the flight of four from No.813. Four Fairey Fulmar fighters from No.807 Squadron also embarked aboard *Eagle* from *Argus*, the remainder staying aboard the latter. To make room for these extra fighter 'planes some of *Eagle*'s Swordfish were transferred to *Argus* who had the primary aerial anti-submarine responsibility while the remainder were put ashore.

The convoy had to undergo several intense air attacks by all arms of the Axis air forces which just swamped the few fighters the Fleet Air Arm could put up against them. The FAA fighters claimed to have destroyed nine of the enemy with two 'probables' but in return they lost one 813 Squadron Sea Hurricane and three of the slower Fulmars. Although totally outclassed by the land-based fighters they met the presence of these dedicated defenders over the convoy during the hard-fought days of 13 and 14 June blunted the edge of many aerial attacks. However there were just too many of the enemy and not enough of the FAA fighters and high-level, dive-bomber and torpedo-bomber assaults broke through on several occasions. There were other handicaps. Both carriers were old and slow and the wind was blowing from astern most of the time. This meant that they had great difficulty flying their aircraft off and on, because to turn into the wind would mean dropping astern and they had not the speed to make up the gap quickly enough.

No more than ten fighters could be kept aloft at any one time. On 14 June the cruiser *Liverpool* took an aerial torpedo and was badly damaged and one of the convoy, *Tanimbar*, was sunk. By dusk that day firstly the long-range Junkers Ju88 dive bombers of the Luftwaffe and then both German and Italian-crewed Stuka dive bombers joined in the assaults along with Savoia Marchetti SM79 torpedo bombers. Both the carriers were selected as prime targets and both had lucky escapes.

Harry Rathbone was transferred to *Eagle* from a very happy ship, the destroyer *Wishart*, early in 1942. He made these observations on the Harpoon operation:

At the time I did not understand why we turned back and allowed the merchant ships with reduced escort to make their way to Malta without our protection. To be honest, I was quite thankful to turn back towards Gibraltar again by that time.

The *Eagle* and *Argus* provided air cover for the convoy but I do remember that the enemy planes still got through to us a lot. I can recall the cool and efficient way the crews in charge of the multiple pom-pom dealt with an Italian torpedo bomber that got too close and also the way that Captain Mackintosh lay on the deck looking into the sun watching the dive bombers and ordering the helm hard over as they commenced their attack dives. (I hope his eyesight did not suffer in later life.) He kept the ship out of trouble by making these emergency turns as late as possible when the Stukas were fully committed. Even so there were some very near misses and I can remember being soaked by one and I was up on the signal deck at the time!

Les Owen remembers that during Harpoon:

> We were very lucky then, as we were missed by a stick of
> heavy bombs from high-flying bombers, and also by an aerial
> torpedo dropped from a Junkers Ju88 which ran right across
> our bows, but we managed to shoot the owner into the sea.

Gordon Drake:

> On our radar set we were able to tell the difference between
> fighter and bombers by the rate of closing etc. but in daytime
> the Chief GI (Gunnery Instructor) in the range-finder used
> to give a running commentary on all the aircraft which were
> attacking us, torpedo-bombers, high-level bombers etc. But
> his description of Stukas, the most-feared of all the enemy
> aircraft, was very good. His voice trembled and he would say,
> 'There is a large group of Junkers 87's otherwise known as
> (Blanking) Stukas directly overhead!' During the Harpoon
> convoy we were under very heavy attack while in the middle
> of the western basin and all the warships were steaming
> round in circles to protect what few merchantmen were left
> to us. It seemed to me just like those old films of Indians
> circling round a waggon train. We had to stay longer than
> planned to give fighter cover until dusk. I always will
> remember the bridge in the heat of the battle coming on the
> headset and asking the Chief GI to 'moderate his description
> of the attacking aircraft!'

Les Goodenough told me:

> It was in the Harpoon convoy that a returning 'plane flew
> towards us. My No.1, AB Tassell, was about to open fire
> when I shouted that it was one of ours. The pilot never knew
> how close he came to being shot down. On these trips certain
> cruisers and destroyers allocated to look after us put up an
> umbrella barrage above us and the shrapnel showered down
> on the flight deck like rain at times. One piece flew between
> us with a whistle. We were less than two feet apart so were
> lucky.

The main force turned back as normal and *Eagle* was due back
at Gibraltar at 0430 on 17 June escorted by the destroyers
*Icarus* and *Onslow*. But having earlier been refuelled from the
fleet oiler *Brown Ranger*, they eventually returned to harbour at
1248 with the rest of Force 'W'.

Here they found that another aircraft transport, *Empire Shackleton*, had arrived with another batch of Spitfires. These were to be flown off to Malta in Operation Pinpoint. The fate of the convoy which was set upon by the Italian cruiser squadron and suffered further losses from both German dive bombers and Italian minefields on the final leg of the journey, led to the postponement of Pinpoint until matters had been clarified themselves somewhat.

*Eagle* finally sailed for this mission on 14 July, leaving Gibraltar at 0552 in company with *Charybdis* and *Cairo* and the destroyers *Ithuriel*, *Antelope*, *Westcott*, *Wrestler* and *Vansittart*. *Eagle* herself had 32 Spitfires embarked together with six Sea Hurricanes for fighter protection.

And so they continued to sail into the jaws of hell. They all knew they were in for a rough time and that while the enemy was at his strongest Force 'H' had rarely been weaker. Nonetheless they could smile from time-to-time despite themselves. The Navy continued to be the Navy no matter what the conditions.

Between 0613 and 0753 next morning, all save one of the 32 Spitfires embarked on the carrier were duly flown off and arrived at Malta safely. The engine of one Spitfire 'cut' while taking off and to avoid going over the bows the pilot swung the aircraft into the protective plating round the forward AA guns and it was seriously damaged. Their new captain, Captain L.D. Mackintosh, DSC, who had relieved Captain Rushbrooke, reported that; 'The leader of the flight was already airborne and a long delay in flying-off the remaining Spitfires could not be accepted.' The crashed aircraft was therefore jettisoned without any further ceremony. There were no other incidents and they secured to No.52 berth at Gibraltar at 1105 on 16 July.

The endless round of flying-off operations continued on 20 July with Operation Insect, *Eagle* with 30 Spitfires embarked, sailed with her old companions the cruisers *Cairo* and *Charybdis*, and the destroyers *Ithuriel*, *Antelope*, *Westcott*, *Wrestler* and *Vansittart* at 0450 and by 0525 were in position 180 degrees Europa Point, three miles steering a course of 082 degrees at 17 knots. A detailed reconnaissance of Italian ports was carried out before they sailed and they were not molested from the air. However, on their first day at sea they sighted no less than nine Spanish merchant ships and before long the Italian submarine

*Dandolo* had ambushed them. She fired a spread of four torpedoes at the *Eagle*, all of which missed. The carrier was in position 37 degrees 48 minutes North, 02 degrees 05 minutes East and the time was 0332 on 21 July. From the British ships four heavy underwater explosions were felt, one very close to *Eagle* and a green flash was seen. It was correctly assumed that these were caused by submarine attack but no asdic contacts or visual sightings of the surfaced U-boat were reported by any ship of the force.

At first light there was still insufficient wind to fly off the fighters and not until 0726 did they begin to take off. Twenty-nine Spitfires were finally got away by 0850. One Spitfire was found to be unserviceable before launch and was struck down again.

Tragedy struck the fourth flight. One of the Spitfires, piloted by Sergeant Pilot J. Evans, took off without a hitch, but once airborne, he found that his long-range fuel tank was defective. Again that old problem still not rectified and this time it was to cost a brave man's life. There was little or no chance that Evans would be able to land a high-performance aircraft like the Spitfire back on the deck of a carrier with absolutely no training and no deck hook on the aircraft. It was considered safest to save the pilot and sacrifice the 'plane. Evans was therefore ordered to bail out over the fleet and the destroyers stood by to pick him up sharply. Unfortunately when he complied with this order his parachute failed to open and he was killed. Again carelessness at home had done the enemy's work for them.

The return of the force was largely uneventful. A further merchant ship was sighted steering north-east at some fifteen miles distance at 0745, presumably a Vichy ship for within a short time it had directed a German Junkers Ju88 reconnaissance aircraft to the scene and she shadowed the force from 0830 to 0850, being fired upon by *Charybdis* each time she ventured too close. As the last flight of Spitfires left, the Junkers followed them presumably in order to aid their interception by German fighters near Pantellaria island as previously.

If so it did not work for all the Spitfires of the first, second and third and what remained of the fourth flight safely reached their destination airfields at Malta later that day.

Shadowing was taken up at 0900 by an Italian Fiat SR14 amphibian which appeared off the starboard beam. Two Sea

*A night air raid on Alexandria harbour, the destroyer* Decoy *was damaged and the* Illustrious *slightly damaged in this attack. Here the battleship* Warspite *can be seen firing her main AA batteries with* Illustrious *silhouetted behind her. (Copyright E. B. Mackenzie)*

*Air Raid Warning 'RED', Alexandria harbour, 1941. Manning the twin Lewis gun aboard HMS* Eagle. *The bridge structure, funnel and mainmast of the battleship HMS* Barham *can be seen beyond* Eagle's *flight-deck. (Copyright 'Tug' Whymark)*

*Seen from HMS* Eagle *the Commander (Flying) 'Beats up' the battleship HMS* Warspite *in Alexandria harbour in one of the newly delivered American-built Brewster Buffalo fighter aircraft. (Copyright E. B. Mackenzie)*

*The Brewster lands on HMS* Eagle *with Commander 'F' at the helm and is manhandled to safety 1941. (Copyright E. B. Mackenzie)*

*Down and out! A blazing Swordfish presents a more grim scene after another crash landing resulting in the explosion of her fuel tanks. HMS* Eagle, *summer 1941. (Copyright A. W. Leyster)*

*A full range on the deck of HMS* Eagle *prior to the Mediterranean Fleet's attack on Tripoli, 1941. The small cruiser seen astern is the famous HMS* Ajax. *(Copyright E. B. Mackenzie)*

*The German blockade runner* Elbe *on fire amidships after being bombed by* Eagle's *Swordfish, South Atlantic, June 1941. (Copyright E. B. Mackenzie)*

*Ferrying Spitfires to Malta in the dark days of spring 1942 was the main preoccupation of HMS* Eagle. *These reinforcements probably saved the island as much as the vital convoy operations and* Eagle *made more of such trips than any other carrier.*

*Here is one of the very few that failed to make it off the flight deck. A Spitfire is pictured going in over the side. (Copyright Gordon Drake)*

*The destroyer HMS* Laforey, *flotilla leader of the 13th Flotilla working from Gibraltar at this time, comes alongside HMS* Eagle *to transfer a ditched pilot she had plucked from the sea. (Copyright Gordon Drake)*

*The classic aerial view of HM aircraft carriers* Eagle, Victorious *and* Indomitable *in line abreast entering the Mediterranean at the start of the epic 'Pedestal' convoy, August 1942. The ship beyond them is the cruiser* Charybdis *with the battleship* Nelson *steaming away from the camera in the far distance. (Copyright Geoffrey Jones)*

*The Sea Hurricane fighter of No 801 Squadron makes her final approach over the stern of HMS Eagle. Almost immediately after this photo was taken four torpedoes struck the ship. (Copyright Fleet Air Arm Museum, Yeovilton)*

*Hit by four torpedoes from an undetected German U-boat during Malta Convoy operation 'Pedestal' in August, 1942, HMS Eagle rapidly heels over to port cascading men and aircraft from her flight deck into the Western Mediterranean. (Copyright R. A. Dakin)*

*After the initial burst of smoke and soot from her funnel uptakes as the torpedoes hit HMS Eagle's list rapidly increased. She was still underway and white smoke from the fires was left astern as she slewed round under helm. (Copyright R. A. Dakin)*

*Within a few minutes HMS* Eagle *has fully capsized and the rescue tug* Jaunty *can be seen chugging her way to the scene of the disaster to pick up survivors. (Copyright R. A. Dakin)*

*Kapitanleutnant Rosenbaum, captain of* U-73, *on his return from sinking HMS* Eagle. *(Copyright O. J. Barritt)*

Hurricanes were flown off down-wind and managed to get enough height to catch and engage this snooper before it could get away. They made several beam attacks and it was clearly seen to be damaged before both fighters expended all their ammunition. It was seen to hit the water with one float but recovered and flew on.

At 1225 *Antelope* reported an asdic contact of an approaching torpedo and an emergency turn away was made but no enemy submarine claimed an attack at this time so the report was probably false. Nonetheless two Sea Hurricanes had to be flown off as an anti-submarine patrol for *Eagle* had no Swordfish embarked and the RAF patrol failed to turn up.

The steering gear of the old *Vansittart* broke down in the early hours of 22 July and she dropped astern of the force. It is remarkable that the western end of the Mediterranean at this period of the war had only two old carriers of 1920s vintage and a handful of destroyers, half of which were the old 'V' and 'W' classes which dated back to World War I. Only *Charybdis* and *Ithuriel* were brand-new ships. One wonders why the Italians with their huge modern fleet did not try conclusions with Force 'H' while it was at such a low ebb, one can only conclude that the sound drubbings administered to it in 1940 by both Cunningham and Somerville had knocked what little stuffing there was completely out of the Italian Navy.

The *Eagle* finally returned to Gibraltar at 1035 on 22 July, escorted by the destroyer *Westcott*.

More exercises were conducted with *Charybdis* and destroyers on 31 July and a Hawker Sea Hurricane embarked in *Eagle* reported sighting a U-boat in position 35 degrees 55 minutes North, 44 minutes West between 0930 and 2030 on 31 July. The exercise was cancelled the next day.

Planning now began for the biggest convoy ever organised to raise the siege of Malta, the famous Operation Pedestal. *Eagle*'s destiny was fast approaching.

\*

The complete story of Pedestal is to be found in my book of the same name, for which I had full access to the official records. Apart from the salient facts of this, the greatest of the Malta convoys, I do not intend to repeat myself, but to concentrate almost exclusively on the role of HMS *Eagle* as seen from those records, both Allied and Axis, and from her own ship's company.

Operation Pedestal was the largest convoy assembled to relieve Malta, so serious was the island's position considered in London. As the Axis powers had an overwhelming air, submarine and surface ship strength with which to oppose the fourteen ship convoy if they so chose, the Admiralty assembled the strongest force it could muster to defend this convoy. The whole escorting plan was complex and the various participating warships were divided into various forces and sub-divided again, but overall command was given to Vice-Admiral Sir Neville Syfret, the commander of Force 'H'; and ships from all over the world were added to his strength. That the Admiralty could assemble such a force at a time of grave disasters at sea elsewhere is yet another fact glossed over by its post-war critics. The First Sea Lord, Admiral Sir Dudley Pound has been almost universally written off as a semi-invalid with no will-power against Churchill and little ability to delegate or organise. The assembling of the Pedestal squadrons gives a lie to all these assertions.

The backbone of the force was the battleships *Nelson* and *Rodney*, slow, but powerfully armed with the nine 16 inch guns and more than a match for the battle-shy Italians should they risk a close encounter. They also mounted formidable AA batteries and served as HQ ships.

In the air where if the Axis ran true to form, they would concentrate their efforts, the Fleet Air Arm could not hope to match their opponents, either in numbers or in modern equipment, but a credible force was assembled; *Eagle* was reinforced by two modern carriers, *Indomitable* and *Victorious*. They could carry between them more than 50 fleet fighters, Hawker Sea Hurricanes, Fairey Fulmars and the new Grumman Martlets (Wildcats in the US Navy). In addition they could embark several squadrons of Fairey Albacore TSR's for torpedo striking forces and anti-submarine work. There was a fourth carrier added, *Furious*, but her role was not defensive but to fly off two sets of further Spitfire reinforcements to Malta under the cover of the convoy proper. A force of Western Approaches destroyers was allocated to her defence; *Keppel*, *Malcolm*, *Amazon*, *Venomous*, *Wolverine* and *Vidette*.

Each fleet carrier was allocated its own protective cruiser, *Charybdis* (and not *Scylla* as in one account) of course remained associated with *Eagle*. They had worked together for so long now they were highly attuned as a team. The *Phoebe* and *Sirius* were given similar roles with the other two carriers while a powerful destroyer force included *Laforey, Lightning, Lookout, Quentin, Somali, Eskimo, Tartar, Ithuriel, Antelope Wilton, Zetland, Vansittart, Westcott, Wishart*, and *Wrestler*.

A fourth anti-aircraft cruiser, *Cairo*, joined the light cruisers *Nigeria, Kenya* and *Manchester* as part of the close escort to accompany the convoy right through to Malta. *Cairo* and *Nigeria* were equipped for fighter direction to help guide the Malta Spitfires to their aid on the last lap of the journey. They were accompanied by the destroyers *Ashanti, Pathfinder, Penn, Bramham, Bicester, Derwent, Ledbury, Intrepid, Icarus, Foresight* and *Fury*, the last four fitted out for minesweeping.

There was also an oiling force with three tankers with seven corvettes and a rescue tug. The *Argus* was on hand with a spare complement of six Sea Hurricanes.

The *Eagle*'s aircraft strength for this operation comprised 16 Sea Hurricanes of Nos.801 (whose acting CO was Lieutenant-Commander R.A. Brabner) and 813 Squadron's (whose CO was Lieutenant (O) C. Hutchinson), plus four partly-assembled spare Sea Hurricanes in reserve. They were hung from the hangar beams out of the way until required. Under the overall command of Captain L.D. Mackintosh, DSC,RN, was Commander W.G.C. Stokes, (Commander Flying) and Lieutenant-Commander (O) C.E.A. Owen, DSC was Air Staff Officer.

A preliminary Fleet Air Arm exercise, (Operation Berserk) was conducted on 5 August in position 35 degrees North, 14 degrees West. This was mainly to enable various air groups and carriers as well as the complex radio and radar nets to be worked out together before the main battle. Two valuable days were spent by the aircraft conducting high and low fighter protection. *Eagle* and *Indomitable* were to maintain high level cover for the whole force as well as their own CAP (Combat Air Patrol).

Some extra crew had to be embarked at Gibraltar prior to her sailing to cope with these extra duties. They were among those with the briefest memories of all of *Eagle*, one of them being a young Air Mechanic (Ordnance), R.C. Cosh. He was to write in his own memoirs:

The Naval Air Maintenance Unit in the dockyard at Gibraltar was our destination. It comprised a few wooden huts as living quarters, a mess hall, and a large

hangar/assembly shop in which we worked. After a few
weeks here I was attached to 801 Squadron whose aircraft
now consisted of Hurricane fighters and who were all
embarked.

The *Eagle* was very crowded. Mess decks were shared, and
there was no room to sling a hammock in the recognised
areas. I slept the first night in the hangar, and lay there in
wonder. Rats were trotting along the steel girders at the deck
heads. Earlier, on the mess deck we had found the bread was
infested with insects. The following day a Royal Marine, who
seemed very old and wise, assured me that although we were
in for a rough time there was no need to worry, because this
ship had blisters a foot thick below the water line, and no
German torpedo would ever sink her!

On the morning of 11 August there was an early intimation of
the presence of U-boats when the corvette *Coltsfoot*, in position
37 degrees 56 minutes North, 01 degrees 49 minutes East,
screening the RFA oilers, sighted the tracks of two torpedoes,
evidently fired at her. From that point onward sightings of
submarines, their periscopes and their torpedoes, and
counter-attacks on submarines and contacts, was more or less
non-stop. The Axis had deployed seventeen submarines, two of
them German, in readiness for Pedestal. The early attacks were
by Italian ships but lurking not far off was an old friend of the
*Eagle*'s from her China Fleet days.

The commander of the German submarine *U-73* was
Kapitanleutnant Helmut Rosenbaum. He was a very experienced submariner, having served in that élite arm of the
German Navy since October 1936. He already had a string of
victories to his credit. However nine years earlier, as a young
naval cadet making his first voyage aboard the light cruiser
*Köln*, Rosenbaum had sailed to the Far East. At the Chinese
port of Tsingtau his ship had anchored close by a British
aircraft carrier, none other than the *Eagle* herself, and
Rosenbaum and his fellow cadets had been invited aboard for a
social evening with their British opposite numbers. Now he was
to return British hospitality in his own special way! He had left
his base at La Spezia some days before and his precise
instructions had come down from the Commander-in-Chief of
U-Boats, Admiral Döenitz himself. Sink the aircraft carriers!
With these vital ships destroyed or damaged, the main weight

of the Axis attack, which was to be delivered from the air, would meet no resistance in the sky. The plan was logical and Rosenbaum determined to carry it out if he could. When, therefore, he picked up the huge British convoy earlier that morning he had ignored the serried ranks of merchantmen which normally would have occupied his eager attention. He was looking for bigger prey.

Thus as the submarine admiral was later to say in connection with this episode, *U-73*'s attack was no 'chance success', but was 'the last link in a chain of deliberations and decisions'. The positioning of the submarine in this location was, 'the most effective use of the U-boat in the most promising position'. We can also agree with Döenitz's description of Rosenbaum's approach and attack as 'a classic'.

In an interview with *Volkischer Beobachter* reporter Edgar Schroder the story of the German submarine's tracking of her quarry was given in graphic terms:

'I never saw so many British flags before.' Rosenbaum was recorded as saying on his first glimpses of Pedestal through his periscope. One of his crew members related that, 'I only once saw the Captain excited and that was when the great aircraft-carrier came into sight, but he had himself in hand again in an instant and from then on every movement was the controlled action of a man completely concentrating on his target. This outward calm had its effect upon all of us. It was an experience to see how exactly and how surely the orders of the captain and of the engineering officer – the latter responsible for keeping the boat at periscope depth – came swiftly following one after the other, especially at the time when the destroyer dashed past us only eight metres away and we had to go deeper as quickly as we could.'

Air activity commenced around 1235 that afternoon when a large group of enemy aircraft had been reported approaching from the southward. *Eagle* flew off four Sea Hurricanes of No.801 Squadron in response to this threat. The pilots of this flight were Lieutenant-Commander Rupert A. Brabner RNVR and Temporary Acting Sub-Lieutenant (A) Peter James Hutton, RNVR, of Red Sub-Flight and Acting Sub-Lieutenant (A) Douglas John McDonald, RN and Temporary Sub-Lieutenant (A) Michael Hankey, RNVR of Yellow Sub-Flight. They joined four others from *Victorious*. Another four were 'spotted' aboard *Indomitable* ready to fly off from a position parallel to and half-a-mile from *Eagle*. Aboard the latter ship the ship's company went to Action Stations and they remained closed up there for about twenty minutes. R.C. Cosh recalls that:

> During the morning we flew off several aircraft patrols and apart from the routine deck landings we spent the time on the flight deck in the warm sunshine. Our aircraft were fully armed, fuelled and serviced and we were waiting for something to happen. It did.

Cyril Williams recalls exchanging words with the fighter squadron's CO as they sailed eastward in the sparkling sunshine of a glorious summer day. 'Will these guns fire, Williams?' 'Maybe, sir!' 'Well, they'd better or I'll have you on Jankers!' 'If they don't you won't be coming back.'

*Eagle*, as part of Force 'F', was in position some 8 cables astern of the starboard wing column of a five column convoy (See Diagram 2) on the morning of 11 August. Like the *Indomitable* and *Victorious*, the *Furious* were operating independently astern of the convoy turning into the wind to fly off and recover their aircraft; the three fleet carriers had the light cruisers *Charybdis*, *Sirius* and *Phoebe* and the destroyers *Ashanti*, *Fury*, *Penn*, *Icarus*, and *Intrepid* keeping guard on them. Joining the convoy from astern but not yet in sight was Captain Jack Broome's flotilla from Gibraltar: *Keppel*, *Malcolm*, *Amazon*, *Venomous*, *Wolverine*, and *Wrestler*.

Eagle herself was zig-zagging at a speed of only thirteen knots. Her precise location was 38 degrees 05 minutes North, 03 degrees 03 minutes East, course 090 degrees. The force was some sixty miles off the coast of French North Africa and still out of range of Axis bomber aircraft and still some 585 miles west of Malta. The *Furious*, screened by *Lightning* and *Lookout*, had moved out to the port quarter at 1229 and had commenced the flying off of her first batch of Spitfires, Operation Bellows. Eight were already airborne and at 1309 she commenced flying off another batch while the other three carriers were operating independently with their attached cruisers and destroyers.

Refuelling of the destroyers was actually in progress and at 1100 the *Laforey* had just been relieved by *Westcott* for this

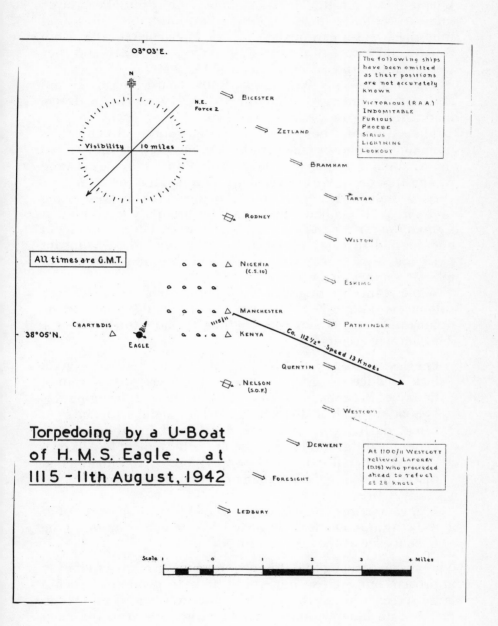

03°03'E.

N

N.E.
Force 2

Visibility  10 miles

The following ships
have been omitted
as their positions
are not accurately
known

VICTORIOUS (R.A.A)
INDOMITABLE
FURIOUS
PHOEBE
SIRIUS
LIGHTNING
LOOKOUT

BICESTER

ZETLAND

BRAMHAM

TARTAR

RODNEY

WILTON

All times are G.M.T.

NIGERIA
(C.S.10)

ESKIMO

MANCHESTER

1115/11

PATHFINDER

CHARYBDIS

38°05'N.

Co. 112½° Speed 13 Knots

EAGLE

KENYA

QUENTIN

NELSON
(S.O.F.)

WESTCOTT

## Torpedoing by a U-Boat of H.M.S. Eagle, at 1115 - 11th August, 1942

DERWENT

At 1100/11 WESTCOTT
relieved LAFOREY
(D.19) who proceeded
ahead to refuel
at 28 knots

FORESIGHT

LEDBURY

Scale  1      0      1      2      3      4 Miles

purpose. Captain R.M.J. Hutton took *Laforey* out ahead at 28 knots to refuel from *Brown Ranger* but, inevitably, for a brief time there was a gap in the convoy's immaculate order. Both convoy and escorts were carrying out zig-zag No.10 and they were on the starboard leg of this at 1115.

The final seconds ticked away. Both aboard the carrier and aboard the submerged submarine the chief actors in the drama made their final moves and comments.

The German newspaper report quotes Rosenbaum's momentous announcement to his waiting crew as they closed the final miles to their intended vitim: 'Put on life-jackets and escape apparatus! We are attacking. Our target is the *Eagle*!'

*U-73* stalked her prey for two-and-a-half nerve-racking hours in all. Rosenbaum had asked for a brandy when he first sighted the carrier and another two later on. The sea was slight and he had to exercise the greatest caution when using his periscope lest it break the surface and give him away with a tell-tale 'feather' in the water.

While concentrating his main approach on *Eagle* the submarine skipper kept his other options open lest he lose the opportunity and be left with nothing to show for his efforts. The German account went on:

> On this occasion there was that most desirable thing – good luck wedded to good management. Mere words cannot describe Rosenbaum's achievement, that of bringing his U-boat through a double screen of warships to *Eagle*, in broad daylight, at periscope depth and in circumstances generally unfavourable to him. The achievement had its own reward. When the ring of ships was pierced, Rosenbaum had placed his boat only 500 metres distant from *Eagle* – he was ready to fire.
>
> *Eagle* was zig-zagging, as the whole formation was, but at the critical moment her zig-zag brought her beam on to the U-boat even as she fired her torpedoes.

There is no denying that Rosenbaum made a skilful and daring approach, but even so how could he have penetrated such a large screen without the slightest detection, and been able to pick out an independently moving target astern of the main convoy itself in such a precise manner without hinderance? It was a puzzle that the anti-submarine department of the Admiralty gave considerable thought to later, but their conclusions were little more than intelligent guesses which they subsequently summarised thus:

(1) Owing to shortage of escorts, due to the fuelling programme, the ships on the wings had been opened out to 2,000 yards.

(2) At 1100 *Laforey* turned over the escort to *Westcott*, the latter relieving her in position 'O'. *Westcott* had come from the starboard wing position and *Laforey* proceeded ahead at 28 knots on completing the turn-over.

(3) Position 'O' was approximately four miles ahead of *Eagle* and therefore, if the U-boat passed through the screen near this position it is reasonable to suppose that it would have done so at about 1100.

And here we should note that Rosenbaum stated in the interview that as he was closing in the final attack phase at periscope depth, a destroyer 'dashed past' at a distance of 80 metres (88 yards); also that she torpedoed *Eagle* from a distance of 500 metres (550 yards). It is therefore not unreasonable to assume that the destroyer was *Laforey* speeding off to refuel at 28 knots, at which speed her asdic and hydrophones would not be working to the optimum effect. The report continued:

(4) On this assumption, the temporary disruption of a portion of the screen at 1100 might explain the failure to detect the U-boat.

(5) The oilers (Force 'R') were in a position some miles ahead of the convoy. The asdic efficiency of the screen was thus reduced at this time by the number of wakes left ahead of the convoy by destroyers proceeding to and from the oilers at high speed.

Criticism was also levelled at the use of the 'very simple' zig-zag pattern employed. Also that: ' ... all ships, including cruisers and above, conformed with the movements of the convoy, except when carrying out special operations or dealing with air attack. It is considered that the anti-U-boat security of Force 'F' would have been increased had the more complicated zig-zags been used and varied frequently and had the heavy ships zig-zagged independently and at higher speed. It is not known, however, to what extent such action would have been compatible with the requirements for defence against air attack, but, judged by results, the air menace, though more serious for the convoy than U-boat attack, was less so for the escort and covering Force.

They concluded, with refreshing candour, that:

Whatever the causes, the fact remains that the U-boat was able, in this case, to penetrate the screen, pass at close range a number of ships in the convoy and at least one heavy ship, carry out its attack, and escape scot-free without at any time being sighted or detected by asdic or RDF. This was a failure, not only of the screen but also of the ships being screened. Judged by the number of sightings of U-boats or their periscopes which took place immediately after the attack on *Eagle*, it is clear that the standard of lookout in Force 'F' was raised as a result of the attack.

At 1317 precisely a heavy muffled explosion was experienced on the port quarter of *Eagle*. This was quickly followed by three similar explosions within ten seconds and splashes were observed at 40 foot intervals going forward. The first explosion occurred abreast P3 gun. The other three explosions occurred between P3 and P2 guns. No torpedo tracks were observed from the bridge or gun positions nor indeed did *any* ship on the screen obtain asdic contact or pick up hydrophone effects. Despite several claims both at the time and since then that torpedo tracks were seen this has never been verified. Captain Mackintosh was to state quite clearly that:

It was originally reported to me by Lieutenant (A) G.P. Hewson, RN, that he and some ratings standing on the flight deck observed some streaks 50 feet from the ship's side which they assumed to be torpedo tracks. Lieutenant Hewson now admits that he saw these supposed tracks after the fourth torpedo had struck, and that they definitely were not the bubble tracks of which he had seen many during his previous service. It is considered that this report of tracks is unreliable and cannot be substantiated.

The four explosions all threw up splashes of water, but the fourth vented vertically more than the other, throwing up a considerable quantity of debris, the signal boom and other gear stowed in the nettings. It was not possible to gauge the precise depth at which the torpedoes struck her, but the small amount of water thrown up by the first explosion indicated that they were running deep.

In Captain Mackintosh's opinion the ship's armoured belt prevented explosions occurring in the magazine which were in the vicinity of all four explosions, but he was not clear on why he thought this should be so. Presumably he felt that this belt was not pierced by the torpedoes which all exploded below, in a similar manner to those which sank the battleship *Royal Oak* of similar vintage earlier in the war.

Immediately after the first torpedo hit her the *Eagle* listed about 5 degrees to port. By the time of the fourth hit she was over to 15 degrees and continuing to heel over rapidly to 30 degrees, settling bodily in the water. Reduced damage control parties were closed up in accordance with the damage control handbook at this time and the ship was in the three-unit system for steaming. Owing to the speed which she went down there was no possibility either of exercising damage control or of investigating the area of the hits.

Everything happened very suddenly so it is not surprising that different survivors remember those traumatic moments in widely differing ways. Leading Stoker Alfred Carpenter wrote in his own memoirs how he was fortunate enough to have been selected for the HPE party:

> This was the high power electrical party, formed from Engine Room personnel to take pressure off the actual electricians by carrying out the less complicated electrical tasks of fault finding in the boiler rooms and engine rooms. The *Eagle* had four boiler rooms – 21 boilers – and three engine rooms. Each of these spaces, besides the traditional means of ladders for entry and exit, also had electric lifts. Two leading stokers were attached to the HPE party, but as they were first and foremost members of the engine room branch, the requirement was that while at sea one of the leading stokers was needed to join up with the boiler room crew for watchkeeping. As I had carried out those duties throughout the previous trip, it was the turn of my counterpart to carry out the watchkeeping duties on the Pedestal convoy. This was just one of the many 'extraordinary circumstances' which meant I was not below on this occasion.
>
> I myself was in a smallish fan compartment, it housed one of the enormous ventilation fans that supplied fresh air, through trunking, to the main engine room. It was large

enough to have a desk and it was where the electrical records and reference books were kept. At this particular time I was getting ahead with my letter writing because, like the sleepers on the messdeck above me, sleeping while they could, I knew that there would be little enough opportunity for anything like that later on. I remember I was writing to my mother and back at the desk had commenced the sentence – 'had to break off there for a while, approaching aircraft caused us to go to action stations' – that was what I intended to write but it was never completed. I was interrupted by a terrific thump followed by an almighty bang. At first the cause of this puzzled me, then I thought the ship had suffered a near miss from a large bomb. My next thought was that, whatever the cause, it would certainly mean action stations again, so putting down my pen I reached for my lifebelt but before making contact with it, two more almighty explosions occurred deep down in the ship beneath where I was sitting. The ship seemed to lift bodily upwards about twelve inches and as she dropped back down the resulting thump tripped all the generators, plunging the ship into total darkness and at the same time she began to list to port. Of course it was now obvious we had been torpedoed.

All this took far less time than it takes me to write it; it all happened within a few seconds. As this was happening I had to make a lightning search for my lifebelt, which because of the upward lurch had moved from where I had put it. Fortunately making a rapid wider search I located it and then made my move towards safety. I knew that my way ahead was to leave the fan compartment, take three paces forward, a sharp turn right and a further ten paces which would take me to the ladder up which I could reach the stokers' messdeck, about ten feet above.

If it seems that I am being too precise in my description perhaps I should explain that having been aboard *Eagle* for three years I had become so familiar with her layout I was not troubled by the darkness. It would have been a very different story had I been among the newcomers who had only joined the ship a few weeks earlier. My passage from the fan compartment to the ladder crossed the engineers' workshop. This was quite a large compartment occupying almost the whole width of the ship and was about 9 metres wide. The workshop contained three large lathes and a couple of smaller ones, plus several workbenches, cupboards for the numerous lathe tools and engineering spares, and, as is usual in workshops, stowage for all manner of useful odds and ends that 'might come in handy'. When on even keel all this heavy metal paraphernalia was not a problem but the ship was far from on an even keel by now and all the loose lumps of metal, large and small, were tumbling down the sloping deck. The banging and clattering of the falling steel was alarming in the darkness as I groped my way towards the ladder. A far more ominous sound spurred me on, however, for I could hear sea water bubbling into the workshop. My time and *Eagle*'s was fast running out!

Unbelievable though it seems in retrospect, as I hurried to reach that ladder through that cascading metal debris not so much as a single nut or bolt struck me. It wasn't until hours later, when recalling my own personal experience, that the significance of this sank in, and I offered up a prayer of thankfulness for my incredible fortune.

Quickly I climbed the sideways sloping ladder, emerging into the stokers' messdeck above. It was a very comforting sight to see daylight coming through a hatchway diagonally from where I was. This led to the upper deck and safety. The ship was continuing to list more and more, and the sloping messdeck with its covering of corticene, a special hard cork-based linoleum, made it difficult to get a grip. So, kicking off my shoes allowed my socks to obtain a reasonable grip and, aided by the chained-down mess tables, I was able to haul myself hand-over-hand within reach of that ladder. Here I joined about six other stokers all waiting their turn to scamper up. There was no panic, no shouting, in fact I clearly recall the absolute silence from the whole party. Up they went one-by-one and when my turn came I too rushed up to fresh air.

The part of the upper deck we emerged at was known as the starboard waist or the waist deck and was a walkway from for'ard to aft. When I arrived there I found many others already who had also had the good fortune to make it from down below. Again there was no panic and no mad dash to abandon ship, even though on looking over the anti-torpedo bulges which normally were totally submerged, we could see them fully exposed.

I scanned the faces of those who had preceded me to see if

any of my chums had managed to escape. The only familiar face I remember seeing in that quick glance around was Reg 'Jacko' Jackson, a leading stoker, who like me had been a member of *Eagle*'s ship's company since August 1939 and was one of my special mates.

Again looking back over the years to that moment, it now seems uncanny that with the ship listing so badly there appeared to be no urgency to leave the ship. I have many times tried to arrive at an explanation why this was so, and the one answer that seems reasonable is that none of us had experienced anything of this gravity before, and the shock was taking a few moments to sink in. Besides we had some doubts whether the ship would actually go down so fast and I think it more logical to accept the fact that a sailor doesn't abandon his ship until so ordered. The consequences of abandoning a ship that eventually stays afloat are that serious charges can be brought and no one was keen to put himself in the position of being the first over the side. A young engineering sub-lieutenant, not appreciating the situation, forced his way past the men on the upper deck shouting orders, 'Get away to your action stations' and disappeared down the hatchway from which I had emerged only moments before. He was not seen again.

Then a tubby seaman, more concerned with survival than consequences, dived over the side and as he surfaced he looked up at us and in coarse but persuasive naval language got the message over: 'Get off of it, she's going down.' Immediately everyone else sprang into action and there was a mass evacuation.

He records other tragedies. A certain young stoker, with a bad attitude to discipline, was always in trouble. When they sailed from Gibraltar he was once again in cells. It was assumed that his punishment was due to end sometime during the trip or else he would have been locked up ashore in HMS *Rooke*. But he wasn't and went down with the ship still locked in his tiny prison. Another stoker, from 'D' Boiler Room, had just begun his ascent in one of the electric lifts when the torpedoes struck and all electrical power ceased to function. The lift jammed and despite his piteous cries for help the darkness and sloping deck made his rescue impossible.

Then there was the torpedo artificers' workshop, which,

because of the necessity to transport the Swordfish torpedoes to and from the workshop, was fitted with a large hatchway. However, the hatch had a cover of such dimensions that its extreme weight made a chain-block necessary to enable the cover to be raised or lowered. The cover was raised at the time of the first torpedo hit and an artificer running up the ladder was almost at the top when the shuddering of the next two torpedoes shook and released the catch holding the cover which allowed this massive chunk of metal to fall. It cut the artificer in two.

A stoker petty officer got out of the ship completely unscathed. Having done so he just slid down the ship's side where he sat on the anti-torpedo bulge, rolled himself a cigarette and, despite pleas from those in the water near to him, continued to sit there smoking until he vanished from view in the swirl of *Eagle*'s final plunge. He could swim, so his reasoning will remain forever a mystery. Leading Stoker Whymark who found a skin complaint that had defied all medical efforts to heal, vanished completely after his being immersed for several hours in the oil fuel of *Eagle*'s demise!

There were no survivors from 'B' boiler room, the stokers on duty there dying to a man. As there were no survivors from the port wing engine room it appeared that this took one direct hit while the centre and starboard wing engine rooms were undamaged. 'A', 'C' and 'D' boiler rooms were damaged and flooded but some survivors got out of all three. In each case the port wing bulkheads collapsed.

The ship's standing orders called for the engines to be stopped by the engine room staff if the ship was ever hit and listing and this was promptly done. The bridge gave direct orders to stop both engines and to put the wheel port 30 degrees, but after the fourth torpedo all normal means of communication failed abruptly. As the ship listed the operator of the sound-powered telephone slid off his seat and in so doing parted the 'phone lead, thus cutting off communications from damage control headquarters to the bridge. No time was available to start up the diesel dynamos, and at least one of them was out of action due to the torpedo explosions.

Again, in the opinion of *Eagle*'s captain, the U-boat that carried out the attack must have passed down between the two starboard outer lines of the convoy and fired electric torpedoes.

Only six minutes elapsed between the torpedoes hitting and

the old ship vanishing beneath the waves. When the *Eagle* received her death blows the whole ship's company was still on the move going from action stations to defence stations. This was a stroke of luck and resulted in an above average number of survivors for such a quick sinking.

It soon became apparent that the ship was going over and under rapidly and officers in their respective stations gave the order to abandon ship. A large majority of the Carley floats and floatnets floated free as she went down. The port side of the flight deck was under water within three minutes so no boats could be got away while the boats on the starboard side were equally useless due to the list.

J. Milne had a lucky escape for his watch that day was the afternoon watch in 'B' Boiler Room. He told me what happened:

I could not take my watch at the appointed time due to Action Stations being sounded off, which meant other duties taking priority until the 'Clear' sounded. Not until then could one proceed to one's normal duties. When the 'Secure' sounded I made my way between decks to the part of the ship where my locker was located, opened the locker for some gear and then proceeded down towards 'B' Boiler Room to relieve my shipmate. There was a small lift nearby which I had opened to travel in style to the boiler room but little did I know at that very minute the U-boat's torpedoes were already on their way. Suddenly I heard what I thought was the sound of gunfire until everything went dark between decks and the ship suddenly lurched over quickly and steeply. My locker door was still open and my gear tumbled out. For a second I crazily commenced to gather all this stuff up until it finally sunk in that the situation was serious.

I somehow made my way to the upper side deck. There was nobody around this part of the ship but I believe the rum ration which I had drunk just about an hour before, helped subdue my fear and, at 18 and not being well-educated, I believed I could cope with any danger. Ignorance is bliss and my attitude saved me as I remained calmer than I would have done had I realised the worst had already happened!

Even without a lifejacket I wasn't worried. The rum was still helping me. I found my way out of the darkness of the canteen flat and somehow scrambled to the upper deck. By this time the ship was on her side with the keel showing where I was standing waiting to leave the ship. It was fortunate for me that the water was quite warm and the sun was shining because I left the *Eagle* in just my underpants only.

I therefore almost enjoyed the swim and easily trod water without any help until order was restored and the destroyer *Lookout* picked me and others from the sea. It was only later that it hit me that all my pals from 'B' Boiler Room had gone down with the ship and had made the supreme sacrifice.

R.C. Cosh remembered her final moments in this way:

At around 1300 a terrific explosion shook *Eagle* on her port side. She shuddered and took on a bad list. At this time, in company with others, I was abaft the bridge on the starboard side of the ship on the flight deck. My immediate reaction was to look around the sky and reach for my tin helmet. Nothing was to be seen. The convoy moved sedately on. The *Eagle* seemed for a moment to right herself. There were three more violent explosions in rapid succession and the old ship took a dangerous list to port.

The aircraft ranged at the stern of the ship broke away from their lashings and went sliding and crashing over the side. Men from the port side netting who were scrambling up the deck holding on to the arrestor wires went with them. Aircraft chocks, tool boxes and a host of other movable objects went cascading down the flight deck, by now at a pronounced angle, and into the sea. I could see figures climbing down the bridge and over the starboard side as the ship continued to roll sideways. There seemed to be no point in hanging about. I slithered over the starboard side and looked down. It was a long way to jump but there seemed to be little future in staying put. I jumped!

The water was pleasantly warm and I quickly surfaced, only to go smartly under again as a very heavy weight landed on top of me, and a very large boot hit my left ear. The owner of the boot shouted his apologies. 'Sorry mate, are you all right?' He continued; 'This is the second time in six months for me, and the last time I waited a month to get a pair of boots to fit me in barracks!'

We swam quickly from the doomed *Eagle*, and turned to look back. Only her bottom was showing now and there seemed to be a lot of figures still scrambling around. With a hiss and rattle from her innards, and hardly a murmur of protest otherwise, the old ship slid beneath the waves. The whole incident had taken no more than six or seven minutes.

The convoy sailed serenely on and from the duck's-eye view that I had of the Med at that time, it wasn't all that encouraging. I floated around on my back for a while, but was quickly disturbed from any reverie by a mighty loud explosion, which sounded much too close for comfort. The noise became louder, and much nearer. Two destroyers were charging up and down dropping depth charges and their obvious priority was submarines, and not us. The sea seemed to shake and so did I! A few dodgy minutes of this and peace returned, which gave me time to take stock of the situation. There were several groups of people in the water, not too far away, and one or two heads bobbing around here and there. One or two dozen, probably, but I wasn't in a very good position to count. Away in the distance was the outline of a ship, which didn't seem to be moving. The destroyers had gone.

I began to swim towards it, hoping that it would stay put, and pausing now and again to flop over on to my back to take a breather. After a while the swimming became less and the breathers more. I had a fair amount of fuel oil over my arms and face, not to mention a pint or two down my throat, which didn't help matters very much. It seemed to me that my luck would need to be extended just a little bit more that day for me to make it. I drifted around on my back again and it felt quite pleasant. The sun was warm. I felt relaxed and didn't care very much what happened next.

What happened next was fortunate. I drifted into a group of three fellows, paddling around with their arms hooked into a ship's lifebelt. There was just room around it for another arm and I accepted the invitation and joined them. A hundred yards away was a destroyer – stopped – men climbing up the side on ropes and ladders. Other men jumping and diving into the water to help them. Salvation! We set a steady course for her bows, paddling our lifebelt along at a fair rate of knots.

I could see the name of the ship and she was beautiful, but her name now escapes me [either *Laforey* or *Lightning*]. I grabbed the rope hanging invitingly before me, soared upwards and was on my way. That, at least, was the intention. Something went wrong with the message from head to arms and in no time at all I hit the sea for the second time that day. Another rope came down in a loop this time, and I sat in it and held on. It was a rough, bumpy, but successful ride and a dozen strong arms pulled me inboard. A mug was held out and I took it and had a mouthful. It was neat rum and the effect was catastrophic. I threw up, several times, and collapsed in a heap. Dozens of others, in varying degrees of fatigue, were strewn around the deck, but we were, for the moment, safe.

Ken Pierce recorded events in this way from the moment the torpedoes struck:

Being an old ship she listed almost at once; and it was obvious that she was sinking. All lighting had failed, so I made my way to the starboard waist deck, where the commander was giving orders for lines to be put over the side so that we could slide down shipside to the underwater bulges, which were now visible. The ship listed again and the commander gave the order to abandon ship, so away we went, down the ropes, up and over the bulge and into the water. I remember seeing someone, I believe it was the senior engineer, sitting on the 'A' bracket and one of the lads calling out, 'Doing a quick inspection, Chief?' He laughed and jumped into the sea.

After swimming away I looked back and saw what I thought was a very novel way to abandon ship. Two men had crawled along a very sloping flight deck and got into a Carley raft which was secured to a ring bolt by a rope. One of them cut the rope and they slid down the flight deck as if in a toboggan only to disappear under the water. However, they appeared again a few seconds later, paddled away and I believe picked up some more swimmers.

I saw three of the main galley cooks supporting one of their mess mates who could not swim, a fine brave thing to do I think you will agree. Words of encouragement were shouted to them telling them that we should be picked up soon, but the non-swimmer seemed more concerned that he had lost his 'choppers' (dentures) than getting rescued. They all survived as far as I know.

Les Goodenough was one of the 'toboggan team' and he recalls:

I had just turned to my mate and said, 'It's my turn to get my head down', when a crash, a spurt of water followed by three more. As soon as we were hit the ship took on a list and we could see it was hopeless. The chief GI, A/B Tassell and myself were in the vicinity of the Carley rafts. The Chief said, 'Give me your knife, Goodenough,' and I found that in the rush to actions stations earlier I had left it behind in the mess. Despite our predicament he gave me a right dressing down (but to this day I *always* carry a knife with me). Many of the rafts were smashed on the starboard bilges and I was brought back to reality by someone half way down the flight deck sitting in a Carley raft held by a ring bolt. He was shouting for someone to release him. At this time the port side of the flight deck was under water with the ship still underway. I slid down to him and, as I released the raft, I jumped in. We slid down the deck into the sea.

Les Owen had closed up at his action station just before, the forward multiple pom-pom. Earlier that morning, on impulse, he had taken all his paper money out of his money belt and put it in his locker for safe keeping. It is still there!

It was when we had dropped astern of the main convoy to take on our returning aircraft that we got hit amidships by four torpedoes. I cannot recall personally hearing any orders to abandon ship but she immediately started to go down on her port side and our aircraft were skidding overboard along with a number of the ship's company, including one of my close shipmates, Ginger Gerhard, the ship's barber, never to be seen again.

I tried to close the ammunition locker of the pom-pom before going over the ship's side to prevent the shells from spilling out so they would not hit my mates coming up the flight deck. When I decided that it was time to go I almost walked down the ship's side on to the bulges with a lot of the ship's company. I blew my lifebelt up, took off my seaboots and jumped in. At first I was dragged down by the suction of the ship sinking. When I finally came to the surface I managed to get hold of a mess deck stool floating in the sea, with about six others. We all got fairly shook up by the depth charges dropped by the destroyers. But eventually I was picked up by the tug *Jaunty* and then transferred to the destroyer *Malcolm*.

'Tug' Whymark was closed up on S2 6 inch gun when the torpedoes hit:

> She immediately started to capsize to port and smoke was issuing from the upper deck air vents. One of the younger gun crew said to me, 'Hear those bombs dropping on us?' I replied, 'Those are not bombs; blow your lifebelt up and follow me, we have been torpedoed.' If I remember rightly, the young lad came from Liverpool and was a non-swimmer. I recall I was concerned about him anyway. *Eagle* was almost over on her beam ends in seconds, still slowly underway. As she turned I kept going forward also following her under. She was almost bottom up and so, my life jacket at the ready, I jumped into the sea and made as much headway from the ship as I possibly could. I looked around. What remained visible of the *Eagle*, her bottom, soon became lost forever. I guess the twenty-odd boilers in her just blew out. There was a loud hiss and she was gone, my home for almost three years had vanished in about three minutes. The water was getting heavily polluted with crude oil seeping from her hull.

Cyril Williams recalls that:

> It was felt by many of the lads that it was inevitable that we would 'cop it' on one of these dangerous runs down into the Med. When it did finally come I had just sat down on an ammunition locker. 1-2-3-4 torpedoes. I recall a shipmate stood by me asking, 'What was that?' I answered by just turning towards him and blowing up my lifebelt. That said it all!
>
> I ran to my abandon ship station. All the Carley floats were stuck in their positions and we could not move them. Somebody threw a rope over the side. It was short for our requirements but nonetheless, down I went, burning my hands on the way down. I hit the water, went down a few feet, came up with a bellyful of oil and sea water, fighting for air only to be taken down again by somebody on my head. Second time up I was fighting for breath when a shipmate who surfaced with me, William Burgess, grabbed hold of me. 'Ginger, help me, I can't swim.' 'OK, don't panic, Bill,' I said. 'We'll make it.' I settled him down and we got into a rhythm. Depth charges were being dropped which was a little worrying plus the thought of sharks crossed my mind. I

didn't fancy losing my legs having just acquired a new pair of shoes!

Like so many others E. Kenward, a seaman attached to 824 Squadron, at first thought the explosion heralded a sneak air attack as so often before.

As the ship failed to right herself afterwards I realised that it was no bombing this time. Already the flight deck was underwater on the port side and aircraft were sliding into the water.

I managed to get to the edge of the deck on the starboard side which by now was quite some distance out of the water as she heeled. I scrambled down and dropped into the sea. I was a reasonable swimmer and managed to get away as far as I could. On looking back I saw the ship was well over and sinking fast, with many people still clinging to her hull as she went down. I can only assume that they were non-swimmers. Indeed I found the biggest hazard apart from the oil on the surface, was non-swimmers asking for help. After what seemed an age I was picked up by the destroyer *Laforey* and later transferred to *Keppel*.

Gordon Drake was very lucky to survive:

I was on the second deck below (the communications mess) and we had just reverted from action stations. There were three of us, myself, a telegraphist and a boy telegraphist. The three of us had been left out grub and grog and we gave the boy 'sippers' (which most probably saved his life). Suddenly, Bang, Bang, followed after a few seconds by Bang Bang!

Immediately we were swimming and the ship had gone over to an alarming list to port. Lights were out and the cortecine which had been polished 'Navy-style' for over twenty years was so slippery it was impossible to get to the hatch. I whipped off my shorts and shoes and with more luck than anything else got to the ladder. I shouted to the others not to touch me and when I had secured my arm through the ladders rungs they were able to climb over me. Then the telegraphist just stood on the ladder and did the impossible, which was to pluck all 12 stone of me clear of the water and onto the ladder. We thus made it to the seamen's messdeck.

The ship smelt of cordite and was shuddering violently and the list had increased to about 30 degrees. One slipped under messdeck tables, while fire and smoke were the worst problems with minor explosions taking place and the ship kept on taking water. Some were laying injured and you would help where you could but you knew all the time she was going quick and that ray of light you could see through the hatch to the upper deck was the only thing that kept you going. We made it, pushing the boy telegraphist in front of us. I can honestly tell you that I will never be afraid of depths after that. Outside it was so peaceful from the bedlam below.

We were joined on the upper deck by an officer who was telling the unfortunates who had scattered about there to keep going and abandon the ship. Shouting 'Every man for himself', he left us by climbing up the starboard side to get a clear jump into the sea. Many left on the upper deck must not have made it.

Harry Kempshall was Band Corporal of the Royal Marines Band. He had only married the previous September and had also got over the shock at finding that his action station aboard *Eagle* was in the spotting top on top of her famous tripod mast:

When torpedoed we had just cleared down from action stations and half the RM Band went down to the TS (Transmitting Station) on cruising watch and were never seen again. Of the other half who were on the mess deck port side, six of us managed to get out.

This was difficult, being on the port side; the ladder from mess deck to waist had collapsed and the bulkhead door aft to the wardroom flat was buckled and immovable.

I got out by jumping up and catching hold of the hatch cowling and on rolling over onto the waist deck found it already awash with oily water. I remained at the hatch briefly, helping a few others out until the water reached the top of the cowling and began pouring into the mess deck.

With a friend and mess-mate we went up the straight ladder to the boat deck with the idea of reaching the flight deck, but this was not to be, for she was by then listing so badly that the flight deck heeled into the water, which washed in and swirled us up into the underside of the flight deck.

Being a good swimmer in those days, I was able to pull myself out using the nets under the flight deck like a spider on a web, and I remember how, as I struggled to the surface it became lighter, so much so that I thought it must be a fire, but on reaching the surface thankfully found it to be the sunshine. The flight deck was half submerged and absolutely perpendicular; I must have been one of the last to get out of her.

Thus passed the gallant old *Eagle*.

# CHAPTER NINE

# Aftermath

The reaction of the escorts to this sudden and unexpected attack was immediate but proved largely ineffectual. The tug *Jaunty*, which had been dropping steadily astern of the convoy and it was obvious she was never going to make the distance, was in a good position to steer directly for the mass of men in the water and start rescue work. The AA cruiser *Charybdis* (Captain G.A.W. Voelcker) was stationed 4½ cables on the starboard quarter of *Eagle* but did not obtain asdic contact, although after the torpedoing of *Eagle* she steamed at 15 knots along the probable tracks. No depth charges were dropped owing to survivors in the water.

The destroyer *Lookout* also crossed the probable position of the attacker soon after the torpedoing but she did not obtain any contact either, but she commenced dropping depth charges to keep the enemy down.

Finally Captain Broome's six destroyers only arrived on the scene some three-quarters of an hour after the sinking and observed other destroyers picking up survivors. They were immediately spread in line of search abreast and conducted a short hunt for the submarine. All these vessels were Western Approaches veterans with a good reputation as highly skilled asdic ships, but they too made absolutely no contact at all. Indeed considering the time that had elapsed theirs was but a forlorn hope of extracting vengeance.

Aboard *U-73* all this furious counter-activity and frenzy concentrated against them proved just how successful their salvo had been. As reported in the *Volkischer Beobachter*:

The death throes lasted for two minutes and then *Eagle* went down. Her sinking was heard in the U-boat, a nerve-racking noise, which those who heard it will never forget, the crackling rustling sounds of bursting bulkheads, the noise of boilers exploding under water – and then the quiet after the hull had sunk down past the U-boat and had reached the bottom.

The hunting craft were so startled that they dropped their depth charges more or less at random. It would have been a bad day for us if the torpedoes had missed and there had been no men swimming about in the water to be rescued distracting the attention of the destroyers.

The U-boat was extricated from the danger area by every artifice that our skilful U-boat men are capable of. Soon the depth charges are being dropped fairly far away and then stillness returns to the sea. In the U-boat all has been still since that first muffled outburst of joy.

The submarine had been crash-dived to a depth of 500 feet, which was close to the limit her hull could withstand. Here she lay doggo with the auxiliary machinery closed down and the bilge-pump left idle, despite risks. Leaks were being found by the water pressure in both the already defective cutout and through the periscope. She was losing oil which found its way to the surface, but fortunately for the German crew this mingled with the far greater amounts from *Eagle*'s riven hull and so did not give *U-73*'s presence away. They lay still for three hours by which time all sounds of pursuit had long since vanished.

Rosenbaum therefore cautiously took his boat up to periscope depth and made a scan of the area. The sea and horizon were empty of all shipping. A brief signal was sent to Admiral Kreisch, the Commander-in-Chief of German submarines operating in the Mediterranean. Rosenbaum reported the composition, speed and bearing of the convoy. He added the proud postscript that he had sunk the *Eagle* and that he himself was undamaged. That same night a special broadcast was sent over the airwaves by the *Deutscher Rundfunk* announcing the news and *Eagle* joined *Courageous*, *Royal Oak*, *Ark Royal* and *Barham* as major victims of Germany's U-boat arm in this war.

Rosenbaum was duly to receive the *Ritterkreuze* from the hands of the Führer for this exploit, ' ... a decoration which he thoroughly deserved', according to the British analysis of the time.

Meanwhile among the hundreds of men struggling in the water many unrecorded acts, both heroic and tragic, were being played out. Oliver Barritt remembered a few snapshots while he got away and was picked up:

Both my friends Leading Stoker Darby Allen and stoker Jimmy Wald were trapped in the catapault hydraulic power room when *Eagle* turned upside down, four decks below the main deck. Stoker Milligan dived into a sea of burning oil several times to save members of the crew after being picked up by the destroyer *Lookout* and he couldn't swim. Jock Simpson was thrown into sea as a doctor had pronounced him dead. He was later picked up by the tug *Jaunty* where another doctor revived him.

When they had hit the water in their raft after their toboggan ride down the tilting flight deck Les Goodenough and his companion found they were still too close for comfort to the bulk of the carrier:

I said, 'Paddle, we don't want to get sucked down.' Within no time at all it seemed the ship was still turning to starboard and going down. The last thing I can recall is seeing an explosion aft, no doubt a boiler blowing up.

I was picked up by HMS *Lookout* and, after reporting our names, I was immediately greeted by Lieutenant Gibbs, my gunnery officer, who fetched a glass of rum for me and a towel to clean myself up. That was the last time we met. When we returned to Gibraltar later I still did not know whether my brother had survived or not. (He did!)

Gordon Drake again:

We could not have been two hundred yards from her when she went right over. We were swimming in inches of oil and the black smoke was being blown all across the sea in front of us. After swimming for a few minutes more we saw her stern suddenly vanishing and soon after she had gone there was a minor tidal wave from the suction that made us think she wanted us to join her.

Destroyers could be seen converging from all areas at speed when you were on the crest of the waves. Then suddenly three came in at full speed. One old timer shouted 'depth charges' and everybody turned and swam the other way if they were able. Then it happened, they must have been half-a-mile away and they parted, each destroyer letting

go her own pattern of charges. No sooner had one explosion
shattered the sea, lifting men out of the water, than another
would follow. Having done their duty they reduced speed
and reformed again to pick us up.

While they swam and waited for rescue the men made
jokes. A commander was seen swimming with his gold
braided cap still on, with seamen shouting, 'I was told to
report to you, sir!' as he passed them. Others yelled, 'Here's
the bus conductor. Two return tickets please: 'That's no
good. It's too early, my old lady will be in bed with the
postman now'. 'Which is the way to Malta?' while all the time
helping mates and urging them not to despair.

Not everyone loved her and not everyone that day felt in any
way sad about the old *Eagle*'s final plunge. Dick Greenwood, for
one, relates:

I know it is an awful thing to say but when I was drifting
astern of her in the water and she was sinking I was glad she
was going. She rolled over with her backside upward and as
she took her final plunge, with her propellers the last things
to be seen, I just thanked God my boiler-room watchkeeping
days on her had finally come to an end. The boys dying on
her at that moment were not on my mind at all. It was only
many years later that I wanted to meet those that were left.

Ken Pierce told me how:

One of our aircraft which was airborne at the time circled
around and dropped his small inflatable raft to a group of
swimmers. I'm sure it was appreciated as very soon the
swimmers were like bees round a honeypot! He circled again,
dipped his wings as if to wish them luck and went off to land
on another carrier.

During a lull in the action, ships were sent back from the
main convoy to pick us up, one of them being HMS *Lookout*.
She was the one I made for, although I had no idea of her
name at the time. As I got near to her stern, I saw several
men throwing heaving lines to lads in the water and pulling
them on board. When I was near enough I shouted for a line
and one was thrown, which I gratefully grabbed. As that
seaman began to pull me in I saw it was a pal from the next
village where I lived as a lad whom I had grown up with. What
a small world! I don't know who was more surprised, him or

me! Dennis Ridley is his name and he survived the war, and
indeed lives quite close to me now. After he got me inboard
(he had some difficulty in getting me over the rail as I was
nearly exhausted) we went to the mess deck where there was
some pretty gruesome surgery taking place on injured
survivors. (That doctor was doing a grand job.) Dennis and I
talked for a bit and he produced 'one out of the bottle' which
went down well!

It wasn't long before action stations were sounded and he
went to his station (Gun crew). It was another air attack
which lasted some time. After the all-clear, we were told that
we were to be transferred to another destroyer as *Lookout* was
required to rejoin the main convoy. HMS *Venomous* came
alongside and we were duly transferred. Being an old 'V' and
'W' class destroyer there was not much room for all us
survivors. I believe there were about five hundred of us
packed like sardines. Still we made the best of it. The crew
did all they could for us; we all got a tot, smokes were handed
round, tea was made.

In all 67 officers and 862 ratings were saved, including Captain
MacIntosh, out of a ship's company of 1,160. The *Lookout*
rescued Captain MacIntosh, 48 officers and 487 men, the
*Laforey* nine officers and 186 men and the tug *Jaunty* had saved
thirteen officers and 185 men. Later these ships transferred
their survivors to the destroyers *Malcolm*, *Keppel* and *Venomous*
respectively, whereupon the two 'L' class destroyers hurried on
to rejoin the battle now developing to the eastward. Captain
Broome's destroyers formed screen on the *Furious* which was
returning to Gibraltar to embark further Spitfires. During that
night they gained some revenge when the *Wolverine* sank the
Italian submarine *Dagabur*. The tug *Jaunty* also returned to
Gibraltar as being too slow to maintain the convoy speed. The
final casualty list was two officers and eleven men killed and
118 missing believed dead.

For the majority of the survivors the ending of the story was
similar to that of R.C. Cosh:

Our only possessions being the clothes we stood up in,
usually underwear, and a pair of overalls, oily and tattered
after three hours in the water. We were given food, names
and numbers were taken and, as the *Laforey* moved to rejoin
the convoy we curled up and tried to sleep.

Later that day we were transferred to another destroyer, *Keppel*, and returned to Gibraltar. The actual timing of these events and the way it was done I cannot remember correctly, but we ended up in the submarine depot ship *Maidstone* at Gibraltar. Having been given a casual payment, food, and a shower, and certain items of essential kit, we felt ready for a run ashore, and that is exactly what we did.

Arrangements were made for us to send telegrams home to our next-of-kin, as apparently the news of the sinking of the *Eagle* and other ships had been released in the UK. The following day we were taken to the airfield at North Front and what remained of 801 Squadron was mustered – minus aircraft of course – and minus all our tools and personal belongings. It was a ramshackled outfit that remained, deflated, but not depressed and we waited, impatiently, for the next move. It came fairly quickly as we were shipped aboard the ancient aircraft carrier *Argus*, to return to the UK. It was a slow and tedious passage. The smell of fuel oil was still strong in my nostrils and very nauseating to me and during the ten days that followed I did not move far away from the upper decks.

At Greenock we were greeted by the ladies of the WVS, with tea, buns and cigarettes. No matter that our improvised kitbags were full of tickler tobacco and duty-frees. Those lovely ladies were there to greet us. They were pleased to see us. We were wanted, we were home, though, in the end, it wasn't to be for very long.

\*

Although *Eagle* herself had gone, a part of her was still fighting the enemy and helping Pedestal battle its way through the strongest concentration of Axis aircraft ever thrown against a Malta convoy. Those 'posthumous' heroes were of course the four Sea Hurricane fighters that had been airborne when the ship had been so quickly despatched.

Having dropped his float to help the struggling crew, Sub-Lieutenant F.J. Hutton landed aboard the *Victorious*. He was quickly refuelled aboard that ship and later that afternoon was again airborne on patrol over the convoy. At the end of that patrol he landed on again, this time aboard the *Indomitable*. After three carriers in three hours Hutton decided to settle down and spent the night on this ship.

The next day when the enemy mounted their all-out air strikes, Hutton flew against them and flew, in his CO's words, ' ... with energy and courage'. He shot down one enemy aircraft and damaged another. That same afternoon Hutton witnessed the loss of yet another of his floating 'homes' when *Indomitable* herself was given the *Illustrious* treatment by a squadron of Junkers Ju87 Stukas and left heavily on fire and damaged after two direct hits and three near misses from these dive bombers which had lost none of their accuracy or skill. Hutton was therefore forced to return to the only operational carrier, *Victorious*, once more. Her deck was naturally crowded and it did not prove easy to organise and take off on the last covering patrol of the day. Sub-Lieutenant Hutton continued to be eager and ready to get airborne yet again, and did so, despite the fact that he had been consistently flying in heavy combat for two solid days.

Hutton, like his three comrades, had, in Brabner's own words, ' ... seen his ship sunk – he was cut off from that moral support which is so necessary in a single seater fighter squadron and which comes from flying among close personal friends.' He added that, 'These officers were cut off from their base, disturbed by uncertainty as to the fate of their friends in HMS *Eagle*, cut off from their squadron and, while receiving a hospitable welcome, were flying in strange squadrons among new colleagues in the heat of an extensive battle.'

Sub-Lieutenant Hankey landed aboard *Victorious* and flew with 885 Squadron from that carrier. He did not long survive his ship for he lost his life while attacking a huge swarm of enemy bombers the next day. He was believed to have been shot down by superior numbers of enemy fighters.

Sub-Lieutenant MacDonald landed aboard *Indomitable* after *Eagle* was sunk and here he was immediately incorporated into 880 Squadron and flew consistently in that squadron in the subsequent battles under Lieutenant-Commander Judd.

Lieutenant-Commander Rupert Brabner, their CO, performed equally gallantly in the days that followed and was commended for his inspired leadership in the air battles of 12 and 13 August. He had been awarded a DSO for his work on an earlier Malta convoy and Rear Admiral A.L.St.G.Lyster commented that, ' ... from what I saw of him on August 12th I think that he earned at least a mention, if not a bar to his DSO. Brabner was leading Hutton, Hankey and MacDonald, who all

got the DSC!' After much argument from the chairbound
warriors in Whitehall, Brabner was also awarded the DSC for
his work on Pedestal. And so, days after she had departed the
field of combat, representatives of HMS *Eagle* continued to
inspire. One of the Sea Hurricanes was wrecked in a dusk
landing mix-up aboard *Victorious* on 11 August and a second
when Hutton was killed the next day. Only two of her entire
fighter outfit therefore survived *Eagle*'s loss. Also lost with the
ship was the Italian standard from the sunken destroyers in the
Red Sea and many other unique and valuable mementoes from
her long life.

*

The grave of HMS *Eagle* is located at 38 degrees, 05 minutes
North, 03 degrees, 02 minutes East in the western basin of the
Mediterranean Sea.

The final word, as is proper, should be left to one who served
aboard her and who loved her despite all her many faults. So let
the words of Lieutenant-Commander (A) Rupert Brabner
convey the achievements, not only of the young pilots he was
quite rightly praising, but of all who failed to come back from
the loss of HMS *Eagle*: 'They all did honour to themselves and
were not unworthy of the ship from which they came.'

Marine Harry Kempshall adds a last postscript for those who
did not come back:

> Most years I attend the Royal Marine Band Service Re-Union
> at Deal, and on the Sunday morning Church Service a page
> in the Book of Remembrance is turned and the name of the
> ship and those lost are read out, and of course, 'we do
> remember them.' Currently there is a project for kneelers in
> the Barrack Church at Deal, and my wife is embroidering
> one which will have the inscription 'HMS *Eagle* 1942'.

# Source Notes and
# Select Bibliography

# Source Notes and Select Bibliography

*Aerei Italiani nella 2 Guerra Mondiale, Bombardierie*, (6 Vols) Edizioni Bizzarri, 1972.

Bragadin, Commander (R) Marc' Antonio, *The Italian Navy in World War II*, Naval Institute Press, Annapolis, 1957.

Brown, David *HMS Eagle*, Profile Warship 35 – Profile Publications, Windsor, 1973.

Chatfield, Admiral of the Fleet, Lord. *The Navy and Defence*, Heinemann, London, 1942.

Chatfield, Admiral of the Fleet, Lord. *It Might Happen Again*, Heinemann, London, 1947.

*Correspondence* re Award to Lieutenant-Commander R.A. Brabner, RNVR, dated 30 April 1943/8 June 1943/11 June 1943. (ADM1/14275)

Cunningham of Hyndhope, Admiral of the Fleet Viscount, *A Sailors Odyssey*, Hutchinson, 1951.

*Despatch*, Admiral Sir Andrew B. Cunningham, dated 29 January 1941, issued as a *Supplement to London Gazette*, 27 April 1948.

*Far Eastern Policy*, War Cabinet, *Report* by Chiefs of Staff, dated 27 July 1940. (Cab.66/10)

Ishimaru, Lieutenant-Commander Tota, *Japan Must Fight Britain*, Paternoster Library, London, 1936.

*La Marina Italiana nella Seconda Guerre Mondiale*, (2 Vols), Ufficio Storico della Marina Militare, Rome, 1960 and 1976.

Muggenthaler, August Karl, *German Raiders of World War II*, Robert Hale, 1978.

*Recommendations for Honours and Awards* – 801 Squadron, dated 13 December 1942. (ADM/14275)

*Report* on Action taken against German M.V. *Franken*, dated 13 September 1939. (ADM199/969)

*Report* of Bomb Explosion aboard HMS *Eagle*: dated 17 March 1940 (ADM267/60)

*Report* on Air Action against four Italian destroyers off Port Sudan; dated 11 April 1941. (ADM199/609)

*Report* on Interception and Capture of the German M.V. *Lothringen*, dated 19 June 1941. (ADM199/809)

*Report of Proceedings* – Operation 'L.B.', dated 22 May 1942 (ADM199/1240)

*Report* of Attack by Enemy Aircraft, dated 18 May 1942 (ADM199/174)

*Report of Proceedings* – Operation Pinpoint, dated 16 July 1942.

*Report of Proceedings* – Operation Insect, dated 22 July 1942. (ADM199/1240)

*Report of Proceedings* – *HMS Eagle* return to UK., dated 29 October 1941. (ADM199/625)

*Report* – Loss of HMS *Eagle*, dated 15 August 1942 ADM199/2067)

*Report and Analysis* – HMS *Eagle*, Aircraft Carrier, sunk by 4 torpedoes, dated 24 August 1942. (ADM267/73)

*Report of Proceedings* – Operation Pedestal, dated 23 August 1942. (ADM 199/2008)

*Reports, Signals and Summaries*, concerning Operation Pedestal, various dates, 1942. (Admiralty, BSR 52).

*Report of Proceedings* – Operations Calendar and Bowery, Various dates, 1942. (M.06609/42 and M.06976/42)

*Reports of Proceedings* – Operation MA5 and Battle of Calabria, dated 29 January 1941. (ADM199/1048)

*Summary of Signals* concerning HMS *Eagle*, 1939-42, (NHB, London)

Roskill, Captain S.W. *The War at Sea* (4 Vols), HMSO 1954-67.

Santoro, Generale Guiseppe, *L'Aeronautica Italiana Nella Seconda Guerra Mondiale* (2 Vols), Ufficico Storico, Rome, 1957.

Smith, Peter C. – *Action Imminent*, William Kimber, London, 1980.

Smith, Peter C. – *Pedestal*, Crécy Books, 1994.

# Index